Comfort, Cleanliness and Convenience

New Technologies/New Cultures Series

General Editor: Don Slater, London School of Economics

New Technologies/New Cultures will draw together the best scholarship, across the social science disciplines, that addresses emergent technologies in relation to cultural transformation. While much contemporary literature is caught up in wild utopian or dystopian pronouncements about the scale and implications of change, this series invites more grounded and modulated work with a clear conceptual and empirical focus. The series draws on a wealth of dynamic research agendas, from Internet and new media scholarship to research into bio-sciences, environmentalism and the sociology of consumption.

Series ISSN: *1472–2895*

Previous titles published in this series:

Brenda Danet, *Cyberpl@y: Communicating Online*

Comfort, Cleanliness and Convenience

The Social Organization of Normality

elizabeth shove

 **BERG**

Oxford • New York

First published in 2003 by
Berg
Editorial offices:
1st Floor, Angel Court, 81 St Clements Street, Oxford, OX4 1AW, UK
838 Broadway, Third Floor, New York, NY 10003-4812, USA

Berg is an imprint of Oxford International Publishers Ltd.

Library of Congress Cataloging-in-Publication Data
Shove, Elizabeth, 1959-
    Comfort, cleanliness and convenience : the social organization of
normality / Elizabeth Shove.
        p. cm. – (New technologies/new cultures series, ISSN 1472-2895)
    ISBN 1-85973-625-4 (cloth) – ISBN 1-85973-630-0 (Pbk)
    1. Lifestyles. 2. Health behavior. 3. Consumption
(Economics) – Social aspects. 4. Consumers – Psychology. I. Title. II.
Series.
    HQ2042.S56 2003
    306–dc21
                                                                    2003006204

British Library Cataloguing-in-Publication Data
A catalogue record for this book is available from the British Library.

ISBN   1 85973 625 4 (Cloth)
       1 85973 630 0 (Paper)

Typeset by JS Typesetting Ltd, Wellingborough, Northants.
Printed in the United Kingdom by Biddles Ltd, Guildford and King's Lynn

www.bergpublishers.com

For John and Jocelyn Shove, with love.

Contents

Contents

Contents

List of Figures and Tables

Figures

Tables

Acknowledgements

A Leverhulme fellowship provided me with the time to write this book and the freedom to spend a couple of months at Lawrence Berkeley National Laboratory, California, USA. I am really grateful to both organizations and to Unilever Consumer Science Insight for providing access to much relevant research material.

I might not have applied for the Leverhulme fellowship at all had it not been for Alan Warde and Dale Southerton, and I certainly could not have had such a good time in California without Gail Cooper, Rick Diamond, Bruce Hackett, Mithra Moezzi, Bruce Sinclair and my co-interviewer, Reuben Deumling.

Over the last five years the European Science Foundation's Tackling Environmental Resource Management programme has supported a series of workshops and summer schools on the theme of 'Consumption, Everyday Life and Sustainability'. Discussions of comfort, cleanliness and convenience first surfaced in that context and I owe much to Heather Chappells, Mika Pantzar, Gert Spaargaren, Bas van Vliet, Matthew Watson, Hal Wilhite and everyone else involved in organizing and contributing to those memorable events.

Closer to home, Waterhouses Community Social Club continues to provide a welcome break on Friday nights.

My thanks to all.

1

Consumption, Everyday Life and Sustainability

To outsiders, sociology has a reputation for dealing with the everyday and the ordinary. This is often cast as a thinly veiled criticism: who needs a whole discipline to understand what people do as a matter of course? In the context of this book, such a reputation represents a challenge and an ideal to live up to. Turning the spotlight back on generally invisible forms of practice, its purpose is to investigate the constitution of normality and the dynamics of habit and routine.

It would be misleading to draw too sharp a distinction between the realm of the spectacular and that of the grindingly ordinary. Even so, I'll start by suggesting that the slicing of academic debate reveals a contemporary preoccupation with the explicit, the visible and the dramatic. Analyses of the tangible threats and traumas of risk society and of catastrophes, controversies and high-profile developments in science, politics and technology all illustrate this trend. Although the gleam of novelty gives issues like biotechnology, genetic modification or the future of e-commerce an immediate allure, closer inspection suggests that even fashionable topics have muddy and sometimes extensive taproots reaching back into long-standing programmes of theoretical concern. Familiar questions of social division and cohesion, consumption and production, agency and structure are rarely far away. Although familiar, these foundational questions are, of course, subject to reinterpretation and revision through and in the light of current concerns. It is easy to see why intellectual resources concentrate around themes that sparkle and spike the interest of research funders, the media, the public and fellow academics. Such focusing is to be expected. But what are the longer-term consequences of grounding ideas about contemporary society in the analysis of its more tangible and explicit characteristics? Might the tendency to pursue novel and fashionable topics not lead to the unwitting elaboration of lopsided conceptual frameworks? Would current lines of theoretical development be any different if they were, by contrast, anchored in the study of ordinary habits and routinized aspects of everyday life?

This is a question that runs throughout the book. Along the way, it takes specific forms. How might we conceptualize *inconspicuous* consumption as opposed to that which is overtly wrapped up with questions of style, status and symbolic signficance? Can existing theories and analyses of things, objects and material cultures be bent and adapted to take account of the intangible, immaterial and invisible services they make possible? What does the co-evolution of technology and practice really mean for you and me and for the way we organize our lives? With what means might we explain the creep of convention and the escalation and standardization of conditions and circumstances that people take for granted? This is not to suggest that the social organization of normality is in some way distinctive, or that the processes involved are not also at play in other domains. Rather, the point is to discover what new theoretical challenges the study of a handful of ordinary practices might generate for a discipline that has, on balance, and perhaps to its cost, drifted from the systematic scrutiny of the mundane.

Of course arrangements that are normal for some strike others as being extremely strange. Though I have no intention of defining the ordinary in any absolute sense, the book engages with sets of practices and expectations that constitute the barely detectable gridlines of everyday life. They form what would commonly be seen as a neutral backdrop against which the dramas of contemporary social interaction are played out. In Goffman's terms (1969), this book is more about the production of the scenery, the lighting and the setting than the action itself. These features are, none the less, actively constituted and reproduced in ways that demand the skilful deployment of rules, resources, technologies and other persons.

Despite inhabiting the shadowy region of the back-stage, the themes with which I deal are themselves subject to sometimes rapid development. In Western societies the sense of changing scenery is both pervasive and elusive.

To give just a few examples, expectations of the indoor environment have shifted substantially in less than a single generation: although some people still wake to patterns of frost on the inside of the window, many more have come to take the comforts of central heating and air-conditioning for granted. In this as in other respects, experiences of cosiness and wellbeing are on the move. To give a second quite specific example, the Saturday night bath, once a standard feature of British family life, has given way to patterns of daily showering, a form predominantly valued for its convenience. The valuing of convenience is itself indicative of further transformation. Any number of devices and solutions are sold in the name of convenience and sold to those who feel themselves to be harried, hurried and harassed. Few can pin down just how and when their habits change but again there is a sense that things were not always so.

These instances point to the significance of middle-range concepts like those of comfort, cleanliness and convenience. Such cross cutting terms encompass a variety of inter-linked conventions and habits and as such offer a vocabulary with which to explore and follow the evolution of routine, and with which to show how new arrangements become normal. One ambition of this book is to investigate unspectacular dimensions of daily life along these lines as a means of better understanding the dynamics of social change.

There are several reasons for concentrating on these three Cs – comfort, cleanliness and convenience – in particular. First, these complexes of practice appear to change in ways that challenge established theories of consumption and technology. Second, despite persistent and extensive variation, there is some evidence to support the view that comfort and cleanliness are subject to distinctive forms of escalation and standardization. Escalation here refers to the ratcheting up of demand, for instance for levels of comfort or for degrees of cleanliness. Standardization implies that the reach of what counts as normal is more and more encompassing. Conventions once confined to particular cultures seem to be extending (and eroding) in ways that suggest convergence in both technology and practice. Global acceptance of the business suit, the waning of the siesta and the expectation of always wearing freshly laundered clothing give an indication of this kind of change. Such trends are neither simple nor inevitable: pockets of habit stick fast, old ways die hard and some are obdurately resistant to change. Even so, there is an arguably new and certainly niggling tension between the production, appropriation and maintenance of standardized and localized interpretations of normal practice.

The prospect of exploring processes of escalation, standardization and resistance is appealing in its own right, but it is of more than academic interest. While the three Cs do not represent the full range of ordinary practice, they do encompass the environmental hot spots of consumption. Around half the energy in the world is used in buildings and much of that is devoted to keeping people comfortable. In the UK, cleaning now accounts for approximately 70 per cent of domestic water usage and demand for hot water is rising. The increasing importance of convenience and of devices designed to ease problems of temporal co-ordination relates, I argue, to the contemporary challenge of scheduling valued aspects of everyday life. As well as engendering the multiplication of energy-consuming but time-saving or time-shifting technologies, this trend has further implications for the definition and delivery of normal and necessary standards and services.

These points are not missed by environmentalists, many of whom are concerned about the proliferation of unsustainable ways of life and the consequences of such for climate change and global warming. Environmentally inspired analyses, usually framed in terms of restraint, excess and individual choice, tend to focus on the consumption of energy, water and other natural resources, but not on the services and experiences they make possible. By focusing so exclusively on individual action, such enquiries miss the bigger picture, failing to detect cultural and generational shifts of expectation and practice. In response, and in contrast, I take a different tack: starting rather than ending with a discussion of the sociotechnical transformation of *collective* conventions and thereby generating a more thoroughly social understanding of environmentally significant change.

This book is therefore driven by three ambitions. One is to revisit theories of consumption, technology and social change through an analysis of ordinarily invisible practices. A second is to work out how and why conventions of comfort and cleanliness are on the move. The third is to shift the focus of social environmental research and policy so as to comprehend the collective restructuring of expectation and habit. This involves tracking what have become routinized and inconspicuous practices. It means thinking again about the definition and appropriation of *services*, rather than discrete objects, and trying to understand both the convergence and divergence of everyday *practice*. This is not an innocent exercize. In focusing on comfort and cleanliness and on the dynamics of co-evolution and integration, the book offers and illustrates a different way of cutting the cake for environmental policy as for social theory.

While questions of comfort, cleanliness and convenience have yet to receive sustained sociological attention, the notion of investigating the escalation and standardization of consumption or the reproduction of habit is by no means novel. As a result, there are many resources on which to draw. The remainder of this chapter isolates relevant ingredients from the sociology of environment, of consumption and of technology.

Natural Resources and Consumer Choices

For all the effort invested in analysing consumer culture and consumer society, and despite the view that these concepts are 'central to unlocking some of the mysteries of contemporary societies' (Shove and Warde 2001: 231), interest in energy and water consumption has been largely confined to the environmental field. One somewhat paradoxical consequence is that consumer practices relating to routine forms of domestic reproduction, to washing, drying, cleaning, heating, lighting, cooling and so on, are as likely to have been studied by environmentalists or by feminists as by those for whom consumption is core business.

This has led to a particular bunching of priorities. It comes as no surprise to discover that *environmentally* inspired programmes are guided by a prior interest not in consumption per se, but in what that means for carbon emissions, pollution, waste and the depletion of finite resources. Building on this initial framing of the problem, dominant questions have concerned the ecological limits to growth, the specification of environmental 'carrying capacities' and the figuring out of where the end of the road really lies. In all of this, escalating consumption and economic growth are generally taken to be interdependent, one leading to and being a precondition for the other (Weyant and Yanigisawa 1998; Laitner, De Canio and Peters 2000). Continual monitoring of the resource and energy intensities of world economies, further fuelled by economic modelling and forecasts of future trends, tends to produce a somewhat depressing picture. One can sometimes glimpse the steadying impact of improvements in technological or market efficiency (Romm and Rosenfeld 2000), but projections of future per capita demand for energy generally point ever upwards.

Although purportedly indicating patterns of consumption, such images are uninformative with respect to the *specifics* of how peoples' expectations and practices change. As indicated above, increasing demand is a foregone conclusion and in this style of economic/environmental analysis, people, in so far as they feature at all, do so as the aggregate consumers of socially anonymous resources.

Even so, plotting future trends in the countries of the North and the South is a contentious matter and one that highlights the political significance of consumption in general and of environmentally significant consumption in particular. In response, technically minded policy analysts have taken advantage of the apparent neutrality of economic and environmental modelling. Some have sought to demonstrate the long-term sustainability of a world in which demand is 'allowed' to increase to levels currently obtaining in western Europe, providing the USA scales back to that level too. Other assessments identify the need to reduce the material intensity of consumption and production by factors of four, or ten or twenty. Such assessments have prompted further, similarly intense, discussion about how the dials of demand might be retuned through policy initiatives or technological fixes (Giovannini and Baranzini 1998; von Weizsäcker, Lovins and Lovins 1997). Exemplifying this approach, Schmidt-Bleek, founder of the 'Factor 10 institute' claims that 'Within one generation, nations can achieve a ten-fold increase in the efficiency with which they use energy, resources, and other materials', and advises industry and government on how this might be done (Factor 10 Club 1997). Exercises of this kind are immensely influential not, or not only, for the results they produce but for the questions they cast and the shadows these throw.

By definition, forecasts and projections make assumptions about the extent and character of future consumption. Also by definition, proposed policy responses imply that projected trends can be changed and modified. In this they carry with them an understanding of basic 'needs' and variable 'wants' and of standards of living that might be compatible with a sustainable future. But which elements of anticipated demand should be taken as read, which are negotiable, by whom, and on what basis? Like it or not, environmental models are shot through with questions of inequality, social justice, entitlements, responsibilities for future generations and visions of the good society. Yet the purpose and process of their production tends to disguise this point with the result that the social conditions and circumstances in which needs are defined slips from view. One ironic consequence is that much – although certainly not all – environmental research, policy and academic comment sidesteps explicit engagement with its own social and political assumptions. Despite and in fact precisely because of its *environmental* focus, fundamental issues about the specification of demand fall (or are pushed) beyond the bounds of normal policy debate.

Given the importance of energy and other natural resources, research and policy has focused on their consumption rather than on consumption in general. Accounting tools used to assess the 'ecological footprints' of regions or commodities, to calculate the weight of the 'ecological rucksack' attached to specific lifestyles, or, less commonly, to evaluate the impact of entire ways of life celebrate this resource-based focus (Wackernagel and Rees 1995) as do technical exercizes in modelling household 'metabolism' (Noorman and Uiter-kamp 1998). Having distinguished between the resources currently used and those potentially required to deliver the same standard of living, it is possible – and politically sensible – to promote 'green' ways of life not substantially different from those we have come to expect, but less damaging in how they are achieved and sustained. Initiatives designed to increase the efficiency with which existing services are provided take no account of how standards of living have been established or what they are.

While environmental impact can be added to the list of evils associated with consumer culture, it is just as easily incorporated into that culture itself. A common strategy, and one that again ducks the question of how needs are defined in modern societies, is to commodify the environment. This takes many forms ranging from trade in carbon emissions permits to the labelling of green products. By imbuing ordinary things and practices with environmental signifi-cance, policy makers encourage consumers to make 'the environment' their preferred brand as part of a broader strategy of ecologically modernizing their lives (Spaargaren 1997). Adopting similar methods but for commercial pur-poses, manufacturers use green credentials in pursuit of higher sales, product differentiation and more precise niche marketing.

In keeping with this approach, research into the relationship between environmental commitments, beliefs, actions and lifestyles sustains and reinforces a model of isolated individuals whose variously green identities are expressed through a precisely calibrated and increasingly extensive palate of green consumer choice (Hinchliffe 1996; Stern *et al.* 1997; Moisander 2000; Hobson 2001; Zavestoski 2001). Grounded in the belief that better information will allow consumers to make 'better' decisions, labelling and standard-setting represent important planks of national and international policy. Such initiatives have the dual purpose of stimulating interest in the environment and of offering a ready-made channel for its expression through the purchase of commodities like high-efficiency freezers, ecological washing powder, green electricity and more. Caught within this paradigm, studies showing that generalized environmental concerns do not simply translate into practice have inspired further programmes of research designed to spot intervening factors that complicate and confound the translation of belief into action.

One might of course wonder, as Don Slater does, 'whether "consumer choice" is the best way for a society to go about defining, let alone filling, its basic needs' (Slater 1997: 136), or for that matter responding to its environmental crises. After all, a green freezer is still a freezer and although advocates of voluntary simplicity might worry about whether to use one at all, studies like those reported in *Green Households* (Noorman and Uiterkamp 1998) take the preservation of current practice – including reliance on frozen food – pretty much for granted. Schor (1999) has called for a debate about the 'quality of life and the quantity of stuff' but for the most part environmental policy makers have been unwilling to consider the social construction of routinized needs and wants. They have instead confined themselves to the limited but still demanding task of jogging consumers into thinking about the efficiency with which their needs are met. In keeping with this approach, the OECD has produced a number of reports on sustainable consumption detailing strategies policy makers might adopt in guiding consumer choice in more sustainable directions. As the title of one such study – 'Information and Consumer Decision-Making for Sustainable Consumption' – indicates, the aim is to help consumers 'see' the environment in what they do, and see if there are other more efficient ways of achieving the same result. All else has the negative connotation of 'cutting back' and smacks of government restraint on citizen-consumers' choice.

Sharing these policy ambitions, but offering a solid critique of the simplistic, individualistic and 'decisionistic' paradigms that dominate, Gert Spaargaren recognizes that many environmentally relevant 'choices' do not appear as such. Buried in the realm of routine and what Giddens (1984) terms practical consciousness, Spaargaren notes that water consumption only penetrates the plane of discursive consciousness when it comes out brown, or in the wrong place, or when the utility bill arrives. For Spaargaren, an environmentalist himself, such moments of deroutinization are critical because they enable people to examine and assess their habits from a green perspective (Spaargaren 1997: 28). Borrowing Giddens's ideas regarding the duality of agency and structure, Spaargaren makes the point that citizen-consumers are not just shoppers. They are also implicated in the production and reproduction of structural constraints and opportunities such as those afforded by public utilities and household infrastructures. Though initiated through cycles of deroutinization and reroutinization, he argues that the ecological modernization of domestic practice is neither 'actor driven or system-imposed' but is both at the same time. Convinced that a process of environmentally inspired modernization *is* under- way, Spaargaren concludes that consumers' commitments 'will profoundly affect and alter the organization of domestic consumption as well as the interrelations between households and socio-material-collective systems' (Spaargaren 1997: 30). But will such a move also redefine what people expect by way of comfort, cleanliness and convenience? Not necessarily, and not unless environmental considerations prove weighty enough to displace con- temporary understandings of what everyday life should be like.

Taking an altogether more robust approach to this subject, Michael Redclift (1996) situates his analysis of environment and consumption in the context of an inter-dependent global economy organized around specific packages of commitment and belief. In his terms, the upward paths of predicted energy demand reflect, and are a consequence of, the social values attached to the production and consumption of energy and resource intensive commodities (Redclift 1996: 40).

Redclift suggests that in the normal run of environmental discourse, and especially the discourse of environmental management, goals like those of achieving a higher standard of living are accorded almost existential status. More than that, 'the underlying social commitments which drive our consump- tion, and contribute to waste, are afforded value by being naturalised' (Redclift 1996: 146). Again the point is that the very process of environmental analysis, debate and modelling, including that concerned with green consumption and ecological modernization, contributes to – and takes for granted – ways of life and suites of values that are at the heart of the environmental problem itself. In concluding that 'we will not be able to undo, through environmental man- agement, what we have done through naturalising our consumption' (Redclift 1996: 148), Redclift turns back to the dynamics of convention, commitment and consumption.

This is an unusual and radical move. As indicated above, discussions of environmentally significant consumption typically focus on resources rather than on the services these make possible, they highlight the promotion of environmental awareness and concentrate on excess and restraint at the level of individual consumer (or citizen-consumer) choice. This politically explicable emphasis overshadows prior questions about the framing and formulation of 'normal' practice. Just as important, it misses the point that much consumption is customary, governed by collective norms and undertaken in a world of things and sociotechnical systems that have stabilizing effects on routines and habits. As indicated above, more sophisticated accounts do take note of how choices are structured, but in concentrating on resources and efficiencies rather than expectations and conventions, environmentalists have largely failed to notice or really engage with critical developments in ordinary consumption.

The missing agenda identified by Redclift brings a trail of questions in its wake: how *do* practices, expectations and ways of life become naturalized? What energizes processes of escalation, standardization, differentiation and development? In addition, how do models, ideologies, cultures and ways of life spill over from one country to another: what are the long-term environmental implications of Westernization, modernization and Americanization, and how are these tendencies modified and mediated by local traditions, habits, meanings and modes of appropriation?

To address these questions head on it is necessary to abandon the resource-based focus of environmental enquiry. As Wilhite and Lutzenhiser (1998) have argued, people do not consume energy. In real life they consume 'cultural energy services', in other words, culturally meaningful services that happen to depend on a supply of gas, oil, or electricity. Amongst others, these include services like those of comfort and cleanliness. It is therefore necessary to consider not just the more-or-less green means by which expectations are met, but what those expectations actually are. From this point of view, studies of eco-villagers or investigations into the beliefs and actions of self-confessed environmentalists represent something of a distraction. What counts is the big, and in some cases, global swing of ordinary, routinized and taken-for-granted practice. This implies an up ending of the social environmental research agenda, as conventionally formulated. Only by setting 'the environment' aside as the main focus of attention will it be possible to follow and analyse processes underpinning the normalization of consumption and the escalation of demand.

This is the strategy I propose to take. As already observed, questions about how new practices become normal touch upon familiar themes within the sociology and anthropology of consumption and technology and there is much to work with. In the next section I highlight a selection of potentially useful ideas regarding the escalation of consumption and the direction of socio-technical change.

Cycles of Consumption and Escalators of Demand

In real life, escalators do not run backwards. Neither do the escalators of demand in economic theory. As Inge Røpke, observes, the nature of the market economy is such as to generate perpetual technological change (Røpke 2001). According to Røpke, firms constantly search for ways of making existing products more cheaply and renewing what they produce in order to generate new demand and keep ahead of their competition. The consumer side of this equation is similarly escalatory. Caught up in what Juliet Schor (1992) refers to as the work-spend cycle, people seem to be drawn deeper and deeper into the maw of a market society, selling their labour and producing things they do not want in order to earn money to buy those they desire (Slater 1997: 26). Individual situations differ but in general the proposition is that the more people spend, the more they need to work and the more they work, the more other people need to spend. In short, this family of ideas conceptualizes consumers' changing needs and wants and hence the changing constitution of normal expectation in terms of the productive forces and requirements of capitalist industrial economies.

Mainstream economists tend to assume that needs are exogenous and that they exist independent of the market. Others argue that consumers' aspirations and desires are made, mediated and created by and through the market itself. Either way, the shared position is that the meeting and/or reproduction of consumers' needs constitutes an engine of change that underpins and explains the ratcheting of demand. In all of this, it is strangely easy to argue about the characteristics of demand without taking much notice of exactly what is consumed, how that changes or what these changes mean for the practices and ways of life of those involved. There is a certainty that development will take place and that it will do so in a manner consistent with the requirements of modern capitalist society but there is no strong story here about the substance of desire, whether constructed or predetermined, or about direction of techno-economic change. To learn more about the detail of production and consumption, we would do well to turn to the literature on innovation, a literature that is centrally concerned with novelty and change, with how products are developed and how they become normal.

Analyses of innovation generally focus on the generation of new goods and services or on methods for standardizing and improving production processes. Concentrating on the former situation, E. M. Rogers' (1983) classic work on innovation identifies a standard sequence through which new products and practices are embedded in society. The sequence is one in which the actions of 'early adopters', that is people with a psychological propensity for risk taking are, in due course, copied by others of a more cautious nature. The implied engine of change on the consumer side of the equation relates to risk and novelty (not to capital accumulation, as it does for producers) but the process is again represented as one of inevitable escalation. As a story of how innovation works, this much-criticized account supposes that the link between new technologies and new forms of demand has to do with the psychological fabric of society and the relation between different types of risk taking. The further assumption is that new technologies *will* diffuse through society and that the process of changing consumer expectation is simply a matter of time.

In so far as the production of new goods and services contributes to the escalation of demand, we might expect the centrifugal pull of Schor's work-spend cycle to be somehow linked to the rate and character of innovation. This would suggest that the social embedding of novelty, or in Rogers' terms, the diffusion of innovation, is not simply, or perhaps not at all, to do with psychological propensities for risk taking, but with an essentially more complex relation between production and consumption.

The idea that consumers' pursuit of novelty goes hand in hand with producers' requirement for innovation constitutes one popular explanation for the escalation of demand. There are, however, other more sociological accounts of the dynamics at stake. In reviewing some of this literature, Shove and Warde (2002) isolate a number of mechanisms held to support escalating levels of consumption. These include social comparison (in which consumption contributes to the maintenance and reproduction of social boundaries and distinctions); the creation of self identity (in which the acquisition of goods and services is central to personal psychological wellbeing); mental stimulation and novelty (these desires helping to sustain constant pursuit of new products and experiences); matching or the Diderot effect (in which replacement of one element or item makes others look shabby and so sets off a further round of acquisition); and specialization (associated with the subdivision and demarcation of previously unified activities or singular products). Individually and in combination such mechanisms may well increase the level and volume of consumption in society. But as explanations of change, they focus on the acquisition of conspicuous and tangible objects rather than on practicalities of use.

Although one might analyse the first introduction of appliances like washing machines or freezers in terms of social comparison, novelty, or specialization, this is not an appropriate vocabulary with which to conceptualize the consumption of gas, water or electricity. In practice, few of the mechanisms identified above cope very well with the transformation of invisible systems, with infrastructural developments or with the 'escalation' of practice and service as opposed to the selection of discrete commodities. The limitation here is that goods and objects are analysed in isolation and without noticing the pre- and co-requisite systems and technologies on which they depend, or the reconfiguration of ideas, actions and habits associated with their use and appropriation.

To understand how routinized ways of life are situated and inscribed in tools, devices and material objects, it is necessary to go beyond these theories of consumption and break into territory more commonly occupied by sociologists of science and technology. This also makes sense when considering the *direction* as well as the rate of change. While the accounts of escalating demand sketched above offer more or less convincing explanations of increasing consumption, they have less to say about how it is that some routes are taken and not others.

Trajectories and Transitions

Initially used to explain why economically optimal forms of innovation are not always realized, the concept of path dependency highlights the extent to which existing technologies and practices structure avenues of future development. As defined by Rip and Kemp, 'path dependencies refer to the inter-relatedness of artifacts with other artifacts, infrastructure and routine' (Rip and Kemp 1998: 354). The classic example in this field is the persistence of the QWERTY keyboard (David 1985), a deliberately inefficient format but one that has become established in a manner now difficult to dislodge. Alignments between actors, along with sunk costs of various forms led, in this case, to a hardening of the 'path' such that it has become increasingly difficult to break away from the QWERTY arrangement.

Patterns of path dependency have consequences for change and stability at various levels: between firms, within technological communities, amongst users and across the plane of social meaning, convention and expectation. In making reversals and dramatic changes of direction difficult such configurations have the dual effect of cutting off otherwise plausible trajectories of sociotechnical development while paving the way for others. For present purposes, theories of path dependency and irreversibility have two advantages. First, they build on the idea that technologies and practices inter-relate. Second, they provide a way of conceptualizing and perhaps explaining the direction in which systems, technologies and practices evolve.

The concept of a 'sociotechnical regime' consolidates the notion that irreversibilities and path dependencies occur at different levels. The terminology of regime or landscape is generally used to characterize the rules, paradigms and dominant technologies framing current action and informing beliefs about what is and is not possible in the future. Hughes' (1983) *Networks of Power*, is a classic and compelling narrative of regime construction, detailing the development of the electricity system *and* the social relations and expectations that go with it. Embedded in institutions and infrastructures, regimes enable and constrain what goes on in the lower planes of Rip and Kemp's (1998) multi-level model of sociotechnical change. In this analysis, discussed more fully in Chapter 3, macro, meso and micro levels of sociotechnical change have their own dynamics but are none the less linked together, each being of consequence for the other.

The literature on regimes tends to emphasize technological interdependence and the part material systems and arrangements play in holding social practices together. Dealing more with the symbolism than the hardware of consumption, Douglas and Isherwood (1996) advance the view that social order is defined and reproduced through the rituals of everyday life; rituals that in turn confer meaning on goods, artifacts and even infrastructures. They claim, for instance, that goods are needed 'to make visible and stable the categories of culture' (Douglas and Isherwood 1996: 38), also arguing that relations of consumption are significant not simply because they are implicated in the management of boundaries between social groups or because they function as crucial media of communication but because 'they constitute the very system itself' (Douglas and Isherwood 1996: 49). This is a curiously dematerialized interpretation in the sense that it underplays the potentially constitutive role of things and sociotechnical systems. Even so, Douglas and Isherwood's insistence that practices have meaning alongside each other and as part of a total ensemble has much in common with the representation of regimes outlined above.

Such explanations make some sense of how conventions, technologies and social relations hang together but how do they change? For Douglas, sources of change are typically external to the society in question. Interaction *across* societal boundaries, of one form or another, is consequently critical both to the maintenance and to the redefinition of practice. Others elaborate on the conditions and contexts of change *within* societies.

Schot, Hoogma and Elzen (1994) suggest that new technologies and practices develop within safe havens or 'niches' protected from the demands and rigours of regular market conditions (Kemp, Schot and Hoogma 1998). As they explain, the boundaries of the sheltered 'nursery' extend as innovations are progressively embedded in society, as knowledge develops, as users become enrolled and as new technological and market conditions are formed. The temporal and spatial characteristics of this process differ from case to case, depending on the properties and characteristics of the surrounding sociotechnical landscape. In practice, there is no guarantee of success. Seedling innovations die all the time, in the nursery, in between the nursery and the wider world and in the wider world itself. The character and duration of the innovation journey is, in addition, likely to depend on the extent and nature of the difference between present social relations and those implied by prospective sociotechnical configurations. Developing this point, Abernathy and Clark (1985) distinguish between incremental and architectural innovation, reserving the latter term to describe situations in which the very architecture or framework of skills, competencies and expectations shared and required by users, consumers and producers is transformed. Defined in this way, architectural innovations represent a seismic shift in technology and practice powerful enough to change the landscape of opportunity and generate widespread obsolescence. The question of whether consumer-producer relations are stabilized or disrupted and reformulated by innovation focuses attention on the relationship *between* technological development, the market and society. This move is interesting for it implies that both the rate *and* direction with which demand evolves are the result of a double act involving innovative technologies and reconfigured markets. These contextualized analyses of sociotechnical change have two especially relevant features: they recognize the constant evolution of technology and practice, and they address the transformation of seemingly stable infrastructures and conventions.

Adding these fragments together, it would seem important to ground otherwise abstract sociological and economic propositions about the mechanisms of increasing consumer demand and relate them to specific contexts of sociotechnical change and innovation. After all, there has to be some direction to escalatory trends like those of work-spend or the pursuit of everlasting novelty. Sociologists of technology argue that at least some of this has to do with what has gone before and what scope this leaves for radical or incremental innovation in the future. Meanwhile, authors like Douglas and Isherwood (1996) focus on the restoration of social order, attributing change to external disturbance or to tension within the social system. Whatever their other qualities, these rather generalized accounts tell us little about how peoples' practices and conventions change from one day to the next. Studies of the relation between specific technologies and their users bring us closer to the detail of such transition.

Reconfiguring Practice

Domestic consumption of energy and water depends on the introduction of new consumer durables, on how such devices and resources are used and on the services they provide. For the most part, the sociology of consumption has concentrated on moments of acquisition rather than the consequent adjustment of what people do. So how does the stuff and substance of consumption relate to the ordering of everyday life and to concepts of normal and proper practice? Again a mixing of traditions is fruitful.

Less concerned with the engines of macro-economic change than with the co-evolution of the 'hybrid' objects with which we surround ourselves, authors like Akrich (1992), Latour (1992) and Bijker (1997) have sought to understand the mutual constitution of technologies and their consumers and users. The resulting repertoire of concepts promises to be of value in thinking about the escalation and standardization of comfort and cleanliness. The suggestion that technical objects 'define a framework of action together with the actors and the space in which they are supposed to act' (Akrich 1992: 208), has given rise to further discussion of processes like those of 'inscription', in which designers embed visions of future users in the things they make, and of 'de-scription' in which users react to those inscriptions. Work in this tradition prompts us to enquire how taken-for-granted but environmentally problematic practices are sustained and given form and shape by household infrastructures and familiar domestic technologies.

In an article explicitly concerned with sustainable design, Jelsma (1999) considers the forms of 'green' behaviour built into things like dishwashers, low flow showerheads and water efficient toilet cisterns. He asks how such devices script and thereby enforce an environmental morality upon their unsuspecting users. Can environmental consumption be 'hardwired' into the home? Answers are complicated not least because some technological scripts are more 'open' or 'resistable' than others, because scripts are, in any event, de-scribed in context, and because stories of failure – in which technologies are used in ways other than those intended – abound. For now, the notion of environmental scripting is useful in that it shows how technologies *might* stabilize or generate new practices. The idea of scripting does not, in itself, reveal much about the extent or direction of change or about how specific technologies and practices relate to more encompassing complexes of meaning, expectation and under-standing. In other words, there is still something of a gap between detailed analyses of individual devices and efforts to understand the co-evolution of inter-dependent suites or complexes of technology and convention.

In so far as technical systems and devices do configure their users (Woolgar 1991) it is important, and in social-environmental terms, vital, to think about their reach and the scope of their effect. The global diffusion of standardized appliances brings with it the prospect of correspondingly standardized routines and practices. Or at least it would do so if it were not for the fact that technolo-gies are rarely appropriated wholesale, or in pure form. Silverstone, Hirsch and Morley (1992) describe the process of appropriation as an active exercise in 'domestication'. As they explain, the politics of technology has as much to do with the locally specific dynamics of its incorporation, customization and conversion as with the conditions of design and production. Even so, and perhaps especially with regard to comfort and cleanliness, it is relevant to take note of global patterns of import and export: of where systems and ideas originate, of what messages they carry with them and of how these are constructed and reconstructed through local processes of appropriation. In other words, there is a geography of sociotechnical change to take account of too.

As well as scripting their users' actions, devices like washing machines and freezers inhabit a world of material culture: a world in which they, and the practices they engender, act as carriers and generators of meaning (Meintjes 2001). It is possible, and in fact quite usual, to consider the 'social life of things' (Appadurai 1986) and the symbolic aspects of their design, acquisition and use without reference to the sociotechnical scripting described above. But in thinking about how ordinary practices change, it is important to notice both aspects and to consider the relation between the two.

The reconfiguration of meaning is evidently important when the transformation of practice is not strongly related to technological development. Somewhat different concepts are therefore required to make sense of situations in which already familiar tools and infrastructures are put to different use or in which the social significance of practice is redefined. During the course of its long career, the bath has for instance featured as a symbol of social status, an instrument in the war against germs and a site of luxuriating relaxation. The material culture of the bathroom arguably represents a fluid but none the less concrete expression of societal value systems. Just as the meaning of the artifact has been rewritten over time, so has the practice and 'purpose' of bathing. Rationales and legitimizing discourses move in ways that are often difficult to follow and that frequently invoke complicated chains of scientific, moral and social judgement. Yet these shifting contexts of social and cultural positioning are of immediate consequence for what people do and for how they understand and make sense of their actions. In capturing these aspects of changing practice it will be necessary to borrow ideas and approaches from cultural studies, as well as from history and anthropology.

Having identified some of the theoretical ingredients with which the book works I now explain how these materials are deployed and how the chapters are organized.

Method and Approach

At one level, this book is about the reconfiguration of comfort, cleanliness and convenience. It looks at how expectations and practices change, at what rate, in what direction, and with what consequence for the consumption of environmentally critical resources like energy and water. It is not difficult to identify candidate explanations: the restless needs of capitalism; the co-evolution of sociotechnical systems; the reproduction of social orders and identities; the pursuit of novelty, the rejigging of symbolic structures – all these constitute plausible mechanisms. But not all are relevant for an analysis of routine and practice as opposed to invention, innovation and acquisition, and not all apply in equal measure, or all at once.

Despite being drawn from a variety of sub-disciplinary fields, the ideas outlined above none the less point in a certain direction. Theories of consumer demand have relatively little to say about the course and character of innovation. Concentrating, often implicitly, on demand for things or the meaning of objects, such analyses rarely attend to the uses and practices these goods afford and make possible. Picking up some of these threads, the sociology of technology has much to offer when thinking about pathways of change and the relation between human and non-human actors. However, this literature has been split between the study of large-scale systems and sometimes tiny devices. As a result, much remains to be said about the middle-range dynamics of sociotechnical change and the respecification not just of practice and action, but of more encompassing notions of symbolic order, propriety and service. The book takes up this challenge, linking theories of consumption, technology and practice, and doing so in a way that seeks to capture changes in the reach and scope of what people take for granted.

The environmental sub-plot offers a practical point of entry to what remains an ambitious theoretical enterprise. The decision to concentrate on aspects of everyday life that are moving in increasingly resource intensive directions limits the range of practices on which I might focus. I could have considered evolving patterns of mobility, food provisioning or waste management – all of which would have fitted this bill. But I had other conditions. I wanted to demonstrate the value of thinking about environment and consumption in terms of the collective redefinition of convention and need. I was therefore keen to select examples that, despite being of enormous environmental significance, do not usually figure in environmental debate. In policy terms, comfort and cleanliness constitute fine examples of non-negotiability, their meaning and importance being quite simply taken for granted. In addition, comfort, cleanliness and in a different sense, convenience are composite and complex achievements – a feature that confounds attempts to analyse them in terms of personal choice and individual commitment. The next step was easy. Sticking to the principle of following practices that are changing fast and doing so in ways that are environmentally problematic, I reduced comfort to a discussion of the indoor climate and air-conditioning, and investigated cleanliness in terms of bathing and laundering.

What follows consists of a somewhat eclectic mixture of historical material and evidence from a range of contemporary sources, from interviews and from different kinds of market research. I concentrate on Western societies, and especially on the UK and the USA, but I have no intention of surveying the current state of play in any one country, or of detailing potentially important differences of practice and expectation within the societies from which my examples are drawn. This is because I use discussion of the three Cs as a means of developing theories of social and technical transformation and in the process building an argument about the dynamics of changing practice. It is this that explains the structure of the book, the order in which examples are introduced and the uses to which they are put.

Starting with a relatively straightforward story, Chapter 2, 'the science of comfort: constructing normality', reviews the (re)construction of convention, analysing this as a path-dependent process of scientific development, technical embedding and conceptual naturalization. Told in this way, the specification and reproduction of comfort provides a fine illustration of the standardization and globalization of ultimately unsustainable expectation. Although it offers a plausible and in many ways predictable account of corporate and technical achievement in making as well as meeting consumer need, this analysis stops short on a number of counts. As a provider-dominated, technologically focused narrative it says little about what the scientific specification of comfort means for everyday life, for what people do or for the collective practices in which they engage.

Chapter 3, 'The co-evolution of comfort: interdependence and innovation', takes hold of these issues through a detailed discussion of the concept of co-evolution. The notion that technologies and practices co-evolve makes much intuitive sense, but exactly what is it that co-evolves with what? What is it that energizes co-evolutionary processes and what gives them direction? How do theories that underscore the co- aspect (that highlight various forms of interdependency) relate to those preoccupied with evolution and the explanation of novelty, change and innovation? In detailing the multiple dimensions of co-evolution this chapter has the further ambition of revealing and exploiting commonalities between theories of consumption and innovation. The result is a new menu of questions about how constellations of technology and practice evolve. Subsequent chapters elaborate on different aspects of this programme.

Chapter 4, 'Regimes of comfort: systems in transition', reviews arguments about the dynamics of meso- and macro-level change as represented in 'transition theory'. By relating this work, largely developed within the field of science and technology studies, to debate about the emergence of increasingly global patterns of consumption, this chapter considers the circulation and appropriation of products, practices and taken-for-granted arrangements *between* as well as within societies. Designed to illustrate and detail mechanisms of regime level change, this chapter looks at how conventions converge around the world.

Although the case of comfort is used to develop different strands of thought, Chapters 2 to 4 exploit the fact that in this arena, and in environmental terms, the introduction and diffusion of new techniques and technologies is of defining importance. But how do regimes of normal and ordinary practice evolve in contexts that are not so obviously subject to waves of technological development? The next three chapters work with examples relating to cleanliness, using these to explore alternative, but not necessarily incompatible, ways of conceptualizing change.

Chapter 5, 'Introducing cleanliness: morality, technology and practice' sets the scene by enlarging the discussion to take account of the moral and symbolic significance of practice. The cleanliness-related chapters (5 to 9) emphasize the positioning and repositioning of routine with reference to systems of social order and propriety, cognitive and classificatory systems and systems of meaning. In this they extend the representation of regimes developed in Chapter 4, moving the argument on by paying closer attention to what holds practices together and to how expectations and conventions arise and disappear.

Chapter 6, 'Behind the bathroom door: revolving rationales', analyses a selection of contemporary and historical accounts of personal bathing and showering. While the bathroom is itself a site of innovation, what counts – at least for energy and water consumption – is not so much the development of new technology as how already established devices like the bath and the shower are actually used. This chapter develops the proposition that culturally and historically specific rationales act as guides to practical action and as justifications of it. In looking at what these rationales are and how they fit together this chapter concentrates on the positioning of private practice within and with respect to generic societal concerns.

Chapter 7, 'Laundering: a system of systems', returns to issues of regime formation first raised in Chapter 3 but complicated by the intervening discussion of rationale, order and propriety. The problem is to understand how multiple sociotechnical systems intersect and what this intersection means for emergent understandings of 'service'. In trying to make sense of how laundry practices relate to stocks and types of fabric, to technologies of washing, drying and ironing, to soaps and detergents and to divisions and definitions of labour, this chapter describes different but inter-dependent avenues of sociotechincal change. In emphasizing the relation between co-existing 'systems' it offers another perspective on the definition and reproduction of cleanliness.

Chapter 8, 'Laundry habits: integrating practices' stays with the laundry in order to show how the intersecting systems of Chapter 7 have effect. How have new technologies, fabrics and products affected the routines and priorities of those who do the wash? In following the demise of boiling and the increasing importance of freshness, this chapter is at heart about the symbolic and practical work involved in maintaining and breaking from tradition.

Summarizing the insights and conclusions of Chapters 6 to 8, Chapter 9, 'System and service' takes stock of the different forms of integration – social, technical, symbolic, moral and practical – considered along the way. Adding bits of argument together, this chapter distinguishes between processes involved in the formation of regimes and in the specification of normal and necessary standards of 'service'. But there is one piece missing. How do the activities, injunctions and obligations discussed this far fit into the stream of everyday life?

Chapter 10, 'Convenience, co-ordination and convention', considers the temporal co-ordination and sequencing of ordinary activities on which the reproduction of conventions and standards depend. This proves to be an important move. It seems that new routines and habits are established and that concepts of normal and necessary service are redefined as people confront and cope with increasing pressures of time. While the idea of convenience legitimizes and sustains specific forms of consumption, convenience devices (things like freezers, washing machines and even showers) have the paradoxical effect of fragmenting activity, inadvertently exacerbating the sense of harriedness and generating demand for yet more convenient solutions. This chapter relates the sociotemporal structuring of society to patterns of sociotechnical development, showing how both keep systems of social and domestic obligation in place and how they compel them to change. In this it provides a set of ideas with which to make sense of comfort and cleanliness and of other routinely invisible dimensions of daily life.

This book appropriates and amalgamates concepts from the sociology of consumption and technology in the cause of better understanding the organizing frameworks of everyday life and how they evolve. The resulting mixture does not generate one all-encompassing theoretical model but it does produce a different way of thinking about the transformation of ordinary routines and habits. As the last chapter, 'Ratchets, pinwheels, cogs and spirals' explains, the effect is to focus attention on the formation of regimes and concepts of service, on how meanings, practices and technologies hold together and how integrative processes themselves influence the rate and direction of change.

2

The Science of Comfort: Constructing Normality

There is no doubting the rate and pace of *indoor* environmental change: over the last hundred years or so, conditions inside have changed significantly. Traditional methods of managing climatic variation, such as the siesta, are in decline. Meanwhile, people in cold climates have become used to wearing lightweight clothing all year round. Increasing dependence on resource-intensive heating and cooling technologies continues to drive energy demand and associated emissions of CO_2 and in this there is an ironic but problematic link between the dynamics of indoor climate change (especially cooling and the diffusion of air-conditioning) and those of global warming. Expectations of the indoor environment are evolving and apparently converging around the globe and around a concept of comfort that is immensely demanding to maintain and reproduce. The amount of energy and of artificial cooling required to sustain recognized standards of comfort in the fastest growing cities in the world is truly frightening. Partly because of this, there is increasing recognition that new, more environmentally forgiving specifications may be required. This is tricky because although notions of comfort have changed historically and between societies, engineers and designers are unlikely to flout established technical standards or challenge conditions of comfort that people have come to expect.

This chapter considers the making of comfort as a concept and as a material reality. It looks at how comfort has been defined and how commercial and scientific interests have together led to the specification of standards with which we are now familiar. As represented here, the story is quite straightforward. I argue that despite and partly because of the seemingly innocent goal of meeting peoples' needs, technical research (allied to commercial interest) has contributed to the convergence of indoor environmental conditions and the naturalization of ultimately unsustainable expectations and arrangements. In figuring out why meanings of comfort take the form they do today, I pay particular attention to the assumptions and priorities that have structured the scientific specification of human need. Whose knowledge and interests are embedded along the way and what difference has this made to the sizing and specification of heating and cooling technologies and the design of the built environment? This is not an especially novel line of questioning. Many other studies have taken a similar route, demonstrating how institutional and political factors shape the production of knowledge, the resolution of controversy and the course of technological innovation (MacKenzie 1990).

Taking a similar approach, but taking it a stage further, this chapter goes on to investigate the translation of science into (design) practice and the relation between design and social convention. Standards play a critical role in this mediation. International codes like those developed by the American Society of Heating Refrigeration and Air-conditioning Engineers (ASHRAE) prove to be immensely influential, acting as a common point of reference and as a co-ordinating mechanism powerful enough to align engineering and manufacturing practices around the world (Schmidt and Werle 1998). Also relevant for this discussion, the standards-making process has been built upon a distinctive yet contested genre of scientific enquiry. Representations of comfort as a standardized set of conditions conflict with those informed by 'field studies' demonstrating cultural variation in meaning, experience and expectation. Current controversy over the technical specification of thermal comfort is sociologically interesting on two counts. As well as illustrating the fluidity of a concept that is presented as 'natural' and unchanging, it highlights the close relationship between science, standards, markets and representations of consumer need. It is of further environmental relevance in that a more flexible approach to the definition of comfort promises to justify and legitimize less energy-intensive design solutions and stem the undoubtedly damaging convergence of convention and practice.

In reviewing the history of thermal comfort research and the standardization of the indoor climate this chapter tells a tale of escalating demand grounded in naturalizing and universalizing concepts of human need and sustained by equally global forms of commercial interest and professional expertise. In terms of the architecture and argument of the book as a whole, the chapter's primary purpose is to illustrate the social construction of energy consumption and to describe the historical development of conditions and conventions that are now taken for granted. It starts with the very idea of comfort, showing how its meaning has evolved. This puts contemporary definitions of comfort into context. The chapter goes on to show how human comfort has been specified and to detail the kind of research involved. As I explain, universalizing programmes of physiological enquiry have informed engineering standards that have, in turn, shaped the design of the built environment and the comfort-related expectations and experiences of those who inhabit it. In taking this course the chapter shows the malleability of the concept and how it has been reified and fixed in place. While biological definitions dominate, there are other equally 'scientific' ways of specifying what people need. Widespread adoption of the alternative so-called adaptive approach would involve reconceptualizing comfort (defining it as an achievement rather than an attribute) and would lead to the construction of a different sort of indoor environment. In considering this possibility, I conclude by reflecting on the extent to which scientific and commercial interests literally construct normality – building conditions and conventions at one and the same time.

The chapter concentrates on the design and management of the indoor climate, but begins with a more general review of comfort variously defined as a state of mind, an attribute and an achievement.

Defining Comfort: a State of Mind, an Attribute or an Achievement?

If you are sitting comfortably then I'll begin. These words, familiar to those who enjoyed the children's radio programme 'Listen with Mother', provide as good a starting point as any. Used to introduce the short story featured in each lunchtime episode, this phrase conjures up an image of cosy anticipation: it suggests a state of mind as well as a proper disposition of the body.

'Comfort', from the Latin verb 'confortare', was first 'adopted in Middle English with the meaning of mental or physical strength, encouragement or consolation' (Heijs 1994: 43). Such interpretations live on when giving someone a comforting hug or when writing words of comfort in times of trouble. A bibliographic search on the keyword 'comfort' consequently reveals innumerable references to religious books and pamphlets, many of them dealing with bereavement. Examples include, *To Begin Again: The Journey Toward Comfort, Strength, and Faith in Difficult Times* (Levy 1999), *The Needs of the Dying: A Guide for Bringing Hope, Comfort, and Love to Life's Final Chapter* (Kessler 2000), to pick just a few. These expressions of comfort have to do with sharing and support but there are other more individualistic formulations, as when someone claims to be comfortable with a decision or when they look forward to a comfortable retirement (Salisbury and Robinson 2001). Although comfort is generally a good thing, comfortable complacency is a danger to be guarded against, especially in business. A number of management texts offer advice and guidance on how to spot and eradicate this problem. O'Toole's (1995) book on *Leading Change: Overcoming the Ideology of Comfort and the Tyranny of Custom* positions comfort as a threat to business success as does Bardwick's volume of the same year, *Danger in the Comfort Zone: From Boardroom to Mailroom-How to Break the Entitlement Habit That's Killing*

American Business (Bardwick 1995). Although interpretations of comfort as a state of mind persist, other much more material definitions dominate.

In following the terminology of comfort from its initially spiritual meaning through to its modern incarnation as 'self-conscious satisfaction with the relationship between one's body and its immediate physical environment' (Crowley 2001: 142) the historian John Crowley notices that the explicit valuing of *physical* comfort represented an important shift of emphasis. With this shift, the terminology of comfort was applied to the means by which that state might be achieved as well as to the state itself. As Heijs explains, from being a subject-bound concept having to do with relations between people, comfort, 'developed into a more object bound term, also denoting worldly goods which could enhance mental and physical well-being.' (Heijs 1994: 43). Redefined in this way, comfort had to do with things, conditions and circumstances.

The pursuit of comfort consequently inspired practical programmes of action and enquiry. Writing of the eighteenth century, Crowley observes that political economists, moral philosophers, scientists, humanitarian reformers, and novelists 'sought to evaluate the relations of body, material culture, and environment in the name of physical comfort'. He continues 'They gave the term "comfort" a new physical emphasis as they reconceptualized values, redesigned material environments and urged the relearning of behaviours' (Crowley 1999: 750). Crowley claims that this led to a further naturalizing of the concept and of the conditions associated with it. In explaining that the achievement of comfort legitimized new forms of consumption, Crowley notes that the term was 'increasingly applied to a middle ground between necessity and luxury' (Crowley 1991: 758). As such it provided a useful benchmark for social reform, offering a point of reference against which to assess 'normal' societal entitlements. This implicitly *universalized* understanding of need allowed philanthropic reformers to assert 'a common humanity on the basis of physical comfort' (Crowley 1999: 772). Soon enough, the goal of providing and achieving conditions of comfort required no further explanation. Illustrating this way of thinking, the UK's Chartered Institution of Building Services Engineers (CIBSE) marked its hundredth anniversary with a short volume entitled the *Quest for Comfort* (Roberts 1997). As well as justifying a century of engineering, the title suggests that comfort exists independent of the means and technologies by which it is produced and known.

This is not necessarily the case. Although entitlements to comfort are taken for granted, it is not always clear quite what that involves. When comfort is materialized and defined as an attribute, for example of clothing or furniture, it makes sense for designers and manufacturers to develop and deliberately enhance this feature, selling comfort as an aspect of what they produce. But what is this quality and who defines it?

Writing about the history of the chair, Giedion (1948) concludes that definitions of comfort reflect the relative influence of upholsterers, engineers and scientists. He illustrates this point with reference to French furniture of the 1850s. Upholsterers were, he claims, especially influential in constructing concepts of comfort embodied in a singularly 'boneless' type of chair known as the 'confortable'. Initially unusual in being totally covered in fabric and tassels and in having huge arms but no visible legs, squashy arrangements of this kind dominate the furniture showrooms of today. The fact that conventionally comfortable chairs and sofas rarely provide support of the kind that the human body 'requires' points to a rift between concepts of comfort as represented in the popular aesthetics of furnishing and those based upon the systematic study of backs and bones.

Anatomical and ergonomic analyses of posture and position, twinned with medical research into the causes and characteristics of back pain, has resulted in a wealth of data relevant for the specification of 'comfortable' seating (Cranz 1998). The trouble is that what ergonomic researchers recommend does not translate into chairs that people find comfortable, leading Cranz to reach the ergonomically unhappy conclusion that 'People seem to respond more to their *ideas* about comfort than to their actual physical experience of it' (Cranz 1998: 113). Anxieties about public health, child development and productivity have, however, prompted the development of European design standards and, in this context, science is the undisputed arbiter of need.

Giedion's work raises one other issue important for the specification of comfort. His discussion of the design and function of moveable medieval chests and stools, the specialization of dressers, desks and shaving tables, and the evolution of rocking and reclining chairs is at the same time an account of the societies in which such devices made sense. In other words his history of furniture is also a history of eating, storing and sleeping and of how these practices relate to concepts of well being, propriety and comfort. In a subtle but critical switch of perspective it is possible, and perhaps sensible, to view chairs, dressers, tables, and so forth, not as embodying comfort but as the tools with which this state is *achieved*. It is obviously difficult to specify the relation between objects and the meanings and experiences they make possible. Yet it is clear that the process of being and making oneself comfortable stretches beyond the appropriation and use of individual commodities, even when those objects are imbued with attributes of comfort.

In commenting on the changing meanings of comfort, I have highlighted a number of key developments, starting with the eighteenth-century redefinition of comfort as a physical condition and as something that people have a right to expect. Examples from the history of furnishing show the specification of comfort to be a contested topic. They also show the relevance of scientific enquiry as a means of determining human need and establishing universally applicable standards. The representation of comfort as an attribute, rather than as an achievement, has also dominated the history of thermal comfort research and the design of the built environment. One consequence is that what were 'wide, and in large part discretionary, social variations in consumption patterns regarding heating and lighting' (Crowley 2001: x), have converged around a remarkably narrow specification of normal and appropriate conditions indoors. In the next sections I look at how this has come about and how is it that so many people spend their days in an environment that wavers little around 22 °C and that stays the same all year round, whatever the weather outside.

Playing God with the Indoor Climate

Bellows, spits, trivets, tripods, firedogs and ingle-nooks went through successive rounds of development but it was not until the eighteenth century that heating and cooking attracted sustained scientific and technical interest. Crowley suggests that 'as the value of physical comfort became more explicit and desirable, the technology of its improvement gained intellectual prestige' (Crowley 2001: 171). For this and other reasons there seems to have been an explosion of enthusiasm for redesigning all manner of things about the house. Even the most humble arrangements came in for serious and increasingly systematic study. Driven by a commitment to improving the basic technologies of the home, key figures like Benjamin Franklin and Benjamin Thompson, better known as Count Rumford, turned their attention to the physics of thermal efficiency and the basic principles of the open fire and the stove. Much preoccupied with the causes and cures of smoky chimneys, theirs was a measured and explicitly scientific approach.

Count Rumford's views on method underline his reliance on rigorous experimentation. He writes as follows: 'In attempts to improve, it is always desirable to know exactly what progress has been made – to be able to measure the distance we have laid behind us in our advances' (Roberts 1997: ii). The results of Rumford's experimental work resulted in designs that undoubtedly enhanced conditions for many. The 'Rumford' fireplace, which had spayed sides to throw heat back into the room and a narrow throat to optimize the chimney's draw, increased efficiency so dramatically that some reportedly found it 'too hot' (Wright 1964: 114). The application of experimental method generated new understanding of the processes of convection and radiation and in turn inspired what Heschong describes as a 'flurry of effort to design the perfect furnace' (Heschong 1979: 14).

Despite being hailed as the 'apostle of comfort' (Wright 1964: 113), Count Rumford and other gentlemen scientists of his time were not concerned to detail the optimal conditions and characteristics of the indoor environment. Their more immediate goal was to enhance the performance and output of heating and cooking devices. Such endeavours were guided by a theory of progress and improvement and by ambitions of reducing smoke, increasing efficiency and lowering cost. But at this point the definition of comfort was not itself an issue. The science of comfort, that is the scientific study of comfort conditions, came later and came as a consequence of the capacity to 'play god' with the indoor climate. Partly inspired by the likes of Franklin and Rumford, the development of heating and cooling technologies went hand in hand with new methods of measurement and control and by the 1920s it was possible to chill, warm, humidify, ventilate and modify the indoor climate reliably and with some precision. It was at this point that it became necessary to ask and to answer the question: 'what should the indoor environment be like'?

At the time when this issue first arose, climatological theories about the relation between civilization, progress, performance and human behaviour were the subject of much debate. Huntington's *Civilization and Climate*, published in 1915, was, for instance, concerned to explain why 'people of European races are able to accomplish the most work and have the best health' (Huntington 1924: 6). Given the ideological, political, not to mention racial significance of these ideas, the prospect of air-conditioning was of immense importance: here was a 'tool that would allow all humanity to progress beyond the accidents of climate' (Ackerman 2002: 41). Who knew what social and geographical consequences might follow the artificial cooling of the tropics and the consequent unleashing of mental and physical productivity until then believed to be sapped and stifled by the natural climate?

Although no longer viewed in quite these terms, the capacity to manipulate indoor climates at will generates a number of still disquieting questions about the relation between nature and civilization. Manufactured weather is a key ingredient in utopian visions of the future. A Stram Steel brochure that makes the point explicitly 'Modernism means air-conditioning . . . How refreshing to step into your home and know in advance that the temperature and humidity will be just right' (Ackerman 2002: 87). But at what price do we cut ourselves off from nature? It is one thing to modify the elements but when buildings are constructed as climatic fortresses, the symbolic division between a managed interior and an unruly and unpredictable world outside is ever more strongly pronounced.

Whether at home, in the car, or at work people inhabit a protected bubble of artificial climate, the conditions and characteristics of which have been determined by scientific research. One doesn't have to reach far into the sociological literature to come upon the idea that science, far from being the solution, is at the root of many of society's ills (Beck 1992). Sure enough, the very uniformity of the indoor environment is itself a cause for concern: is it right to keep 'human' animals indoors all the time? What has been lost (the sensation of thermal variation, fresh air, a connection with the natural rhythms of the day and the year, and so forth) and gained (increasing incidence of asthma, sick building syndrome . . .) by constructing the man-made environments in which we spend so much of our day? This kind of lingering unease is given dramatic expression in Philip Kerr's (1995) novel, *Gridiron*. This is a story of a high-tech building, the sophisticated controls of which are taken over by the software of a child's computer game. Consistent with conventions of the game, and the genre, the building turns its considerable armoury of indoor climate controls back upon its unfortunate inhabitants, destroying them one by one. The moral is clear: don't play god with the weather.

This warning acquires other more sinister overtones when we recall the global environmental costs of maintaining what we now think of as comfortable conditions inside. In a prophetic statement, Huntington, author of *Civilization and Climate*, observes that 'each advance in our so-callled control of nature makes us more dependent than before upon the continued existence not only of the artificial conditions which we create, but upon the natural conditions which alone make it possible to create the artificial conditions' (Ackerman 2002: 144). On reflection, it is extremely strange that so much energy and effort should be invested in controlling nature in order to construct conditions that suit the supposedly natural needs of the human body.

The next sections consider the history and the role of thermal comfort research in an attempt to explain how this situation has come about. Initially established in industry laboratories in the 1920s, thermal comfort research was designed to determine and define what conditions should be like indoors. Now undertaken in universities and specialist research groups, the study of thermal comfort involves a range of disciplines including building physics, ergonomics and modelling. It is a complicated field in which debates are full of technical detail. Cutting through many of the subtleties, I show how the idea of comfort as an attribute has been operationalized and specified through successive programmes of mostly physiological enquiry.

Quantifying Comfort

Compared with cold blooded creatures, human beings are soft, thin skinned and vulnerable: things soon go wrong if they get too hot, cold, wet or dry. People none the less live in an immense variety of climatic conditions including the tropical, the arctic and the arid. Protected by shelters ranging from the thin fabric of a tent to the thick ice blocks of an igloo, they have found ways of modifying the thermal variability of the outdoor environment. As Humphreys observes, the management of comfort 'pre-dates by thousands of years the development of the theory of heat exchange' (Humphreys 1995: 5). But because building scientists, architects, designers, engineers and technical experts have come to take an essentially physiological view of human comfort so much for granted, this reminder comes as something of a shock.

The 'heat balance model' to which Humphreys refers describes the physical relationship between a person and his or her environment, comfortable 'neutrality' being that state in which the heat generated by the human body is equal to the heat transferred away. It is worth highlighting two features of this foundational model. First, and as Brager and de Dear explain 'Heat balance models view the person as a passive recipient of thermal stimuli and are premised on the assumption that the effects of a given thermal environment are mediated exclusively by the physics of heat and mass exchanges between body and environment' (Brager and de Dear 1998: 84). Second, and related to this, the model predicts that people will report being comfortable given the right environmental conditions.

With this as a common starting point, physiological studies have led to successive revision of what were initially static and relatively simple descriptions of thermal optimization. Caught up in the seemingly endless quest for better understanding of the dynamic relation between bodies and their environments, terms of analysis have been refined, new parameters included and the scope of enquiry extended to take account of, sound, lighting and smell. Exploiting the potential afforded by the latest computer technologies, physiological models are now able to detail the thermal properties of 9,000 parts of the body and to simulate the dynamics of blood and tissue heat transfer as well as the operation of sensations, nerve endings and layers of skin.

To figure out how and why this kind of research has informed the specification of comfort, we need to reflect on the types of questions it promises to clarify and the sort of knowledge it generates.

Questions and Agendas

In *Home: A short history of an idea*, Rybczynski (1987: 220) argues that mass production, industrialization and the possibilities of indoor climate control transformed the meaning of comfort 'not only qualitatively but also quantitatively'. The possibility of manufacturing just about any kind of indoor environment went hand in hand with the ability to control and measure key (reproducible) parameters like those of temperature, humidity, and ventilation. Since nature offered ready-made models of climatic perfection it made sense to use this new found capacity to analyse and reproduce already idealized environments. To begin with, American air-conditioning manufacturers of the 1920s harboured varied ambitions including those of bringing the 'best of the beach' indoors, or recreating the fresh breezes of a mountain resort (Cooper 1998). But which conditions were 'best'? This was contested territory, especially as the idea of indoor climate control conflicted with popular and medical theories about the value of fresh air and natural ventilation.

Thermal comfort research undertaken at the American Society of Heating and Ventilating Engineers (ASHVE) saved the day, leading to the specification of just one ideal climate defined through the quantitative analysis of mechanically reproducible parameters. The 'Comfort Zone', defined by Houghten and Yaglou (from the ASHVE) in 1923, took into account heat and humidity. This specification had a decisive role in closing debate and doing so in a manner that suited the industry's interests. Summarizing the social and commercial importance of this development, Cooper writes as follows: 'The drive for quantitative accuracy was fuelled not only by the need for accurate information on which to build effective designs, but also by the desire to supply engineers with the surety of quantitative values in the rugged debate before the public in general and regulatory agencies in particular' (Cooper 1998: 70). In effect, scientific study of the human body resolved otherwise endless discussion about what engineers and designers should do, how the fledgling heating and cooling industry should be regulated and how competing technologies might be evaluated.

The research-based quantitative specification of comfort had the further, perhaps more significant, effect of creating and shaping markets. For air-conditioning manufacturers the basic challenge was not so much that of meeting human need (whatever that might be) but of turning comfort into a mass commodity and of making it into a consumer product that could be actively promoted, desired and delivered. In all of this, it was an enormous advantage to invoke scientific evidence. And it was even better when such evidence proved that given the vagaries of the weather just about everyone needed the product in question. Cooper puts it precisely: 'When it was shown that no natural climate could consistently deliver perfect comfort conditions, air-conditioning broke free of its geographic limits. When no town could deliver an ideal climate, all towns became potential markets for air-conditioning' (Cooper 1998: 78). In short, the quantification and specification of an ideal and ideally consistent environment, defined in terms of temperature, humidity and so forth, constituted a really significant breakthrough in constructing comfort as a marketable concept and in the normalization of man-made weather.

Physiology – as a discipline – had two qualities that made it ideally suited to the task of specifying comfort *and* of generating conclusions that would apply everywhere and to everyone. First, it took comfort to be a natural condition in the sense that it could be defined and analysed in terms of human biology. Second, it generated precise, quantitative results that were difficult to contest. The science of thermal comfort, as developed from the 1920s on, has had the straightforward ambition of revealing and better understanding natural physiological responses, but the comments above suggest that this is not an entirely neutral enterprise. Reviewing the field in 1993, Nigel Oseland concludes that the knowledge produced by conventional thermal comfort studies is of a type that legitimizes air-conditioning and that relates to the needs of that industry. Research in this tradition is, he says, of little value to those designing buildings to make use of solar energy. Put simply, 'Passive design requires thermal comfort information of a quite different kind, since the interest no longer focuses on thermostat settings, control bands, and cycling times' (Oseland and Humphreys 1993: 35). This observation underlines the extent to which comfort research has revolved around the taken for granted agendas of those who manufacture and specify equipment and the degree to which questions and methodologies correspond. My next step is to show how the resulting models and concepts of comfort have found their way into the real world.

From Laboratory to Design Guide

Ole Fanger was surely not the first to study the components of comfort but his work has been enormously influential in practice (Fanger 1970). Taking Fanger's equation as a kind of case study, this section follows the operationalization of comfort research and its incorporation into design guides and international standards. Inspired by what he refers to as the 'the basic rule of ergonomics' (Oseland and Humphreys 1994: 12), Fanger's stated ambition was to help designers produce buildings that meet users' needs – no easy matter given individual variations of size, sex, age and fitness and given that these factors have implications for metabolic rate and skin area. No one set of conditions will satisfy the physiological requirements of a variety of human-thermal systems (i.e. people) and as buildings are generally occupied by a variety of such persons, compromises must be made.

Tackling this problem head on, Fanger undertook extensive programmes of laboratory-based research with the aim of identifying the 'quantitative conditions' necessary to obtain not perfect but 'optimal thermal comfort'. His research subjects were exposed to different conditions in carefully controlled climate chambers. As well as measuring skin temperature at different parts of the body, their experience of comfort was assessed by means of a standardized questionnaire. Using this instrument, respondents' feelings were recorded on a seven-point scale ranging from hot to warm, slightly warm, neutral, slightly cool, cool and cold. The laboratory environment allowed Fanger to vary and quantify the relative significance of six dimensions including metabolic rate, clothing, air temperature, radiant temperature, air velocity and humidity. Taking subjects' expressions of thermal 'neutrality' to indicate comfort, Fanger used the results of this research to develop a general equation by means of which he contends that it is 'possible, for any activity level and any clothing, to calculate all combinations of air temperature, mean radiant temperature, relative velocity and air humidity, which will create optimal thermal comfort for man' (Fanger 1970: 15).

Providing the six dimensions of comfort can be controlled (again we see that this line of enquiry assumes the use of mechanical heating and cooling), Fanger's equation makes it possible to predict, specify and so design optimal conditions, that is conditions under which most people will report being satisfied or thermally neutral most of the time. This represents a vital step in the translation of science into practice. Before considering the uses to which such equations have been put, I want to highlight three generic features of the approach.

Although comfort is defined both by Fanger and by ASHRAE's Standard 55 – which is based on his work – as 'that condition of mind which expresses satisfaction with the environment' (Fanger 1970: 14) the body is treated as a physiological system. This being the case, the scientist's role is to identify, with as much precision as possible, the objective conditions that engender thermally neutral, or comfortable, responses. Shifting fields a little, MacAndrew and Edgerton criticize the sort of reasoning that characterizes this kind of research. Their extensive cross-cultural study of drunken comportment leads them to challenge the claim that drinkers lose control of themselves because of alcohol's toxic effect on the central nervous system. Arguing that being drunk is a cultural achievement and not simply the result of chemical or neurological change, they reach the following conclusion: 'if we are ever to understand drunken comportment, we must focus on the shared understandings of the nature of drunkenness that obtain among men living together in societies' (MacAndrew and Edgerton 1969: 171). Turned back to the case in question, the implication is that experiences of heat and cold might be similarly mediated through shared understandings, not of drunkenness, but of comfort. But having framed questions of comfort as questions about the relation between the human body and its environment, thermal comfort researchers are unable to acknowledge or accommodate cultural variation. Personal characteristics (and therefore thermal sensations) may differ widely, but the guiding assumption is that experiences of comfort are determined by the same basic principles of physiology.

Second, Fanger's comfort equation is based on an accumulation of data from a large number of individual cases. The process of averaging in order to achieve a norm is extremely familiar, but is again one that deserves a moments reflection. David Armstrong shows how comparable methods helped construct what he refers to as the 'normal' patient. Careful surveying and quantitative analysis made it possible to identify the mean height and weight of children at different stages of their development. With this statistical benchmark in place, deviance and abnormality came into existence along with the 'normal' child (Armstrong 1983). Standardized comfort equations, also built upon averaged data, have similar effect. They too anchor definitions of optimal or 'normal' conditions in a statistical mean. The result is unambiguous but it is also an artefact of the process of its production. When statistical normality is taken to represent normality in the 'real world', the range of practices and conditions that might be so described is inevitably narrowed. This represents a further mechanism through which science 'creates' normality and is again not unique to this field.

Third, it is useful to recall the purpose and context of Fanger's work. Presented as a general theory of comfort, his research was, as he says himself, designed to inform the specification of air-conditioning systems. This orientation, together with the two features just described (namely, the assumption of social and cultural neutrality and the reliance on statistical normalization), are embedded in Fanger's work and in the engineering standards and design guides that depend on it.

From Design Guide to Practice

One reason for focusing on Fanger's research is that it provides the basis for ASHRAE Standard 55, *Thermal Environmental Conditions for Human Occupancy* (ASHRAE 1992). First released in 1966, this standard informs national codes in Australia, Canada, China, Hong Kong, Jamaica, Malaysia, New Zealand, Pakistan, the Philippines, Singapore, South Korea and Thailand (Janda and Busch 1994). Other internationally relevant standards such as ISO 7730 also incorporate Fanger's Predicted Mean Vote-Predicted Percentage Dissatisfied thermal comfort index. Despite sometimes important differences of detail, for instance, the ASHRAE Standard prescribes a range of acceptable temperatures whereas the International Standards Organization (ISO) provides a method for their calculation, all share and reproduce the core assumptions outlined above.

The consequences for the built environment and for sales of heating and cooling equipment have been tangible. Although ASHRAE standards are not mandatory, American engineers and designers are reluctant to waver from them and since 'it is hard to meet the standard's narrow definition of thermal comfort without mechanical systems' (Brager and de Dear 2000: 22), the effects are predictable. Nick Baker is probably right to conclude 'that the very existence of definable standards for mechanically-conditioned building has been the main cause for the proliferation of air-conditioning' (Baker 1993: 130).

Going full circle, the controlled laboratory conditions of thermal comfort research have generated insights and conclusions that have in turn inspired and justified the development of controlled, laboratory-like, environments in the real world. Reporting on a comparative study of workers employed in international style office buildings, de Dear found that Singaporeans and Danes responded in the same way and in a manner perfectly consistent with Fanger's model (de Dear 1994: 130). This perhaps suggests that the model, and the codes and standards derived from it, really do capture and permit the reproduction of universally comfortable conditions. That is one interpretation. Another, and one supported by de Dear's discovery that in their naturally ventilated homes Singaporeans responded 'quite differently and inconsistently with the prediction of these models' (de Dear 1994: 130), is that employees' expectations have changed *because* of the spread of mechanical heating and cooling. It is at least possible that in determining what people 'need', the science of comfort has allowed designers to produce buildings and systems that meet and at the same time create expectations of comfort.

Before jumping to conclusions about the relationship between science, standardization and consumption it is as well to realize that for almost all its history, thermal comfort research has been in a state of increasingly explosive crisis. The next section considers these tensions and their implications for the theory, practice and future of comfort.

Qualifying Comfort

While there are methodological differences between laboratory-based research and that undertaken in the field, the fault lines of controversy do not simply mirror differences between quantitative and qualitative traditions. The terminology of qualification is none the less appropriate because field studies have the common effect of *qualifying*, that is, of complicating, refining and sometimes refuting the view of comfort as a psycho-bio-thermal attribute.

Although undoubtedly dominant, the tradition of physiological research on which ASHRAE and ISO standards are based is not the only paradigm in town. From Bedford's pioneering work in 1936 onwards, teams of comfort researchers have also been studying people in their 'natural' habitats, that is, in homes, workplaces and the open air (Humphreys and Nicol 1998: 991). Whether designed to check the validity of laboratory results or driven by the conviction that the achievement of comfort is at heart a social process, field studies have shown people to be comfortable (or to be more precise, they show that people say they are comfortable in response to standard survey questions) under remarkably different conditions and under conditions that fall way beyond the margins of physiologically specified comfort zones. To give just a few examples, Nicol found Pakistani workers to be comfortable at temperatures of up to 31 °C (Nicol 1999: 271). At the other extreme, people have reported being comfortable indoors at around 6 °C during an Antarctic winter (Goldsmith 1960). Focusing on European differences, more recent research described by Stoops indicates that Portuguese office employees are content with a much wider range of seasonal variation (up to 5 °C) than Swedes who do not expect indoor environments to waver by more than half a degree (Stoops 2001). As Humphreys' (1976) catalogue of field studies suggests, this list could go on and on.

There are two ways of responding to findings such as these. One is to extend the scope of laboratory-based studies in the hope of resolving or at least accommodating observed discrepancies between actual and predicted experience. The other is to treat insights into how people behave in the real world as relevant and revealing data in their own right. Exemplifying the latter approach, researchers at the more radical end of the adaptive spectrum have sought to understand the social, technical and economic dynamics of comfort. Their approach to question 'what makes people comfortable?' and hence what sorts of buildings should be provided, is best illustrated by Humphreys' (1995) article 'Temperatures and the Habit of Hobbits'.

Adaptive Opportunity

Imagining a trip to Tolkein's Middle Earth, Humphreys speculates on the strategies thermal comfort researchers might adopt to discover, specify and recreate optimal environments for members of Hobbit society. While the driving question – how to meet Hobbits' needs? – resembles that which has preoccupied laboratory researchers, Humphreys advocates a more direct approach, starting with observation. 'We would', he says, 'measure the thermal conditions inside a sample of occupied Hobbit holes. We would observe which rooms they most frequented. We might notice in what circumstances Hobbits opened or closed doors and windows or stoked up the fire to control the hole-temperature. We would notice what the Hobbits chose to wear from their enormous stock of clothing' (Humphreys 1995: 3). 'In the course of our enquiries', he continues, 'we would have learned to know a good Hobbit hole when we saw one, and we would have also learned a good deal about the preferences and adaptive strategies of Hobbits in their quest for comfort' (Humphreys 1995: 4). Happily, there would be no need to subject hobbits to 'invasive measurements or tiresome experimental routines' (Humphreys 1995: 4). In practice, ethnographic investigation should generate all one needs to know to produce comfortable Hobbit accommodation.

The key point is that by 'comfortable' Humphreys means an environment that offers sufficient possibilities for adjustment and adaptation: in other words an environment in which Hobbits can *make themselves* comfortable. This way of thinking involves a fundamental conceptual shift. Instead of being defined and analysed as an attribute, comfort is viewed as an achievement. Accordingly, conditions count as comfortable when they offer varied, flexible and socially as well as technically viable means of avoiding discomfort (Leaman and Bordass 1995: 4). The substance of what people, or even Hobbits, count as comfort (or discomfort) is another matter, and one that might be expected to vary with the outdoor temperature as well as with history and culture.

This way of thinking makes sense of otherwise perplexing observations that people adjust to different (and even similar) conditions over time, not just physiologically, but in the sorts of responses and strategies they adopt. Viewed as a dynamic enterprise, the achievement of comfort is here understood as a creative process of trading, juggling and manipulation whether of clothes, activity, and daily routine, or of building technologies like windows and heating systems. From this perspective, movement between contrasting thermal conditions is not necessarily a problem for designers to resolve. It is simply part of inhabitants' ordinary experience. For Heschong (1979) such variation is in fact an important source of pleasure and 'thermal delight'. Brager and de Dear make a similar point, arguing that 'current control strategies typically adopt a building-centred, energy consuming approach that focuses on creating constant, uniform neutrality-conditions which might actually be perceived by some as thermal monotony or sensory deprivation.' (Brager and de Dear 1998: 93). There are, of course, cultural and conventional limits to what counts as acceptable variety, as well as historically specific material, technological and economic constraints and possibilities. In this regard it is relevant to notice that comfort strategies have changed *because of* the diffusion of standardized mechanically controlled conditions. Taking this as an example of everyday adaptation, Humphreys describes the intersection of social and technical expectation as follows:

> if a building is set, regularly, at, say, 22 °C the occupants will choose their clothing
> so that they are comfortable at that temperature. If enough buildings are controlled

at this temperature, it becomes a norm for that society at that period of its history, and anything different is regarded as 'uncomfortable', even though another generation might have preferred to wear more clothing and have cooler rooms, or to wear less clothing and have warmer rooms. (Humphreys 1995: 10)

Although sociologically plausible, observations about the relative and social status of comfort present practical problems for designers and engineers. What does the adaptive paradigm mean for them, for manufacturers and for the ability to design and specify conditions in which people are (or can make themselves) comfortable? How can designers cope if meanings of comfort vary so from one context to another? Should ethnographic research be undertaken in advance of *each* new building? Is there any role for ASHRAE guidelines or for other such globalizing standards and if so, what might that be?

Taken to heart, the logic and philosophy of the adaptive approach legitimizes the provision of multiply varied indoor climates. As well as extending and enriching expectations of comfort such a strategy would also promote the thrill of difference. In other fields of ordinary consumption cultural diversity is increasingly valued so why not also in the domain of comfort? More modestly, designers might be encouraged to produce buildings that allow occupants control over their immediate environment and enhance what Baker and Standeven have called 'adaptive opportunity' (Baker and Standeven 1995). Despite advocating a spectrum of more and less challenging responses, proponents of the adaptive model generally agree that existing standards are not universally applicable, that they ignore important contextual influences and that it is misleading to view people as passive recipients of given conditions (Brager and de Dear 1998: 83). The general effect of all this is to favour culturally and climatically specific design solutions and to justify more flexible specifications.

In environmental terms, these are welcome developments for it has long been clear that the maintenance of thermal comfort, as enshrined in ASHRAE standards, is an unsustainably energy intensive enterprise. 'Single-temperature standards' are, claim Nicol and Roaf, 'costly to the economy, to architecture and to the environment' (Nicol and Roaf 1996). Something has to change but since ASHRAE's standards are founded on a bedrock of scientific evidence they cannot be abandoned overnight. What is required, and what adaptive researchers are endeavouring to produce, is an equally 'scientific' body of evidence on which to base and justify design guides that are 'sympathetic to the climates and cultures of the world and sustainable in the energy that they require' (Humphreys and Nicol 1998: 1002).

Adaptive Science

However meaningful and relevant, studies of how people make themselves comfortable in different societies do not generate self-evidently generalizable knowledge of the kind on which the standards making process has come to depend. This presents a number of methodological challenges: what sort of evidence is required to justify revising standards along adaptive lines and is the production of such compatible with the basic tenets of the adaptive philosophy? Can adaptive science filter through from research to design guide and so to practice? Put another way, can what Disco and van der Meulen (1998) call 'cosmopolitan' knowledge be abstracted from necessarily localized studies of convention and habit, and if so, how?

One methodological response is to aggregate. Humphreys' meta-analysis of thirty-six field studies is in this tradition (Humphreys 1976). Researchers have subsequently drawn increasingly detailed volumes of data from what they revealingly refer to as 'field experiments' in an effort to isolate relevant variables through careful sifting and comparison (Brager and de Dear 1998). Such exercises have led to a number of conclusions. Humphreys' analysis indicated that preferred indoor temperatures related to the weather outside. Although not the whole story, this simple insight suggested the possibility and the value of producing standards that explicitly 'link the indoor comfort temperature to the outdoor temperature throughout its seasonal and geographical variation' (Humphreys 1995: 9).

A second response is to develop criteria with which to refine and customize standards to suit specific conditions, fashions and customs. By studying how and when people adjusted windows, fans and clothing in response to change across a range of climatic conditions Nicol and colleagues have sought to produce design guidelines appropriate for the specific culture and context in which they were working. The conclusion they draw from this experience is that it is possible to design internationally applicable methodologies for specifying variable-temperature standards that exploit existing knowledge about clothing and climate related habits (Nicol and Roaf 1996; Nicol *et al.* 1999).

Before considering proposals to revise ASHRAE standards along some of these lines it is worth pausing to take stock of the adaptive sciences. What assumptions and ideas do they carry with them and what might therefore be carried through to the built environment? Three features are especially relevant. First, when comfort is defined as a sociotechnical achievement, the human body is no longer the primary point of reference. What matters more are the conventions according to which people order their environments. By implication comfort, like drinking or drug taking (Becker 1963), is an acquired habit and one equally laden with meaning. Observation of peoples' practice may reveal apparently consistent patterns but these are not to be assumed in advance or extrapolated from the laws of physics and human biology.

Second, although research in the adaptive tradition makes use of statistical normalization – as in laboratory studies individual preferences are averaged and note is take of what those averages are – interpretations are typically qualified with reference to the society or context from which data are drawn. Hence it is possible to show that Pakistanis, on average, prefer different conditions to those favoured by Swedes. Used in this way, averaging has the potential to reveal diversity and expand rather than contract definitions of comfort.

Third, and perhaps most important of all, studies of how people make themselves comfortable are methodologically open-ended. Because there are no variables to control, no prior assumptions need be made about the dimensions of optimization or the components of comfort. Researchers need not confine their attention to those features of the indoor environment that can be mechanically controlled: if people make themselves comfortable by other means, that is just as relevant. In the event, field studies *may* show that the achievement of comfort has come to depend upon air-conditioning but research of this kind does not in itself underpin such developments.

Because of these features the adaptive sciences occupy an uncertain and ambivalent position with respect to the industries of the indoor environment, to standards-making bodies and to the markets that both sustain. Humphreys and Nicol themselves recognize that 'a change in the philosophy behind the provision of thermal comfort will result inevitably in changes in the industry that designs, supplies, installs, and maintains the requisite hardware and software' (Humphreys and Nicol 1998: 1002). Wholesale adoption of the adaptive model might render current standards redundant, perhaps creating demand for new codes with which to specify the range of adaptive opportunities that buildings afford, or for anthropological advice on how to tailor designs to suit specific cultures. In effect, the theoretical framing of comfort as an achievement results in a style of thermal research that is, on the face of it, likely to inform the development of a more varied and a more flexible built environment than that constructed according to current ASHRAE standards.

Adaptive Standards

The prospect of rebuilding concepts of comfort along these lines is some way off, if it happens at all. Yet there are interesting developments afoot. Proposed revisions to ASHRAE Standard 55-1992 include an 'optional method for determining acceptable thermal conditions in naturally conditioned spaces' (ASHRAE 2001: 22). This might not sound like much, especially as it will make no difference to the design of air-conditioned buildings, but the very idea represents a significant breakthrough at the level of theory and approach. In detail, the proposition is to introduce guidelines that take due account of research showing how thermal preferences change in relation to outdoor weather and climate (Brager and de Dear 2000). A second less dramatic move is to remind designers that although it is customary to assume buildings' occupants to be sedentary and to be wearing a certain number of clos (the clo being a standard unit of clothing), this need not be the case.

It is not necessary to go into all the technicalites to appreciate that debate about the nature and character of thermal comfort is opening up. Ideas grounded in concepts of comfort as an *achievement* are filtering into standards making processes traditionally based upon concepts of comfort as an *attribute*. This could easily represent the thin end of a wedge ultimately leading to questions about whether it is in any event necessary to specify the indoor environment. If optimal conditions are a function of a building's form, the services it provides and the climate in which it is placed, might not understanding of these features be enough to produce inevitably variable, but locally meaningful solutions (Nicol and Humphreys 2001: 57)? A further possibility, and one that might also spell the end of thermal comfort standards as they currently exist, relates to the development of indoor climate control. Standards have, remember, been developed to cope with the problem of determining and providing optimal thermal conditions for people who have different physiological needs. But what if people could adjust their own micro-environments according to their own fluctuating requirements? On this point, Humphreys and Nicol (1998) and Fanger agree that 'the ultimate solution . . . is individual control' (Oseland and Humphreys 1993: 11). The notion of providing 'personalized' air is the next logical step (Fanger 2001). This might indeed be the perfect design solution for it places responsibility for the specification of comfort as well as for sustainability and energy consumption firmly in the hands of the user. As usual, the designer's task would be to meet users' needs but this time it is the need for choice rather than for comfort or sustainability that must be met.

If ASHRAE and ISO standards were to be revised, radically overhauled or even abandoned it probably would be easier to design more environmentally friendly buildings but would such moves challenge or reinforce unsustainable convergence at the level of ideas, that is, in contemporary meanings and expectations of comfort? Advocates of adaptive standards have so far been keen to stress that they facilitate incorporation of 'energy saving strategies *without sacrificing comfort*' (my emphasis) (Brager and de Dear 2000), in other words, without modifying what people have come to expect. As a political strategy this makes sense: if the aim is to change the standards of professional practice it is as well to be as uncontroversial as possible. But in another way, this brings us back to the more fundamental question of how science, standards and design – adaptive or otherwise – influence what people think of as comfortable environments.

Constructing Comfort

This chapter has been designed as a case study in the making of need – for comfort and for energy. As such, it began by showing that comfort, defined as a physical condition, was 'invented' in the eighteenth century. Subsequent efforts to specify the properties of comfort have proved controversial despite the fact that being comfortable is represented as a normal and in the case of thermal comfort, natural state of affairs. Nature and science stand in tension with each other throughout the chapter. Scientific understanding of human physiology has resulted in the specification of indoor environments designed to meet human need. Meanwhile, critics claim that the resulting uniformity constitutes an entirely 'unnatural' form of sensory deprivation. Nature is a universally relevant point of reference, but it proves to be a sometimes unreliable and often elusive guide to action. There is, in addition, further ambiguity about the natural or artificial status of an indoor climate that is so completely cut off from the weather outside. Are we to think of ourselves as part of nature or as safely protected from it? There is much less doubt that standard conditions of comfort have been naturalized in the sense that they are now simply taken for granted. Needs have been defined and reproduced in an incredibly precise manner and in a manner that takes no account of the historical variability of indoor climates or the range of conditions in which people of different cultures say they are comfortable. Much of the chapter has been concerned to detail how this has come about.

The notion that there are human needs to be met and that the task of science and engineering is to specify and deliver the required conditions has proved central to the normalization of demand. The specification of human need was Fanger's goal, and the ambition of meeting such needs was the reason for developing and producing standards based on his research. In describing the role of science in shaping practice I have highlighted the commercial benefits of a physiological conceptualization of comfort. Reliance on the sciences of heat transfer, rather than those of anthropology or sociology, has permitted the development of generalized, apparently universal conclusions about optimal indoor environments. Such precise and theoretically transferable specifications have favoured and perhaps been essential for the global diffusion of energy intensive heating and cooling technologies. As a result, a growing portion of the built environment is quite literally constructed around these models and concepts.

In this case, international standards have been powerfully effective media for the translation of research into practice and for the worldwide standardization of technologies, building styles and conventions. As represented here, standards are good not just for regulating and controlling practice but for doing business, building mass markets and creating opportunities on a scale that would be difficult to generate in any other way (Krislov 1997). In short, universalizing types of science are especially well suited to the dissection and specification of human need and to the design and diffusion of standards and standardized commodities purporting to meet these requirements.

As promised, I have offered a relatively conventional analysis of the social construction of indoor climate change, providing a narrative written from the top down and from a largely technological perspective. Although much has been learned about how and why the reproduction of comfort has come to be such a resource intensive enterprise, I have said nothing about what this means for the organization of social life, for what people wear or for how they relate to the buildings they occupy. The next chapter has the dual purpose of taking forward a discussion of the co-evolution of the technologies and practices of comfort and of thinking further about the mechanisms of change and the processes involved.

3

The Co-evolution of Comfort: Interdependence and Innovation

In the previous chapter I considered the scientific specification of comfort and the normalization of a very narrow interpretation of need. But what difference has this made in practice and how have conventions and habits changed over the last century or so? This chapter uses the concept of co-evolution as a starting point from which to review different ways of conceptualizing the relationship between material objects, technical arrangements and the ways of life associated with their acquisition and use. In developing the notion of co-evolution I review theories and perspectives drawn from two main sources: from sociological and anthropological literature on consumption, and from studies of innovation in science and technology. In linking these up and identifying commonalties, gaps and discrepancies this chapter identifies themes that are developed in greater detail in the rest of the book. As such, the issues explored here are critical for the development of the narrative as a whole.

Still working with the case of comfort, the chapter begins by describing interdependencies between specific technologies/devices and users' practices, between such objects and the sociotechnical systems of which they are a part and between sociotechnical systems and peoples' expectations and habits. In getting to grips with what these three dimensions of co-evolution mean for the escalation and standardization of environmentally problematic forms of consumption it is important to think about how co-evolutionary processes are energized.

Stripping contending explanations down to the core, I distinguish between theories of change that are, at heart, narratives of difference and those that focus on order, coherence and alignment. This provides a common framework with which to group ideas drawn from diverse traditions. When put into practice with reference to the acquisition and use of air-conditioning, this scheme highlights commonalities between conventionally distinct lines of enquiry, for instance between technical and economic analyses of the 'innovation journey' and cultural studies of social comparison, novelty and fashion. Likewise, discussions of lifestyle and habitus prove to have much in common with the conceptualization of irreversibility and sociotechnical scripting. In combination, these families of thought provide relevant insight into the dynamics of acquisition and use. However, they fail to offer much purchase on two critical issues.

First, and as revealed through a discussion not of air-conditioning but of lighting, technically coherent 'systems' and systems of meaning do not always coincide. One can therefore observe divergent practices and conventions that none the less depend upon 'the same' suite of technologies. What does this mean for the otherwise plausible notion that technologies and practices co-evolve? Might there be different 'levels' of co-evolution? How are new devices incorporated into more encompassing and perhaps more stable concepts of service? In different ways, these questions run on through subsequent chapters.

Second, and again introducing what is to become a central theme, theories of change that help explain the acquisition and even the use of environmentally relevant technologies do not capture collective transformations of everyday life like those associated with the decline of the siesta. These observations and conclusions drive the book on to the next chapter and to an analysis of regimes and systems in transition.

Before getting into a rather abstract conceptualization of co-evolution, it is as well to give a sense of the societal and practical significance of indoor climate control. It is tempting, especially in the light of the previous chapter, to think of thermal comfort as a bounded and primarily technical issue. As the following paragraphs illustrate, different ways of keeping comfortable have implications for divisions within society, for patterns of sociability and status and for the temporal structure of the day and the year, as well as for fashion, furniture, food, interior design and the form of the built environment. To understand how conventions and expectations of comfort have come to be as they are, we need to take note of all these dimensions and more.

Consider the world of the nineteenth-century French peasants so vividly described by Flandrin (1979). In detailing the close relation between material context and the rituals of family life, Flandrin shows how central the day-to-day management of the indoor climate was to a society strongly marked by seasonal variation. During the winter, neighbouring families would gather together in the 'biggest and warmest cowshed', only returning home to sleep at night (Flandrin 1979: 107). These sheds, these refuges from the cold, were also places for conversation, flirtation and work. Within them, complete social hierarchies were mapped out around the fireplace. Each detail of positioning was of social-thermal significance. The master of the house would, for instance, occupy place of honour near the fire surrounded by women to his left and older members of the family to the right (Flandrin 1979: 110). Flandrin uses this material, along with evidence of sleeping and eating habits, to retrace the long-term transformation of domestic life. Skipping centuries and continents, Hal Wilhite describes the role of the Japanese *kotatsu* – a heating device covered with a rug under which family members would tuck their legs in order to keep warm – in similar terms. He argues that the introduction of central heating systems modified forms of sociability associated with the *kotatsu* and redefined comfort in spatial rather than person-centred terms. When the whole house is kept to the same temperature the punishment of being sent to one's room loses much of its bite (Wilhite, Nakagami, Yamaga and Haneda 1996).

Strategies for keeping cool are just as deeply embedded in the social order of society. As Gail Cooper explains, in places like Phoenix, Arizona, 'Folkways of dealing with the heat often involved getting out of the house' (Cooper 1998: 168). Verandas created opportunities for casual observation and social exchange and, for months of the year, people would eat, play and sleep outside. By contrast, air-conditioning privatized comfort. An American woman, interviewed in the mid 1950s as part of a survey reported in *House Beautiful*, was, for example, of the view that 'television and air-conditioning are bringing families together again' (Ackerman 2002: 123). If so, air-conditioning was also drawing people back out of other social networks.

As these examples suggest, the management of comfort makes a difference to who you meet, what you do, and when and how you organize your life. No wonder, then, that divisions of age, gender, class and race are so often reproduced through the day-to-day provision of heat and cool. Deeply routinized options, particularly for the rich have involved the seasonal ebb and flow of whole populations and sometimes of government institutions. Classically, 'the British in India simply packed up during the hottest months and moved business, the colonial government, and all social life up to the hill stations, towns in the Himalayan foothills where the air was cooler' (Heschong 1979: 6). Despite their contemporary invisibility and apparent social neutrality, modern technologies of indoor climate control are of equally penetrating social significance. The USA's National Building Museum (2000), makes no bones about it, claiming that: 'Air-conditioning transformed 20th-century America . . . a defining technology of modern times' it 'launched new forms of architecture and altered the way Americans live, work, and play'.

The chaos caused by even the briefest of power cuts shows just how many institutional interests are involved in the mass production and industrialization of comfort. Such events also show how much consumers rely on the technologies of central heating and cooling and on the utilities that supply them (Shove *et al.* 1998; Guy and Shove 2000). Rybczynski (1987: 220) claims there has been a democratization of comfort with the effect that it is 'no longer the privilege of a part of society, it is accessible to all'. Countering this view, authors like Boardman (1991), Lutzenhiser (1993), Cole (2000), and Graham and Marvin (2001) document the persistence of 'fuel poverty' and the extent of social-thermal inequality. But in so doing they also show how far governments and welfare agencies have come in taking the provision of affordable warmth (or coolth) to be a 'necessity of life' (Boardman 1991: 2). Symbolically and politically, it is now 'normal' to be unaware of the indoor climate, normal that conditions are maintained by 'artificial' means involving resource-intensive systems of heating and cooling, and normal that these conditions are divorced from those outside.

This material suggests that if we are to understand the transformation of comfort, we must also understand the overturning of images, traditions, rituals, skills and responsibilities, as well as the diffusion of standardized equations and the techniques and infrastructures of mechanical engineering. In its simplest formulation, the proposition that relations of comfort are simultaneously social and technical offers a way into this problem for it suggests that they are, to borrow Bijker's terminology, 'two sides of the same coin' (Bijker 1997: 274). The next section reviews different ways of conceptualizing this interlinking and identifies processes thought to influence not the design but the acquisition and use of mechanical heating and cooling.

Dimensions and Dynamics

The notion that technologies and things shape and are shaped by social, economic and political considerations makes good intuitive sense and I want to start by simply accepting the claim that the social and the technical emerge 'as two sides of the same sociotechnical coin during the construction processes of artifacts, facts, and relevant social groups' (Bijker 1997: 274). On the face of it this is a necessary first step in understanding the complexities of comfort hinted at above. A second reason for tapping into these ideas is that they are strikingly similar to arguments put forward by anthropologists, especially those interested in material culture. Focusing more on the relation between objects and people than on the development of new technologies, Kopytoff is, for instance, of the view that societies 'simultaneously and in the same way construct objects as they construct people' (Kopytoff 1986: 90). There are relevant differences in how objects and technologies are conceptualized, but the view that change is a process of co-evolution constitutes common ground for both intellectual traditions. Or does it? It is easy to slip into these seductive terminologies: to talk, quite convincingly, of the sociotechnical co-evolution of comfort and to discuss the hybrid processes of heterogenous engineering involved (Law 1987). But how does this business of simultaneous construction really work? Furthermore, how does the social-symbolic relation between objects and people (including issues of value, exchange and meaning) tie in with the sociotechnical structuring of the same situation? In addressing this question I take the concept of co-evolution apart and specify some of the dimensions and dynamics at play.

Although co-evolution is usually talked of as a two-way process, the poles, or in other words the *dimensions* at stake are not always the same. It is useful to sort these differences out. Sometimes, and especially in the sociotechnical literature, the terminology of co-evolution is used to describe the relation between specific devices and the wider systems of which they are a part. This kind of discussion is especially relevant when considering pathways of innovation and when showing how sets of devices and social arrangements depend on each other within more encompassing macro-systems or sociotechnical landscapes (Rip and Kemp 1998).

In other cases, it is the co-constitutive relation between technical arrangements and material objects, on the one hand, and social relations and practices, on the other, which is at the centre of attention. This interaction is, for instance, of particular significance for scholars interested in the cultural life of things (Appadurai 1986) and the way that artifacts 'make visible and stable the categories of culture' (Douglas and Isherwood 1996: 59). Building on the view that 'social worlds are as much constituted by materiality as the other way around' (Miller 1998b: 3), Miller's discussion of 'why some things matter' is in this tradition as is Akrich's work on social organization of technology 'transfer' (Akrich 1992).

Co-evolution is thus used to describe (1) the relation between technologies or material artifacts and social relations/practices and (2) the relation between specific technologies or material artifacts and more complex sociotechnical systems. In a few cases, *both* dimensions figure in the discussion. This is particularly so for authors who have written about the development of 'infra-systems' like those of electric power, telecommunications or automobility. In such situations the critical axis is that between socoiotechnical systems or landscapes, on the one hand, and social arrangements, practices and expectations on the other. In effect this constitutes a third (3) axis of co-evolution. Others have written about the co-evolution of policy and technology; of technology and the market; of culture and technology, and of artifacts, beliefs and evaluations routines (Rip 2002: 6) but for now I want to concentrate on the three dimensions identified above.

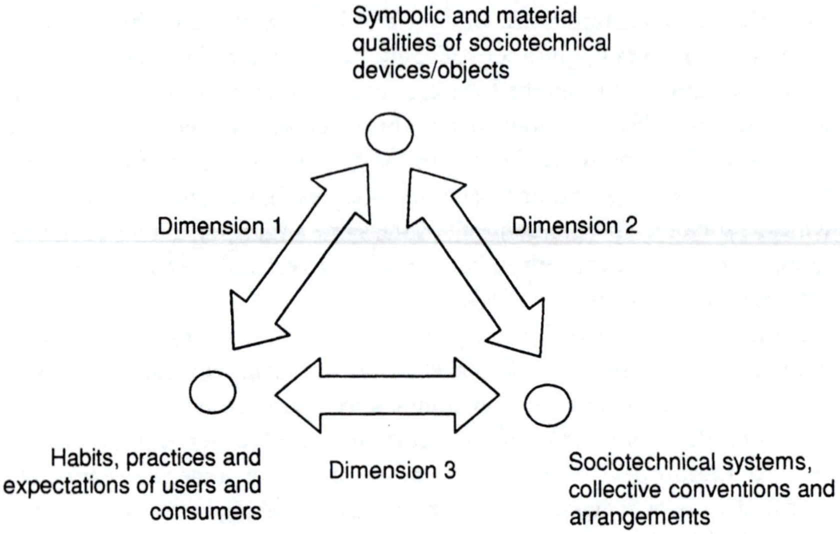

Symbolic and material
qualities of sociotechnical
devices/objects

Figure 3.1. Three dimensions of co-evolution

The triangular framework of Figure 3.1 distinguishes between these dimensions and shows how they might also relate one to another. It is a simple sketch and has the limited purpose of showing that the language of co-evolution is variously used to refer to interdependencies between devices, systems and practices.

As a descriptive scheme this is relatively uncontroversial and as an explanation of change, not especially informative. Where, in all of this, are the well springs of novelty and innovation? What is it that flows through those empty arrows and what are the media and mechanisms of change? So much for the co-, but what about the evolution? Darwin's theory was based on two essential ingredients, variety and natural selection. Although economists and social theorists have sometimes latched on to these ideas with enthusiasm, few sociologists of technology or, for that matter, students of material culture would be entirely happy with the idea that the dynamics of change revolve around the survival of the fittest sociotechnical configurations. That much is clear.

But what then, *are* the proposed mechanisms of change? Although not usually discussed in quite this way, I suggest that there are two dominant if typically tacit accounts. The first has to do with *difference* and with processes of de- and revaluation. This kind of reasoning locates and explains change in terms of the successive revaluation of specific items and practices. To put it concretely, as novelties become normal so meanings change and so the landscape of significance and difference moves on.

The second has to do with *coherence* and so with processes of de- and restabilization. Kuhn's (1970) concept of paradigm is relevant here, as are what Bourdieu talks about as the practice-unifying and practice-generating principles of lifestyle and habitus (Bourdieu 1984: 101). Applied to technical innovation and to consumption the proposition is that dominant designs or conventions exert a form of centrifugal force, holding arrangements together but also creating conditions of instability. Sociotechnical trajectories are, in this analysis, forged through processes of enlisting, enrolling and building coherence.

Although only loosely specified, these two dynamics, one of difference, the other of coherence, connect as easily with the literature on consumption and practice as with studies of innovation. Putting these pieces together, the question is whether these two forms operate independently or in concert, how, and with what consequence for the various dimensions of co-evolution outlined above? The next three sections explore these issues from different angles and in the process fill out this somewhat arid dissection of dynamics and dimensions. They do so with the aid of examples and cases relating to the transformation of the indoor climate. The first shows how theories of difference and coherence might be used to explain the introduction and acquisition of air-conditioning and its positioning within the sociotechnical system of the home.

Difference and Coherence: Acquiring and Using Air-conditioning

Between 1962 and 1992, the percentage of American homes with air-conditioning grew from twelve to sixty-four per cent (Kempton and Lutzenhiser, 1992: 172). This figure disguises important points of detail for it does not distinguish between central air-conditioning systems and individual units and it tells us nothing about the relative costs of energy or the price of the systems themselves. However, it does give a crude indication of escalating demand and as such provides a point of departure for the following exercise in comparing theoretical accounts of the processes involved.

Difference and De/revaluation

The explanations considered under this heading make unlikely bedfellows. Although rooted in the different soils of economics, marketing and sociology, they have in common a shared assumption that processes of innovation involve and are to some extent driven by the revaluation of difference.

Representing just such an approach, Campbell suggests that: 'to understand modern consumerism means to understand the nature, origin and functioning of the processes through which novelty is continuously created, introduced into society and then disseminated through all social classes' (Campbell 1992: 48). Risk taking and the pursuit of novelty need not go hand in hand, yet the supposition that consumer goods, technologies and habits somehow percolate through society has much in common with Rogers' (1983) classic analysis of innovation and the 'S' curves of diffusion: trickling, trail-blazing and emulation being key to both. Although Rogers does not relate the propensity for risk taking to social class or status, the suggestion that the practices of 'early adopters' are in time taken up by more cautious members of society and finally by reluctant 'laggards' invokes a similarly infectious account of social change. By implication, the dynamic is one of de- and revaluation: risky technologies become safe just as initially high-status items acquire new meaning as they filter through the strata of society. The transformation of meaning and so of social advantage is central to this analysis for it is this that generates the need for new sources of innovation and novelty that in turn drive demand. Echoing this view, Wilhite and Lutzenhiser (1998) conclude that efforts to maintain distinctive status-based consumption patterns require constant innovation.

In an article explicitly linking analyses of technological innovation with theories of consumer behaviour, Mika Pantzar (1997) pays serious attention to the evolving character of meaning as novel technologies become normal. Tracking the symbolic trajectories of a range of commodities (the telephone, the computer, the car, the television), he suggests that such items go through distinctive phases of redefinition. Starting their collective career as fashionable objects of desire, the next stage is one in which acquisition is legitimized in rational or functional terms. According to Pantzar, this is followed by a period of routinization. At this point, the technologies in question are so ordinary that their acquisition needs no justification at all. What is distinctive about this analysis is the proposition that the (re)attribution of meaning is itself part of the dynamic both of innovation and of normalization. Even when technologies appear stable, that is, when their design is 'fixed', their acquisition and appropriation remains a process of invention for their 'purpose' and social significance is always on the move (Bijker 1992; Shove and Southerton 2000). In practical terms, this underlines the relevance of paying close and continual attention to the social positioning of objects, to the messages they embody and to the detail of differentiation. To return to air-conditioning, it is clear that much effort has been invested in specifying the social meaning of mechanical cooling and giving value to the possibilities it affords. Answers to the questions: 'What is air-conditioning, what is it for and what does its acquisition mean?' differ over time and from one society to another, and continue to evolve.

Wilhite, Nakagami and Murakoshi's (1996) historical study of Japanese advertising indicates that air-conditioning was associated first with modernity

and then with a distinctively Western lifestyle. Early advertisements emphasized the air-conditioner itself, displaying it as a modern accessory for the
traditional Japanese home. By contrast, later editions show people in Western
dress surrounded by the props of a Western lifestyle including a coffee table
and a glass of whisky. By this stage, the air-conditioner that makes this idealized
environment possible is barely visible in the background. According to Wilhite,
air-conditioning became so tied up with the signification of modernity that
Japanese families acquired and installed such systems even when they preferred
natural ventilation (Wilhite, Nakagami and Murakoshi 1996).

Although not sold on arguments of Westernization, American households
also took some persuasion to abandon old habits and come round to the view
that they actually 'needed' artificial cooling. This was no easy task. As well
as costing money to buy and run, proper use of air-conditioning meant keeping
windows shut and foregoing the pleasures of the pre-cooled life. Justifications
relating to health, cleanliness and family togetherness were used to sell the idea
but with uncertain success. As Ackerman (2002) describes, air-conditioning
followed an erratic course through different 'communities of emulation', often
beset by ambivalence if not resistance. In a typically wry account the author
Garrison Keillor catalogues his parents' objections: 'Mother thinks air-conditioning causes colds'; while father is of the view that 'Air–conditioning is for
the weak and indolent' (Keillor 1985). The contemporary redundancy of such
discourse, at least in America, illustrates Pantzar's point. The fact that these
arguments are no longer needed is evidence itself that air-conditioning has
become an essential part of normal life. It may not last forever but for the time
being, air-conditioning is positioned a rational response to a recognized need
for a particular form of 'comfort', and for a host of other benefits associated
with the ability to manage, control and customise your own environment.

The processes through which things are differentiated and given meaning,
and through which such meanings change are complicated, contested and
surely not influenced by science or advertising alone. Detailing these dynamics,
surveys of consumer culture tend to highlight the relation between acquisition
and *positive* forms of social identity, showing how people make themselves
through what they buy. Offering a negative perspective on symbolic significance, Wilhite and Lutzenhiser suggest that fear of social failure is an equally
compelling force for change. Given social pressure to conform, homes, air-
conditioning systems, cars, freezers and ovens are, they suggest, socially dimen-
sioned and sized to cope with even extreme events. The oven is, for example,
large enough to cook the Christmas turkey, an event that happens but once a
year. Turning this description into a theory of demand, Wilhite and Lutzenhiser
hypothesize a process in which 'spare' capacity is gradually filled, previously
'extreme' situations become normal, new extremes are set, and further 'just

in case' capacity is required. This is an account of social dimensioning that relates issues of self-image to the *collective* redefinition social obligation and of what is involved in meeting them. But again, differentiation and re/devaluation are presumed to be the driving forces of change.

The core idea, common to all positions sketched above, is that people distinguish between themselves and others through the acquisition of new commodities and technologies. As novelties become normal and innovations diffuse, so their social meaning and significance changes and it is this cycle of de- and revaluation that drives the co-evolution of technology and (acquisitive) practice. In essence, difference-based theories of this type focus on the dynamics of acquisition: on why people buy air-conditioning systems when they do, rather than on how such items are used. Second, they deal with the circulation of discrete devices and technologies rather than the co-evolution of complex systems and services.

Summarizing these points, Figure 3.2 shows how such accounts relate to the three dimensions of co-evolution identified above. As the solid black arrow indicates, the first dimension of co-evolution, namely that between objects and practices, is the centre of attention. The more collective orientation of certain difference-based theories, for example those that consider the respecification of social obligation, relates to the third dimension of co-evolution, represented by the arrow shown in grey.

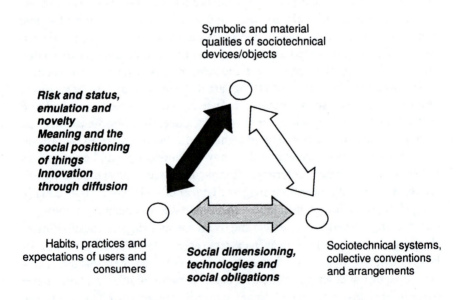

Figure 3.2. Difference, de/revaluation and the co-evolution of objects and practices

What is missing, but crucial to the next group of explanations, is an understanding of how novel objects, technologies and practices are positioned with respect to sociotechnical systems and collective conventions.

Coherence and De/restabilization

Theories of change emphasizing consistency and coherence offer a different but potentially complementary platform from which to explore the co-evolution of comfort.

In their paper on 'Lifestyle, Status and Energy Consumption', Loren Lutzenhiser and Marcia Gossard (2000) make the case for analysing bundles of energy-related practice, showing how these interact to define and reproduce more and less sustainable ways of life. The point I want to take from this concerns the clustering of activity and, in social terms, the practical and symbolic interdependence of apparently isolated actions and habits. The packaging of expectation and practice takes many forms but, to give a practical example, air-conditioning is unlikely to be thought of as optional for someone who lives in a Western country with a hot climate and who also has a large house, a substantial income and a number of cars. Without it their life or, more accurately, their lifestyle would be incomplete. By implication, change is explained in terms of the constant tug of coherence. This has much in common with the 'Diderot effect' already referred to in Chapter 1. In Diderot's case, the acquisition of a new dressing gown made everything else seem dingy, so sparking off a round of updating and improvement. Bourdieu's concept of habitus as a 'structuring structure' and of lifestyle as a 'system of classified and classifying practices' (Bourdieu 1984: 171) points to the existence of much more elaborate repertoires of practice-generating schemes. Not all of these will have the effect of increasing consumption yet the expectation that items or for that matter habits and practices should match or at least contribute to some meta-order has, as McCracken puts it, 'clear "ratchet" implications for consumer expenditure. It helps to move the standard of consumption upward and prevent backward movement' (McCracken 1998: 127). The suggestion here is that new items and technologies are sought after as a means of preserving coherence.

There are, in turn, certain similarities between accounts of symbolic unity and more technologically grounded theories of irreversibility. The notion that past actions and investments enable and constrain future possibilities does not imply stability but like McCracken's representation of the Diderot effect it helps make sense of the lack of backward movement and hence the ratcheting of demand. It is not necessary to work through the literature on path dependency and innovation to appreciate that building technologies are strongly interconnected, that each component has implications for the performance of the whole, and that this has consequences for avenues and thresholds of change. Again air-conditioning is a good example. Air-conditioned buildings do not need such features as overhanging eaves or verandas and by omitting these elements American designers were able to offset the additional cost of mechanical cooling. But without those features in place, 'new houses required air-conditioning to make them comfortable' (Cooper 1998: 153). Details of layout, window design and construction now revolve around the requirements of mechanical cooling to such an extent that the technology is literally built into the architecture of the home. In effect, mechanically cooled properties are designed *for* air-conditioning just as they were once designed *for* natural ventilation.

These observations underline the inter-dependence of design: the inclusion of air-conditioning locked builders into a particular design strategy just as the normalization of such strategies locked them into the use of mechanical cooling. In this case, the relevant dimension of co-evolution is obviously that between specific technologies (like air-conditioning) and the systems (the design characteristics of the rest of the house) into which they are introduced. As represented here, the dynamic animating this process is one of co-dependency. Change in any one part of the system implies change elsewhere and it is because of this that air-conditioning has been quite literally drawn into the fabric of the built environment.

There is a further co-evolutionary relationship to consider, namely that between the air-conditioned house and its occupants' habits. In thinking about how this operates it is useful to refer back to the notion that technologies script the practices and actions of those who use them. Just as the size of the key fob prevents hotel customers making off with it by mistake and just as sleeping policemen silently but effectively slow the traffic (Latour 1992) so houses act on their inhabitants. This happens at a number of levels. The sealed windows of air-conditioned homes prevent occupants from opening them just as the lack of a veranda prevents anyone from sitting on it. Taken together, such features tie homeowners into an air-conditioned way of life, like it or not. In other words, the 'normality' of such a life is established by virtue of its unavoidability as well as through marketing, advertising and social comparison.

Although buildings may inscribe and sometimes enforce certain behaviours, they do not represent a comprehensive hard wiring of meaning and practice nor do they necessarily over-ride comfort-related habits. As a number of authors have documented, there are various ways of using and resisting air-conditioning systems. Some of the householders studied by Hackett and Lutzenhiser went to extreme lengths to let their closed, air-conditioned homes 'breathe' naturally (Lutzenhiser *et al.* 1994). These experiences are worth quoting for they point to other systems of social order and coherence that are also relevant. One respondent, interviewed in Davis, California, felt that 'there is something disturbing about not accepting the climate you live in'. This person goes on to describe what comfort means to them, and how they achieve it: 'your idea of being cool and comfortable changes: it is more flexible. 80 degrees [Fahrenheit] is "cool" in August while 68 degrees is warm enough in December . . . [in the summer] . . . I do things that require energy in the morning when it is cool' (Lutzenhiser *et al.* 1994: 16). These brief insights imply a complete seasonal-diurnal system of organizing activity and of understanding and managing the relation between indoor climate and everyday life.

Kempton and Montgomery's (1982) research on how heating and cooling technologies are operated in practice points to also relevant layers of convention and understanding. Their work showed that folk knowledges of natural and technical systems were often at odds with the understandings of technologists, engineers and designers, and with the 'scripts' these experts sought to construct. People consequently opened and closed windows in ways that made no thermo-dynamic sense but that were consistent with what they had always done. Likewise, complex controls were treated as on-off switches if that was the mental model into which they fitted. Conceptual frameworks and traditions like these hold householders' actions together and constitute a further force for coherence.

These examples suggest that coherence of one kind or another can, and often does, lead to the reinventing and reshaping of technical objects in use. There is, in other words, a technical ordering of the air-conditioned home in which design elements interact and so define the system as a whole. At the same time, inhabitants have their own, also coherent conceptual systems and senses of how life should be. There are different ways of thinking about how these schemes intersect.

The most common is to examine the relative significance of each for the deployment of some new technology. How far do technologies 'configure' their sometimes unsuspecting users (Woolgar 1991), and/or to what extent are they actively adapted, incorporated and converted in the process of what Silverstone refers to as their 'domestication' (Silverstone *et al.* 1992; Lie and Sorensen 1996)? Another route is to think about how complete systems of coherence inter-depend. From this perspective, the work of appropriation that Silverstone describes is work undertaken to resolve discrepancies and iron out differences between the kind of order inscribed in specific devices or appliances, and in prior (but also mobile) systems of social relations and habits.

There is more to say about the resources required to make co-evolution happen, but for present purposes what counts is the simple observation that mechanisms of change are frequently associated with the de- and restabilization of order.

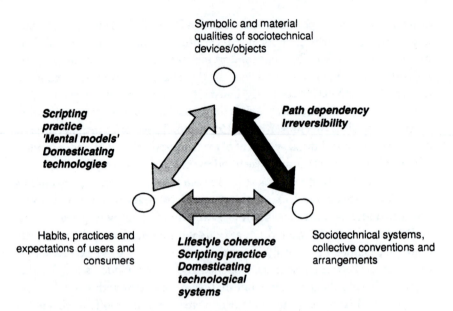

Figure 3.3. Coherence, de/restabilization and the co-evolution of objects and systems

Figure 3.3 positions these ideas with reference to the three dimensions of co-evolution. The solid black arrow suggests that theories emphasizing coherence and the restoration of order are most often invoked with respect to the second dimension, namely the co-evolution of objects and systems. Notions of scripting, configuration and appropriation are more commonly introduced when thinking about how devices and practices co-evolve. Meanwhile, analyses of lifestyle and, in a rather different sense, studies of large-scale technical systems explain change with reference to the pressures of interdependence. It is important to notice that these coherence-based accounts focus on how technologies are used and what this means for the routines they engender and sustain, rather than on when and why they are acquired.

Using the spread of air-conditioning as an example, I have distinguished between the dimensions and dynamics of co-evolution in such a way as to reveal commonalities between what are usually separate theories of consumption and technological innovation. A number of provisional conclusions arise from my attempt to put this scheme into practice. One is that theories of change grounded in the dynamics of *difference* have relatively little to say about the co-evolution of complex systems or the co-determining relation between tools, technologies, and practices and habits of use. Theories of *coherence* are better suited to these tasks. There are, however, different forms of coherence relating to different systems of order (for example, the 'system' of a mental model; the technical 'system' of a fully air-conditioned home, and so forth). Analytically, much depends upon how system boundaries are specified and how intersecting systems are thought to inter-relate. The next section takes up this issue, exploring the development and appropriation of incandescent and fluorescent lighting as a means of addressing the fact that although conventions and indoor environments appear to be converging around the world there are, none the less, important and revealing patterns of persistent diversity.

Diffusion, Diversity and Lighting

Lighting has come in for much the same style of scientific attention as thermal comfort. The stated ambition is to determine optimal conditions in order to produce and provide what people need. Biological and physiological research has again provided a vocabulary and an experimental basis for determining 'which combinations of lighting intensity and color are experienced as comfortable' (Bijker 1997: 243). As with thermal comfort, technical enquiry has helped construct and naturalize need through systematic quantification of the effects different types and levels of illumination have on productivity, health and well being (Loe 2000). In this field too, definitions, specifications and recommended illuminance levels have practical and commercial consequences for the industries and manufacturers involved (Mills and Borg 1999). In the course of his complex and careful tale of how the high-intensity daylight fluorescent lamp came to be as it is, Bijker describes how laboratory-based studies were used in differentiating between incandescent and fluorescent technologies and in shaping markets for a particular version of the latter. It is, he observes, 'intriguing to see how the elaboration of illumination theory and practice, resulting in the ability to make varieties of white light, was used to develop the high intensity fluorescent lamp' (Bijker 1997: 243). Technical research was undertaken to characterize and quantify the benefits of a particular kind of light – white light – in the course of creating a bounded space in which to locate and legitimize the development of high intensity daylight fluorescent lighting. Bijker explains why this move was important and how the interests of utilities and of lamp and fixture manufacturers combined to marginalize other more efficient technologies that used less electricity.

Enlisting scientific research constituted only one amongst a range of technical-political strategies adopted in the course of stabilizing the high intensity solution. However, two aspects of this endeavour are especially relevant for the present discussion. The first relates to the positioning of daylight as *the* relevant point of reference. With this as the benchmark, only high-intensity fluorescent lamps could compete. Second, this specification was associated with studies demonstrating the biological *'need'* for such illumination. 'It was claimed', writes Bijker

> that lighting research had indicated that the human eye functions more naturally above 100 foot-candles than under 15 to 50 foot-candles, which was considered the upper limit of most incandescent general lighting systems at the time. The ultimate advantage of fluorescent lighting to the consumer was therefore to be found in properly designed installations giving at least 100 foot-candles. (Bijker 1997: 243)

One might expect that the successful construction of fluorescent systems, i.e. systems that met this 'need' better than any other would, along with all the other power games Bijker describes, ensure their success. And in terms of the trajectory of technological development this is exactly the story that Bijker tells.

Convincing though it is, this analysis of the politics of technology and of innovation through diffusion stops short of the living room. Back in the world of consumption and use, fluorescent lighting has *not* managed to comprehensively dislodge alternative, non-scientific concepts of comfort. Patterns of use have not simply co-evolved in tune with this technology. Incandescent fittings and bulbs continue to be produced and sold, and qualitative images of cosiness and warmth continue to be sold along with them. The puzzle is that in some societies interpretations of 'comfortable' lighting have swung in favour of fluorescent fittings. In others, incandescent, habits have stuck tight. How might we explain these rather dramatic differences of lighting convention and how might we do so in terms of the co-evolution of technology and practice?

Wilhite, Nakagami, Yamaga and Haneda's (1996) comparative study of householders in Fukuoka, Japan and in Oslo, Norway is instructive in that it reveals diametrically opposed interpretations and contrasting uses of 'the same' lighting technologies. Norwegian respondents, who had an average of 9.6 sources of light in their living room, had strong views about how homes should be lit. Several were of the opinion that 'it is too cold with a ceiling lamp' and that ceiling lamps 'give such cold light'. Their overwhelming preference was for incandescent lighting. Elaborating on this, one interviewee explained that it felt 'more cozy with small lamps'. Another noted that 'I like to have the table lamps on so there will be a special glow in the room', also concluding that a home with only one light on must be a 'sad' house (Wilhite, Nakagami, Yamaga and Haneda 1996: 799).

Meanwhile, Japanese respondents, who had an average of 2.5 lamps in their living rooms, subscribed to a very different aesthetic. As one put it, 'Europeans and Americans seem to feel that the incandescent light is warm. But I think what is warm for Japanese are the natural features', here meaning the ability to see the natural features of one's companions. Rather than being warm, incandescent lighting generated what was described as a cold atmosphere. One respondent reports feeling 'blue with it [incandescent] because it is too dark' (Wilhite, Nakagami, Yamaga and Haneda 1996: 799). In both countries, homes were equipped with a mixture of fluorescent and incandescent lighting. However, Norwegians reserved fluorescent fittings for bathrooms and kitchens, these being precisely the locations in which the Japanese used incandescent bulbs. As this example indicates, switching on the light has many meanings other than those of simply lighting the room (Moezzi 1998).

Bijker positions his work as an analysis of sociotechnical change and in keeping with this approach claims that: 'All stable ensembles are bound together as much by the technical as by the social. Social classes, occupational groups, firms, professions, machines – all are held in place by intimate social and technical links' (Bijker 1997: 273). But what is it that connects lighting technologies and their consumers? It would be a shame to abandon the logic of co-evolution and at the last minute reach for merely 'cultural' explanations of the differential appropriation of incandescent and fluorescent lighting in Japanese and Norwegian homes.

To do otherwise requires further discussion of those intimate social and technical links but from the perspective of consumption and use. Bijker's own discussion of 'obduracy' offers a useful way forward. He uses this idea in various ways but one is to describe situations in which relevant social groups have 'invested so much in the artifact that its meaning has become quite fixed – it cannot be changed easily, and it forms part of a hardened network of practices, theories, and social institutions' (Bijker 1997: 82). Thus hardened, artifacts tie social groups, including producers and consumers, together.

In practice, and as with fluorescent and incandescent lighting, the substance of these linkages may differ from one situation to another. As a result, what looks like 'the same' artifact might become obdurate through different routes, and through routes that have long-term consequences for the meanings that are consequently fixed. Closer inspection of Japanese and Norwegian societies might reveal relevant variations in traditions of wiring and house building, in the balance of power between utilities and lamp manufacturers or in the sociotechnical landscape within which electric lighting emerged. Wilhite edges toward this conclusion, noting historical differences in home lighting traditions and observing that Japanese ceiling lights can be traced back hundreds of years. But there is still something of a tension. While the technological meaning of fluorescent lighting is uniformly fixed on the global stage (at this level the technology is both standardized and established), it is, at the same time, fixed at the local level by specific and highly variable configurations of consumer-producer relations. Far from reaching closure, the semiotic status of fluorescent

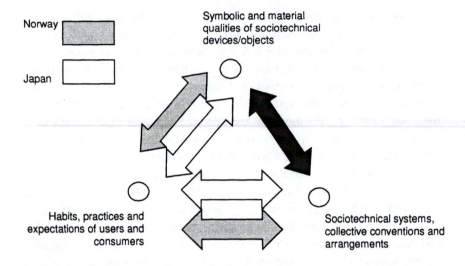

Figure 3.4. Co-evolution and the local configuration of standardized technologies

and incandescent lighting remains open. In some situations, fluorescent lighting means lighting that is good for living rooms, in others its meaning is stabilized in an entirely different manner.

Figure 3.4 represents these multiple possibilities in terms of the three dimensions of co-evolution. In this case, the dark arrow makes the point that the development of fluorescent lighting can be analysed in terms of a co-evolving relation between the artifact and the sociotechnical context of its production. This is the story that Bijker tells (Bijker 1997). Yet this same technology is differently implicated in co-evolution of comfort in Japan and Norway. The two pairs of parallel arrows indicate that fluorescent lighting has co-evolved along contrasting lines with respect to individual habits and lighting practices and with reference to collective conventions and aesthetics of comfort in these two societies.

Although it captures the points made above, this is a puzzling image. How can fluorescent lighting be 'the same' if the mechanisms of co-evolution are genuinely bi-directional? An obvious solution is to argue that the technology is not really the same because it is appropriated in very different ways in Japan and Norway and since its meaning is established through contrasting processes of domestication. Another option is to distinguish between different levels of co-evolution. We might therefore argue that, yes, fluorescent lighting has co-evolved with the networks of industrial power in which it was enmeshed (as indicated by the dark arrow and as described by Bijker) and, yes, there are also other more localized dynamics of co-evolution that stabilize consumer-producer relations. One way of thinking about how these multi-level arrangements work out in practice is to take note of the relationship between specific devices (lamps), and the services they make possible, these being lighting, cosiness and comfort. This is an option explored in the following section and developed through the rest of the book.

I have so far reviewed theories of change and of the development and appropriation of air-conditioning and lighting from different angles on the grounds that such an exercise might help explain the reconfiguration of what people count as comfort. To some extent this has been a good strategy, perhaps especially because it has revealed that certain elements are missing. It has gradually become clear that when dealing with such a composite service as comfort, suites of technology operate together and together co-constitute the collective conventions of everyday life. From whatever perspective, careful research into the design, development, acquisition and use of any one device is likely to miss this bigger plot. In addition, the Japanese and Norwegian examples remind us that that certain traditions of comfort endure despite the global diffusion of standardized technologies. This observation raises further questions about the units of co-evolution and the scales on which such processes occur. These themes are pursued in subsequent chapters but by way of concluding this discussion and introducing the next I want to comment briefly on the waning of the siesta, using this as an example with which to consider the (re)specification of comfort as a collective practice.

Comfort as Collective Practice: the Siesta

The sociologist Eviatar Zerubavel claims that 'time is among the major parameters of the social order and that social life is structured and regulated in accordance with it' (Zerubavel 1979: xxi). I would add that means of maintaining conditions and conventions of comfort have a vital role in configuring the sociotemporal rhythms of society. In much of southern Europe, shop shutters drop at noon only to re-open in the late afternoon. Schools and offices follow suit for the temporal order of these societies still revolves around the siesta. Giving up and retreating during the heat of the day is a simple, low-cost method of managing climatic variation. It is a long established tradition and one that structures the distribution of traffic jams, the scheduling and duration of meal times and the co-ordination of social interaction.

The idea that the working day runs from eight or nine in the morning through to five or six in the evening is a relatively recent convention but one that has spread from its point of origin in northern Europe and become a model now recognized around the world. These are what people think of as normal working hours. One of the benefits of air-conditioning is that it maintains the same temperature throughout the day and, with mechanical cooling in place, people are climatically free to work when they want. However, air-conditioned companies would put themselves out of synch with everyone else if they were to work from nine to five in a siesta-based society. As shift workers know only too well, it is hard to co-ordinate with friends and family members when lives are organized around different time frames. But if working from nine to five becomes the norm, it is those who persist in resting during the middle of the day who run the risk of social exclusion. The 'need' for air-conditioning is likely to increase if people accustomed to taking a siesta adopt a 'normal' working day for the sake of sociotemporal co-ordination. Cumulative pressure of this kind is here described by a lawyer working for an international firm in Barcelona. She explains the problem as follows: 'we used to put on the answering machine and leave for a two-hour break, but clients started calling more often and hanging up on the recording' (Los Angeles Times, 28 March 2001). The solution, in her case, is to stay open all day. And of course the more offices that do so the greater the incentive for the rest to conform to this regime.

These observations suggest that the value of having or lacking an air-conditioned office is at least partly related to the temporal structure of the surrounding society. Although the waning of the siesta is of considerable significance for the management of comfort (and vice versa), it has proved difficult to find any reliable evidence on where and at what rate sociotemporal socioclimatic arrangements like these are changing. There is one rather well documented exception. In April 1999, the Mexican government officially announced the end of the siesta for its 1.6 million employees. Citing modernization, efficiency and synchronization with NAFTA partners as reasons for ditching the traditional lunchtime break, this was a move that brought government schedules in line with those of the private sector (Moore 1999). Air-conditioned buildings generate standardized indoor climates by mechanical means but as these siesta-related examples indicate, air-conditioning is also implicated in the standardization and synchronization of sociotemporal regimes, regimes that are, as Zerubavel observes, major parameters around which social life is organized. Whatever their other qualities, none of the co-evolutionary theories and arguments rehearsed this far have the reach or range required to illuminate collective societal transformation on this scale.

Reconfiguring Comfort

Starting with the idea that technologies and practices co-evolve, this chapter has taken the study of comfort beyond the science of temperature, ventilation and humidity control. Co-evolution is a slippery concept and one that is used in different ways. In an effort to make sense of the these variations I distinguished between three dimensions with respect to which objects, systems and practices are thought to co-evolve. I then identified two usually tacit accounts of what drives these co-evolutionary relations. The resulting scheme provided a convenient framework with which to organize and compare proposed mechanisms of change. The case of air-conditioning showed that theories concerned with the dynamics of *difference* or of *coherence* emphasize different dimensions of co-evolution and offer alternative ways of thinking about how expectations and technologies of comfort change.

This exercise also identified two limitations, or at least two issues deserving of further attention. The case of incandescent and fluorescent lighting raised questions about how the dynamics of change (and obduracy) work out across international, national and local 'arenas' of co-evolution. It also pointed to important differences between the development and use of specific technologies (lamps) and the reinterpretation of more encompassing concepts of service (meanings of comfortable lighting). On this point, it is not sufficient to conclude that lamps are differentially appropriated depending on the lighting cultures in which they are 'domesticated'. Instead, the task is to understand how concepts of lighting and comfort themselves co-evolve. This means paying attention to the relation between individual devices and entire complexes or suites of sociotechnical order.

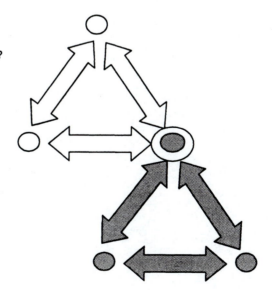

By what means do the systems, conventions, technologies and habits of one sociotechnical regime turn into another?

What are the mechanisms of system level change?

Figure 3.5. Reconfiguring comfort

Finally, brief consideration of the siesta indicated the need to reach beyond the triangle of co-evolution, however it is understood and analysed and whatever the engines of change. Something more is needed if we are to understand how entire cultures and conventions of comfort are redefined and reproduced.

Figure 3.5 provides a graphic illustration of this challenge. As represented here, the task is to show how complete co-evolutionary frameworks move from one state (indicated by open arrows) to another (in which the arrows are shown in grey).

The next chapter takes this discussion forward with the help of 'transition theory' and the arguments of those who have written about the transformation of sociotechnical regimes.

4

Regimes of Comfort: Systems in Transition

Chapter 2 offered a relatively conventional account of the construction of need, focusing on the universalizing role of science in defining a uniquely standardized concept of what people require. Although important, the top-down specification of need is but one step in the making of demand. Chapter three went on to look at how standard concepts of comfort have been realized and normalized through the acquisition, use and appropriation of key technologies. The ensuing discussion of co-evolution explored different ways of thinking about the relation between technology and practice. In the process it became clear that there was more to be said about how regimes of comfort are constructed and how they change. Building on these ideas, this chapter concentrates on the dynamics of global convergence and the transformation of complex sociotechnical systems.

It begins with a description of two Cypriot houses. One was constructed around a hundred years ago and is located in a village some fifty kilometres outside Limassol. The other is a modern town house situated in the centre of that city and built in 1993. These are both unremarkable properties interesting only for the fact that they are occupied by different generations of the same family. During the course of his degree in building surveying, George Papadopoulos, the grandson of this family, gathered technical data about the two buildings. Some of this is summarized in Table 4.1.

Golton uses this material to calculate changes in energy intensity over time but it is the background descriptions accompanying the quantitative data in which I am interested. These dry narratives do a brilliant job of illustrating different ways of defining and achieving comfort and of showing what these mean for the organization of everyday life.

The description of the grandparents' house in the village runs as follows: 'The wall stones are bedded in mud mortar and built in two skins with small stones to fill the cavity ... The internal surfaces are finished with a layer of mud and a gypsum slurry ... It is a simple but not inelegant technology. The

Table 4.1. Two Cypriot homes

Features	Grandparents' house	Parents' house
Area per person	18m^2	66.5m^2
Roof	Timber, mud, straw	Reinforced concrete
External walls	Stone and mud	Reinforced concrete frame, brick and cement mortar
External openings	3 timber doors	14 doors and windows with aluminium frames and imported glass, 1 door of imported timber
Internal finishes	Natural gypsum	Processed gypsum, vinyl paint, ceramic
Floors	White soil	Ceramic, terrazzo and carpet
Internal services	None	Copper, galvanised steel and PVC pipe, PVC covered copper wire
External services	None	Copper, galvanised steel, salt glazed earthenware and PVC pipe, aluminium wire
Lighting	Animal oil	Electricity
Space heating	Wood burning fire	Diesel oil
Space cooling	None	Electricity
Cooking and washing	Wood burning fire	Gas, diesel, oil, electricity, solar
Control of comfort	Inhabitants experience a wide range of conditions	Inhabitants experience a narrow range of conditions
Control of lighting	Limited control	Extensive control
Servicing the dwelling	Takes considerable time	Takes barely any time
Social network	Local friends and relatives	International networks, electronic communication

Source: adapted from Golton (1994).

thick walls absorb heat in the summer days, releasing it in the cool nights. In the winter they dampen the rate of temperature drop at night as the heat is released' (Golton 1994: 2). Even so, warm clothing is required to keep out the cold. Building services are limited and much time is spent gathering wood for cooking and heating, collecting water and generally keeping the house going. Golton concludes that the grandparents' lifestyle, 'is equally reflective of local relationships, running with the grain of the seasons' (Golton 1994: 5).

The parents' town house has a 'reinforced concrete frame founded on reinforced concrete pad foundations . . . External walls infilling the frame are of 200mm thick brick bedded in cement and sand mortar . . . Internally the wall finishes are gypsum plaster with vinyl emulsion paint or ceramic tiles. Floor finishes are ceramic tiles or terrazzo and in some places carpet' (Golton 1994: 6). In this case, building services are extensive for 'the role of conditioning the internal climate is passed to a sophisticated, relatively energy hungry technology'. Water comes in pipes, oil is delivered by tanker and the air-conditioning runs for several hours a day during the summer months. Though George's parents still take a siesta, their pattern of entertaining, their aspirations and their leisure activity indicates a lifestyle which is 'equally reflective of international relationships running without much heed to the grain of nature or the seasons' (Golton 1994: 8).

This little study of two generations of Cypriot family life helps clarify questions that previous chapters on the science and co-evolution of comfort have yet to address. There is no denying the existence of powerful commercial and professional interests in standardizing building materials and services. Should it be needed, the comparative table provides further evidence of what this has meant for the practicalities of design, construction and use. As detailed in Chapter 2, the universalizing paradigms of physiological research have helped determine and specify parameters of thermal comfort, here reproduced in the design and sizing of the heating and cooling systems with which the town house is equipped. Golton's descriptions of related ways of life in turn support the notion that technologies and practices somehow evolve together.

All this is relevant for thinking about how concepts and practices of comfort change, yet comparison of the two homes points to a further challenge. This relates to the fact that the grandparents' way of life was uniquely adapted to the conditions and circumstances of a specifically Cypriot environment. By comparison, the parents' expectations and comfort-related practices are not radically different from those of people living in any number of other countries and climates. In other words there are two issues to deal with. Picking up the threads left dangling at the end of Chapter 3, one is to better understand the transformation of macro or societal level concepts of comfort. The second is to say something about the direction of change and about how and why conventions might be converging around the world.

The following account recognizes the material anchoring of practice and the possibility that standardizing technologies might script and order correspondingly standardized expectations, but it also recognizes that this is not inevitable. Engaging with the substance as well as the process of change and with the meaning as well as the provision of services like comfort, this chapter makes a case for locating analysis of cross-cultural convergence in terms of a more systemic theory of sociotechnical change.

Levels, Layers and Landscapes

Chapter 3 reviewed different ways of conceptualizing the co-evolution of systems, devices and practices. Whether grounded in the sociology of consumption or of technology, these ideas failed to provide an entirely satisfactory account of the societal reconfiguration of comfort. This was partly because discussion of the dimensions and dynamics of co-evolution took relatively little note of the levels at which such processes take place, or of what Rip and Kemp (1998) characterize as a multi-layered system of innovation. Rip and Groen's (2001) three-tier model of sociotechnical change helps in making sense of the relation between new technologies and the sociotechnical environments into which they are introduced. It also gives an indication of how meso-level regimes and macro-level landscapes are formed and how they change.

Figure 4.1 shows (micro-level) local practices developing against a (meso-level) backdrop of regimes and (macro-level) landscapes. Novel 'configurations that work' are defined and constrained in various ways by the rules and characteristics associated with these higher levels. At the same time, these constraints and rules evolve as new sociotechnical configurations develop. The layering aspect is such that regimes are built on a raft of more and less irreversible configurations that stabilize and are stabilized by macro-level landscapes of sociotechnical order. The dynamics of de- and restabilization on any one plane are consequently shaped by the properties of the system as a whole.

In some instances, as when thinking about the introduction and use of the car, these three levels and the relationships between them are relatively clear. Cars depend upon and generate co-requisite arrangements including networks of roads, garages and petrol stations, driving skills, regulatory systems and laws. Such systems in turn produce and maintain societies that presume and rely upon high levels of automobility. This kind of hierarchical analysis implies that it might be possible to intervene deliberately and steer events in such a way as to reshape the course of longer-term transitions. Theories of this kind are especially appealing to policy makers and such ideas have informed programmes of research designed to identify ways of stimulating the development of more sustainable regimes and landscapes (Elzen *et al.* 2002).

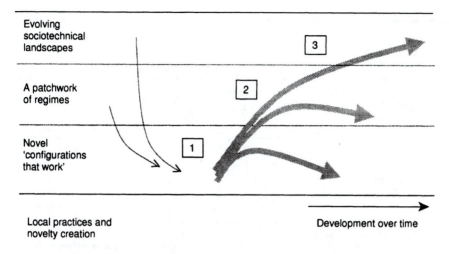

Local practices and   Development over time
novelty creation

1 Novelty, shaped by existing regime
2 Evolves, is taken up, may modify regime
3 Landscape is transformed

This figure is from Rip and Groen (2001) 'Many Visible Hands' in Coombs, R., Green, K., Richards, A. and Walsh, V. (eds), *Technology and the Market: Demand, Users and Innovation*, Cheltenham: Edward Elgar and is reproduced with the permission of the authors, editors and publisher.

Figure 4.1. The dynamics of socio-technical change

However, two features of this model limit its ready application to the rather fuzzier case of comfort. First, novelty is held to originate 'within existing regimes, starting at the micro level of local practices' (Rip and Kemp 1998: 389). The weaker dotted lines indicate that novelty is also shaped by existing regimes, but the thick arrows head upwards, suggesting that this is the dominant direction of change. It is important to remember that this scheme was developed to describe the dynamics of technological innovation, not to conceptualize social change in general. This is one reason why it does not quite mesh with Wilhite *et al.*'s description of the 'arrival' of air-conditioning in Japan (Wilhite, Nakagami, Yamaga and Haneda 1996).

In Japan, *imported* themes of modernity and Westernization represented powerful forces shaping the construction of a regime of mechanical cooling. In other words, images of what buildings should be like along with scientifically inspired visions of ideal comfort conditions flowed back down the layers to influence novel configurations and local practices. It is unfair to criticize the three-tiered model on these grounds; after all, the story of Japanese air-conditioning has to do with the *acquisition* not the development of technology.

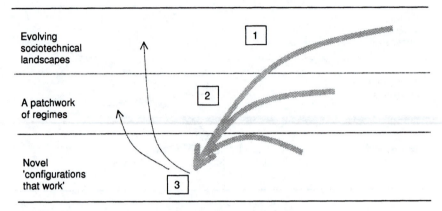

1   Western/American science and technology of comfort
2   modernity exemplified by standardised air-conditioning systems
3   novel technologies of artificial cooling introduced; traditional methods of construction
     abandoned

Figure 4.2. Reversing the irreversibilities

Yet the example raises relevant questions about the generation of novelty *between* as well as within societies, and about how irreversibilities are built. These figures should not be taken too seriously but if the large grey arrows were to be turned around such that they converged to a point, Rip's model could be modified and perhaps misused to illustrate the dynamics of standardization or the diffusion of American influence and technology on other cultures and practices. Figure 4.2 sketches the kind of thing I mean.

Recognizing the ratchet-like effects of irreversibility, the layered scheme supposes that sociotechnical landscapes are sustained and reproduced by the patchwork of regimes of which they are constructed. Again certain comfort-related examples resist such sequential, multi-layered interpretation. In Japan and Norway, divergent styles of lighting coexist within an apparently similar transnational landscape built around established infrasystems of electric power, shared expectations of an artificially lit society and the ready availability of standardized technologies. Does this imply that societies might have landscape-level features in common, but differ with respect to the way these co-evolve through the layers of regime and local practice?

Figure 4.3 explores such a possibility. As the image suggests, society (a) and society (b) share the same sociotechical landscape (represented by the black cell which they have in common) but differ in what this means for the operation and future of specific regimes, and local practices.

Again, this exercise takes the original model out of context, this time referring to the *use* of novel products in place of technological novelty per se, but

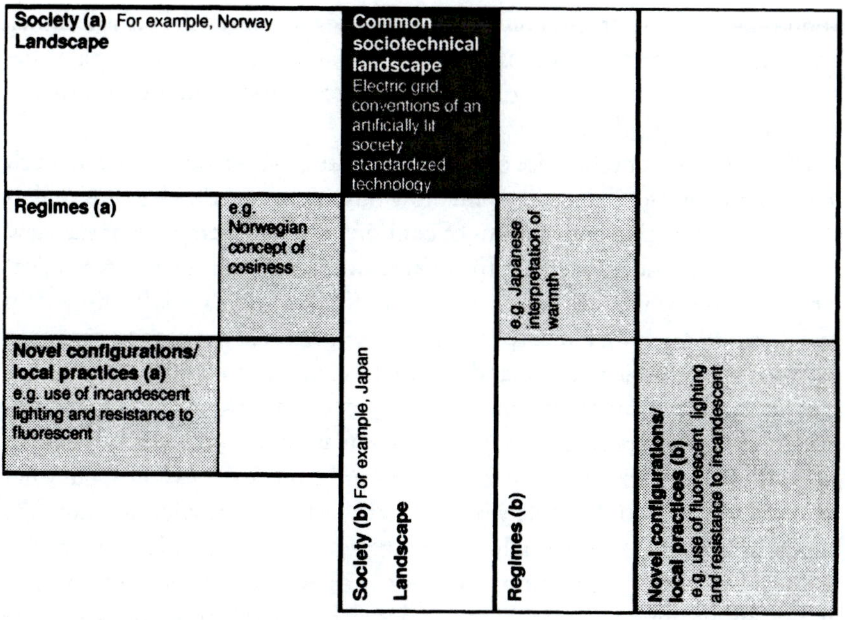

Society (a) For example, Norway Landscape		Common sociotechnical landscape Electric grid, conventions of an artificially lit society standardized technology		
Regimes (a)	e.g. Norwegian concept of cosiness		e.g. Japanese interpretation of warmth	
Novel configurations/ local practices (a) e.g. use of incandescent lighting and resistance to fluorescent		Society (b) For example, Japan Landscape	Regimes (b)	Novel configurations/ local practices (b) e.g. use of fluorescent lighting and resistance to incandescent

Figure 4.3. Shared landscapes, divergent regimes

again the result is of wider significance. The persistent variety of certain comfort-related practices suggests that the relation between the three tiers is more complex than has so far been allowed. While meso and macro levels clearly accommodate combinations of dominant and marginal micro-arrangements, the upward arrows of irreversibility disguise the extent of diversity within each plane, and obscure relevant differences in the fixity or flexibility with which the various levels interlock. To give a specific example, while cars have arguably had the common effect of engendering cultures of automobility, the meanings and practices they sustain vary widely between different cultures and contexts (Miller 2001).

Although Rip's model is immediately useful in understanding the transformation of comfort and routine in Cyprus over the last century, some adaptation is required if it is to be of value in explaining how Cypriot, Japanese and American families have come to share similar expectations of the indoor climate.

Convergence, Abstraction and Reversal

One possible response, already anticipated in Figure 4.2, is to show how standardized concepts and technologies have, as it were, imposed themselves upon previously divergent cultures and regimes of comfort. This is a rather unsophisticated explanation of globalization and not particularly plausible given the extent to which comfort-related practices are so engrained in so many aspects of everyday life.

The emergence or otherwise of a global culture has been the subject of much debate and it is useful to think about how this might contribute to our understanding of changing conventions of comfort. Rip and Kemp are of the view that there is considerable overlap between what they call the sociotechnical landscape and what anthropologists might think of as material culture (Rip and Kemp 1998: 338). However, there are significant differences of orientation between 'transition theories' and efforts to characterize and conceptualize cross-cultural consumption. For a start, authors writing about cultural homogeneity and/or diversity tend to study the circulation of commodities (Featherstone 1990; Hannerz 1996). There is, for instance, much discussion about what happens to goods and people when they cross cultural boundaries: does the export of Western and especially American products (Coca-Cola, soap, barbie dolls and so forth) lead to global convergence? How are things appropriated and given meaning in 'local' contexts (Howes 1996)? This emphasis on the flow of objects and meanings (how is it that the same thing has different meaning in different contexts, how is it that the same meanings can be reproduced through new and different things?) has two implications.

First, relatively little attention has been paid to combinations and complexes of artifacts, let alone to such composite enterprises as the built environment. Although cities feature prominently in discussions of globalization, they do so as concentrations of capital and communication, as melting pots of culture or as focal points of style and identity (King 1990), but not as technical systems or human habitats.

Second, the cultural dimension of the material is routinely given priority. In drawing attention to the dynamics of indigenization (Appadurai 1990) and the embedding of commodities in local contexts of production and consumption (Miller 1998), writers in this tradition suppose a measure of interpretive flexibility. Commentators more interested in how material objects, or non-human actors, script their users' practices would almost certainly have more to say about the practical and physical embedding of 'global' technologies within established sociotechnical systems. That is not to deny the importance of indigenization, but it is to make the point that such processes are likely to have material, political and economic as well as symbolic properties. One would, for example, expect local histories of path dependency, irreversibility and lock in to be of some significance for processes of appropriation.

In exploring some of these issues Appadurai (1990) distinguishes between what he terms ethnoscapes, mediascapes, technoscapes, finanscapes and

ideoscapes together constituting a 'landscape' of pretty much the same conceptual status as that described by Rip and Kemp (1998). Appadurai's investigation
of five dimensions of 'global cultural flow' and his suggestion that 'the complexity of the current global economy has to do with certain fundamental
disjunctures between economy, culture and politics' certainly maps onto the
three-tier model rather better than other more selective studies of material
culture. Appadurai is more interested in how these various 'scapes' fit together
(or not), in how global 'flows' work out, and how they are translated from
context to context than in the hierarchical layering of innovation. These ideas
about circulation and flow are potentially useful when thinking about how
comfort-related tools and meanings move between societies.

How does this work in practice? There are various accounts of how needs
are cultivated and naturalized and of how the culturally specific appropriation
of new products and ideas works in these terms (Wilk 1995, 1999). Although
useful in thinking about how conventions of comfort change within any one
society, generic accounts of this kind tell us little about standardization and
convergence *between* societies or about the relation between that which circu-
lates and that which is forever localized. Switching fields, similar issues are
of interest to those studying the relation between 'expert' and 'lay' knowledges.
Working in this arena, and doing so in a way that resonates with some of the
global-local debates alluded to above, Disco and van der Meulen (1998) have
written about the relation between 'cosmopolitan' knowledge which is explicit,
codified, and free to circulate widely (scientific knowledge being the prime
example), and local knowledge that is, by contrast, tacit and context specific.
They suggest that cosmopolitan knowledge and generalized insights are
abstracted from necessarily localized experience, and that cosmopolitan knowledge is in turn appropriated and given meaning through context specific
processes of *reversal*. Taking these ideas out of context, and blurring the
distinction between knowledge and practice, I want to apply them to the
discussion of comfort.

Reinterpreted along these lines, Chapter 2 provided a rather detailed account
of the production of cosmopolitan knowledge and of its embedding in standards and technologies, these being key media of circulation. Laboratory-based
studies of thermal comfort exemplified a particular form of abstraction.
Methodological differences aside, field researchers also shared the ambition
of producing generalizable conclusions through the study of local experience.
Meanwhile, Chapter 3 documented moments of reversal, that is instances in
which standardized understandings of comfort were made real in specific
contexts: as when Japanese and American families invested in air-conditioning
or when Mexican office workers abandoned the siesta. This suggests the
availability of a common, cosmopolitan repertoire – a global techno-ideoscape

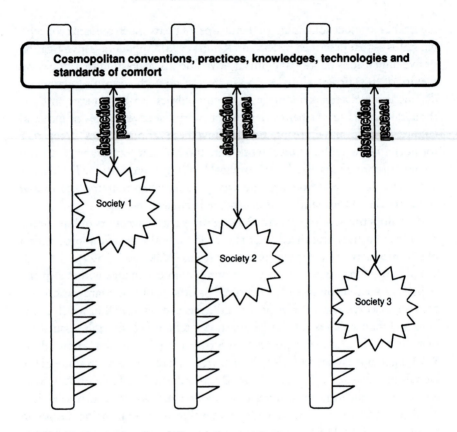

Figure 4.4. Convergence, abstraction and reversal

of comfort-related technology, practice and convention – which is reversed and appropriated (perhaps through the processes of naturalization and cultivation that Wilk describes) in different ways in different societies.

Taking ASHRAE standards and the meanings of comfort associated with them as an example, it is immediately obvious that the distance between such singular definitions and existing culturally specific comfort regimes is immensely variable. Capturing these ideas, Figure 4.4 makes the further point that while societies as varied as Japan, Norway and Cyprus may be moving towards a mono-culture of comfort they do so from extremely different starting points. In Figure 4.4, society 1, society 2 and society 3 each have their own 'local' configuration of comfort but each is edging toward a common model. The little teeth on the edge of the 'tracks' introduce the further point that processes of abstraction and reversal are not merely symbolic. Consistent with arguments developed earlier, movements of this kind are likely to have a trajectory of their own, punctuated by points of sociotechnical irreversibility.

By combining ideas about the relation between cosmopolitan and local comfort-related practices with the tiered models of sociotechnical change discussed above, we can begin to make sense of the experiences of George Papadopulos' parents and grandparents, *and* of the similarity between his parents' expectations and mine.

The elements fit together as follows. As described in Chapter 2, the production of cosmopolitan concepts of comfort went hand in hand with the development of standardized and standardizing technological systems. In understanding the appropriation of these devices and the practices associated with them, it was necessary to conceptualize the specification and reproduction of comfort as a collective social achievement. Changing expectations of what constitutes comfort evidently involve more than the development and diffusion of individual technologies, hence the relevance of reflecting upon the characteristics of system-level change and the mutually determining relationship between sociotechnical landscapes, regimes and innovative practices. This has the advantage of offering a more encompassing vision of what is at stake in any one society, but it does not help in understanding the transnational standardization of comfort.

By appropriating the distinction between cosmopolitan and local knowledge/ practice and acknowledging a further dynamic, namely that of abstraction and reversal, I was able to describe and position the diffusion of shared concepts of comfort *and* their context-specific appropriation within different societies.

The case of the two Cypriot houses illustrates all aspects of this story. In the town as in the country, the day-to-day meaning and practice of comfort is strongly influenced, scripted even, by the nature of the household infrastructure. In both situations, sociotechnical regimes and landscapes of convention frame and contextualize individual actions and expectations. The difference is that in the parents' case, these expectations reflect and reproduce a cosmopolitan concept of comfort shared by their contemporaries in other cultures but not by the older generations of their own family. These cosmopolitan concepts are to some extent embedded in the design of the parents' town house, in what it is made of and in the air-conditioning and other systems it contains. In retaining the siesta they retain some of the comfort-related practices they have in common with their own parents and with other members of Cypriot society, but not with their son George who has become accustomed to a 'normal' nine-to-five working day.

Escalating and Standardizing Concepts of Comfort

The last few chapters have explored the question of how comfort becomes normal from different angles. In environmental terms the message is clear.

Escalating consumption is directly attributable to the specification and global standardization of 'comfort zones' the maintenance of which depends on energy intensive systems of heating and cooling. In working out how such a narrow definition of comfort has been naturalized, it has been important to take note of the science and engineering involved, of the technologies that have been developed and the ideologies they have carried with them. As described here, the rate at which standard concepts of comfort have spread and taken root, and the apparent ease with which they have displaced what seemed to be entrenched regimes and ways of life has to do with their grounding in a particularly universalizing form of science, their embodiment in a handful of codes and equations, and their materialization in the form of equally standard-ized commodities. Air-conditioning and central heating systems are bought and sold around the world and this is a very important part of the story. So too is the narrative of ratcheting and path dependency. Technical developments have made it possible to define and reproduce indoor climate conditions, which have in fact become 'normal', and since the management of comfort is so deeply embedded in the structuring of social activity, this has endless consequences for a vast array of climate-related practices: for the scheduling of society, for when, where and what people eat, for what they wear and for how they organize their day.

Although these chapters have also dealt with diversity, reversal and domesti-cation, the core of this account has to do with the standardization of conven-tion and technology. This has implications for the longer term, especially because much of the 'necessary' hardware (the built environment) is already with us, and because our sense of future possibility is bound up with what we have become accustomed to. The buildings we inhabit today consequently contain within them important scripts for the future for they are, like it or not, helping to build what will become the traditions and conventions of tomorrow. At the same time, this has helped illustrate just how fast things can change. If science and technology are as pivotal to the specification of comfort as I have suggested, battles over the development of 'adaptive' standards for natural ventilation may be of real significance, perhaps heralding a radical redefinition of what comfort means and how it might be achieved. The Chartered Institute of Building Services Engineers' quest for comfort, referred to in Chapter 2, now seems real enough, not in the sense that there is an end in sight but in that the pursuit is indeed endless. Despite and even because of the standardizing influ-ence of science and engineering, regimes of comfort are unlikely to ever finally stabilize.

More abstractly, the case of comfort has provided a context in which to review and explore theoretical accounts of escalating and converging patterns of consumption. I began with a story in which the standardizing power of scientific knowledge took centre stage: it was this that generated a universally applicable (or at least universally applied) concept of comfort, and this that set the scene for global convergence. I then concentrated on ideas relating to the mechanisms of sociotechnical change, to the hard-wiring of present and future possibilities and to the mutual structuring of social and technical systems. In this chapter I have tried to put the ratcheting of demand into context, considering the relation between different regimes of comfort and thinking about the dynamics of change between as well as within societies. Throughout, the specification and appropriation of technology (heating, cooling, lighting and so forth) has been important. The next chapters are similarly concerned with the dynamics of escalation and standardization. However, they deal with practices that are not so obviously structured or scripted by the technologies and material properties of the built environment. Partly because of this, other theories are required to make sense of how and why conventions change.

5

Introducing Cleanliness: Morality, Technology and Practice

This chapter marks a change of direction or at least a change of emphasis in the course of the book. Up to now I have been dealing with the indoor environment, using that as a case through which to examine the co-evolution of practices, technologies and conventions. Although the reconfiguration of habit remains a dominant theme, the switch from comfort to cleanliness takes me into new territory. While failure to conform to contemporary standards of comfort might generate feelings of sympathy, concern or even shame, it is unlikely to engender disgust and revulsion. By comparison, notions of cleanliness are more laden, more weighed down, with symbolic and moral import. Concepts of what is right and proper are unavoidable when thinking about how cleaning practices come to be as they are and how it is that weekly patterns of bathing and laundering have turned into daily routines. Although much of what has been said about the co-evolution of technologies and practices and the cross-cultural convergence of convention still applies, the discussion of cleanliness introduces new challenges. For example, how might we explain the development of routines that are more resource intensive but that make use of existing technologies and infrastructures? Why should more energy and water be required to sustain and reproduce what people take to be normal, ordinary and necessary standards of cleanliness? In this context, much depends upon changing ideas about how things should be and what people should do. It is therefore important to examine the movement and convergence of dominant discourses and rationales and their relation to collective, 'structural' anxieties of the time (Warde 1997). Ideas do not translate directly into action and there is more to be said about this relation between morality (meanings of right and wrong), technology and practice. In short, it is necessary to work themes of social order and propriety into the analysis of sociotechnical co-evolution.

Questions of Cleanliness

This chapter provides an introduction to some of the ideas (social, medical and scientific) entangled in the making of cleanliness and in it its contemporary reproduction. As before, I am interested in the escalation of demand and the standardization of convention. As will become clear, however, there are relevant social and material differences in how comfort and cleanliness are specified and achieved. Because of this, somewhat different processes are involved in the normalization of standards and practices. Part of my aim is to detail these variations and consider their implications for theories of change, and in particular for an understanding of regime-level transition. This might seem like a rather academic exercise and to some extent it is. On the other hand, better appreciation of *how* conventions of comfort or of cleanliness develop is of practical relevance for those seeking to steer related practices in a more sustainable direction.

The habits I consider under the heading of cleanliness differ from those relating to the provision of comfort on three counts. First and as already mentioned, they are more obviously soaked with moral, social and symbolic meaning. Second, cleaning often constitutes a form of work. The fact that this can be organized and arranged in different ways (at home, with the help of a commercial laundry, a washerwoman or a launderette) is of some significance for how 'standards' evolve. Third, the achievement of cleanliness generally involves the co-ordination or synchronization of multiple sociotechnical systems. What difference do these features make to the way that conventions and practices of cleanliness evolve? That is one question.

A second ambition is to revisit and, with the help of these new examples, develop the following themes. In Chapter 3 I distinguished between theories of difference (and a dynamic of de- and revaluation) and of coherence (and a dynamic of de- and restabilization). This was useful in conceptualizing the acquisition of new technologies like air-conditioning. Can such ideas also be applied to the appropriation of new discourses and rationales or to new ways of using the same technologies?

Chapter 4 considered regime-level transformations in the meaning and provision of comfort. Much of that discussion concentrated on the embedding of heating and cooling technologies and on the path-dependent consequences of standardization for the indoor environment and peoples' expectations of it. The concept of a sociotechnical regime is certainly useful when trying to figure out how complexes of technology, practice and convention co-evolve, but more is required in order to understand the redefinition of services that can be delivered in different ways. In addition, and as demonstrated in Chapter 7, the production of fresh laundry depends upon the effective integration of multiple technological systems, each having its own more-or-less path-dependent narrative. How might we conceptualize transitions in practices that are so multiply anchored? That is another question. Finally, the relation between regimes and the services they sustain deserves further investigation, as do mechanisms of integration: how do suites of systems and practices hold together and how does that affect the rate and direction in which routines change?

Consistent with the approach outlined in Chapter 1, I take these arguments on with reference to practices that are currently on the move and that appear to be moving in more resource intensive directions. This imposes significant limitations. Although much could be said about the multiplication of household cleaning products (Thomas 2001), cultures of de- and re-odorization (Classen, Howes and Synnott 1994) or the cultural and religious significance of the toilet (Reynolds 1943; Wright 1960; Lambton 1997), I focus on personal bathing and showering and on the domestic laundry for the following reasons.

After space heating and cooling, the production of hot water generally represents the second most significant use of energy in the home (Weingarten and Weingarten 1998). Bathing and clothes washing account for 37 per cent of domestic water usage in the USA (American Water Works Association 1999) and around 30 per cent in the UK (Environment Agency 2001; Shoulder *et al.* 1997). More specifically, models and forecasts of future water consumption in the UK anticipate a fivefold increase in the number of litres used for showering between 1991 and 2021 and an equally dramatic decline in the use of the bath (Herrington 1996: 35). As people are expected to shower more and more often and to use more powerful showers, this shift threatens to increase the total amount of water (including hot water) used for this purpose by something like 30 per cent over this period.

As an environmental issue, clothes washing is more delicately poised. Although the horizontal axis washing machines used in most of Europe consume roughly half the water required by the vertical axis models that dominate the American market, both formats are now more efficient than they were twenty or thirty years ago. In the UK and the USA technological improvements are just about keeping pace with changing patterns of ownership and use. Market penetration is already at saturation levels of over 90 per cent in both countries, so such increases relate to the growing number of separate households and to the frequency with which people wash. A number of commentators expect this balance to tip in the direction of escalating consumption. The UK's Centre for Alternative Technology, for instance, estimates an 18 per cent increase in the energy used by UK domestic washing machines by the year 2020 (Centre for Alternative Technology 1997).

Patterns of resource consumption do not simply follow developments in the acquisition and design of new technologies. Changing habits are also critical.

Over the last thirty years in Britain, the quantity of washing laundered at 90 °C or above has dropped from 25 per cent to 7 per cent (DEFRA 2000). Meanwhile, the total volume of domestic laundry has been slowly but steadily rising to the point that domestic machines now handle an average of 1,332 kg of laundry per year in the USA (Biermeyer 2001) and 822 kg per year in the UK (DEFRA 2000).

Despite what Vinikas (1989: 615) describes as a 'net drop in dirtiness' associated with mains water and sewerage systems, paved streets, the use of cars rather than horses as normal means of transport, the introduction of electric power and decreasing dependence on coal, contemporary conventions of cleanliness demand more and more frequent washing. Before discussing the detail of why this might be so, I take a look at how writers on cleanliness have characterized the relation between morality, technology and practice.

Morality, Technology and Practice

Mary Douglas argues that concepts of defilement are the outcome and the consequence of the routine policing of social boundaries. In describing complex categories of who can and cannot touch what (untouchables are, for example, literally beyond contact), and in detailing rules and procedures for purification and decontamination, Douglas makes the point that 'where there is dirt there is system' and that 'dirt is the by-product of a systematic ordering and classification of matter' (Douglas 1984: 36). Developing an essentially social theory of dirt, she writes as follows: 'As we know it, dirt is essentially disorder. There is no such thing as absolute dirt: it exists in the eye of the beholder. If we shun dirt, it is not because of craven fear, still less dread of holy terror. Nor do our ideas about disease account for the range of our behaviour in cleaning or avoiding dirt. Dirt offends against order' (Douglas 1984: 2). For Douglas, the mundane business of washing and wiping is as revealing of social order as any of the more dramatic rituals and taboos surrounding birth, death and sex. Having explained that in chasing dirt, people are basically involved in making their environments conform to an ideal order of society, Douglas concludes that 'when we honestly reflect on our busy scrubbings and cleanings in this light we know that we are not mainly trying to avoid disease. We are separating, placing boundaries, making visible statements about the home that we are intending to create out of the material house' (Douglas 1984: 69).

More obviously than comfort, cleaning is the stuff of division and demarcation. By implication, *new* practices of cleanliness indicate a reconfiguration of social ideals and orders within, but perhaps also between and across societies. As Douglas puts it, 'the same impulses which bring definitions of dirt into existence can be supposed to be continually modifying and enriching them' (Douglas 1984: 5). Accepting Douglas's view that cleaning is at heart about the symbolic reproduction of order, questions remain regarding the specification of order-maintaining activities and how they change. Dealing with similar themes, Elias relates the differentiation of manners to the structure of society, detailing what he describes as long-term structural changes leading 'toward a higher level of social differentiation and integration', mediated through increasingly privatized forms of self-control (Elias 1979: 223). Again the implication is that practices like those of cleaning mirror and constitute the ordering of society. As that becomes more fractured and complex, so do the means and manners through which divisions are reproduced and maintained.

This is all very well, but how do meanings and significances become attached and why to some but not other practices? While recognizing the symbolic significance of cleaning, authors like Cowan (1983) and Forty (1986) show how the development and introduction of new technology has changed the metaphorical terms and phrases with which those 'visible statements' are made. As the next four chapters demonstrate, certain devices and appliances have rescripted the meaning of cleaning, effectively imposing 'their own' classifications of dirt, disorder and propriety. In this respect there are parallels with comfort. Like ASHRAE standards, washing machines and soap powders have the potential to create and sustain conventions that are difficult to avoid. Jelsma suggests that domestic technologies script their users' behaviour in more-or-less environmentally benign directions and thus act as 'moralising machines' (Jelsma 1999). But there is more to it than that for the tools and technologies of cleanliness inform definitions and classifications of dirt. In addition, they configure the knowledge and skills of those who use them and thereby structure the moral landscape in which actions have meaning. For example, and as discussed in more detail in Chapter 8, the introduction of an automatic washing machine or a tumble dryer changes the fine grain of what it means to wash and dry properly. In this it has the potential to transform the social import of both the process and the outcome. In so far as cleaning technologies are enmeshed in a landscape of moral and social distinction, their development has the further effect of reconfiguring that terrain.

On a more macro scale, the fabric of the urban environment serves to stabilize and standardize definitions and expectations of normal practice. Infrastructures of electricity and water have been immensely influential in shaping the meaning and practice of washing and in constituting what Melosi characterizes as the 'sanitary city' (Melosi 2000). Studies of the civic institutionalization of cleanliness tend to focus on the material embodiment of changing medical and scientific theories. Adopting this method Melosi organizes his history of the sanitary city with reference to dominant theories of public health. He therefore details differing strategies associated with miasma-based and bacteriological concepts of disease. Dealing with habits of cleanliness rather than the development of underground infrastructures, Nancy Tomes (1998) takes a similar line, also relating new routines of hygiene to advances in scientific and medical knowledge.

Authors like Melosi and Tomes suppose the management of dirt to be a functional and essentially utilitarian enterprise, the details of which reflect the latest thinking about disease and infection. As scientific understanding changes, so behaviour follows. By contrast, Elias and Douglas take cleaning to be a predominantly symbolic matter bearing little necessary relation to the science of the day. For them, science represents one amongst other means of legitimizing social division and dirt-related discrimination. The division between these two positions is not as wide as might at first appear. After all, the moral and symbolic significance of dirt and disease has frequently shaped the course of scientific and medical enquiry. Sontag's (1991) work on *Illness as Metaphor* does a fine job of illustrating this relationship, demonstrating the social power of ideas and images of health and wellbeing and their effect on the course of scientific enquiry, the practice of medicine and peoples' responses to it. Latour (1988) makes similar connections when arguing that the 'discovery' of microbes and their identity and status depended on the means through which they were known and the strategies and practical measures adopted in response. The distance between Tomes and Douglas therefore depends on how we conceptualize the relation between scientific knowledge and the symbolic (but also structural and sociotechnical) ordering of society.

This debate is of some significance for an understanding of change. If cleaning is at heart a matter of policing social boundaries and restoring order, change can explained in terms of the shifts in the structure of society and in the distinctions that are to be maintained. In concluding that domestic technologies have ordering properties of their own, writers like Jelsma, Cowan and Forty suggest that concepts of cleanliness are in part, and in addition, bound up with a narrative of technological innovation. By implication, moral regimes are to some extent commodified, scripted and embedded in the tools and infrastructures on which we rely. Quite how these social-symbolic, moral, scientific and technical 'dimensions' run together also depends on the social organization of the practices involved.

What cleaning entails, and for whom relates to the social division and organization of labour, its location within domestic or commercial systems of provision (Fine and Leopold 1993) and its positioning within systems of gender, status and identity. For cleaning, more so than comfort, changing expectations and standards have to do with the definition and allocation of constituent activities and the terms in which these are judged.

Whatever the beliefs and technologies of the day, doing what people think of as cleaning, whether of the person or of clothing, generally requires a rather high level of active participation. Cleaning consequently involves the routine reproduction not just of classificatory schemes of delicacy, propriety and gender, but also of performance. Taking practices to be themselves constitutive of the ends they purport to serve, Hackett (1993) argues that rather than being a predefined goal or something that people strive to achieve, cleanliness is best understood as the outcome of whatever it is that people do in its name. Following this kind of reasoning, it is the everyday activity of laundering or showering that convinces people there is dirt to remove.

The following chapters draw on all these ideas in exploring the relation between morality, technology and practice. Chapter 6, on personal bathing, is built around the proposition that discourses and contemporary rationalities legitimize and guide practice. Some of these discourses invoke scientific understanding, some are more transparently judgemental and others have little to do with cleaning at all. In tracking the ebb and flow of ideas about what bathing is about I pick a course between the positions represented by Elias, Douglas, Sontag, Tomes and Melosi. In discussing laundering (Chapters 7 and 8) I pay more attention to the relation between technology and practice, examining the reproduction of social order and categories of propriety and service through the active deployment of (co-constitutive) arrays of materials, tools and technologies.

I do not want to imply that technologies and products tag along behind or that habits and classificatory structures mirror the latest scientific knowledge. But by way of background, it is useful to provide a brief review of humor, miasma and germ-based theories of disease on the grounds that a number of related ideas are still in circulation. I then take stock, equally briefly, of how classifications of cleanliness have been (and still are) bound up with distinctions of class, race, age and gender. Again the intention is to indicate how activities like bathing and laundering position people and how such practices are positioned within other systems of order. The last section of this chapter considers the commodification of cleanliness, showing how ideas of dirt and social order have been materialized and how products and technologies have given form to the business of cleaning.

Humours, Miasmas and Germs

Although there is an extensive literature on body image and style, much less has been written about keeping clean. Vigarello's little book on *Concepts of Cleanliness: Changing Attitudes in France Since the Middle Ages* is an important exception. In it he pursues the notion that such concepts are inti-mately related to beliefs about the body. It is, as he says, 'as if the image of the body had a determining effect' (Vigarello 1998: 20) on habits of washing, wiping, and laundry. Three such images are particularly important.

The first has to do with the concept of the body as a system in which different humours exist in a state of relative equilibrium. These ideas, popular in the sixteenth century, went hand-in-hand with a belief that the body was porous and subject to penetration by heat and water. On the positive side this meant that carefully controlled bathing could be used for therapeutic purposes: to restore balances, moisten the body and even 'correct certain sour or vicious humours' (Vigarello 1998: 11). But at the time when these concepts were particularly pervasive, the dangers were much more apparent. By subjecting the body to water and opening up the pores, one ran the risk of letting in all manner of evils, not least pestilential air. Fear of the plague is a constant point of reference in Vigarello's discussion of deep-seated and durable anxiety about the 'wide open' skin through which vital substances leak out and dangerous elements seep in. No wonder that bathing went out of fashion and no wonder either that clothing was viewed as a second skin, hermetically sealing weak bodies and protecting them from unwanted infiltration. According to Viga-rello, 'Clothing in times of plague confirms this image, dominant throughout the sixteenth and seventeenth centuries, of a body which was completely porous, and which necessitated quite specific strategies: the avoidance of wool or cotton, materials which were too permeable, and of furs, whose deep pile offered a haven to unhealthy air' (Vigarello 1998: 10). Informed by such ideas, sixteenth-century concepts of cleanliness did not favour frequent washing. On the other hand, wiping, and especially wiping with clean fabric, promised to mop up excesses of bodily humours. In a formulation now difficult to compre-hend, laundry was important precisely because of the dangers of bathing.

The second cluster of ideas associates danger and disease with decay and smell. Those subscribing to miasma-based theories of illness believed air to be the key medium of transmission: just as dangerous odours percolated up from the bowels of the earth so they might be absorbed back into it. Corbin's (1986) compelling social history of smell, appropriately titled *The Foul and the Fragrant*, provides a subtle account of the miasmic mindset and of a seventeenth-and eighteenth-century world in which stenches emanating from cemeteries, cess pools and marshes were again believed capable of penetrating the fragile margins of the body. Preoccupation with the circulation and flow of vapours and gasses and with the odours of bodies, the smell of their humours, and the details of putrefaction and excretion dominated social and medical discourse for over a century (Corbin 1986: 36).

As danger lay not with filth and dirt as such, but with the odours arising from it, the priority was to remove smell. Buildings and even cities were consequently designed to maximize ventilation and circulation and minimize risks posed by pockets of stagnant air like those trapped in dead-end streets or under staircases. An alternative but also viable counter strategy was to fight smell with smell. As Corbin explains, 'To use excessive amounts of perfume was to protect oneself and purify the surrounding air'. Perfumes, fumigants and aromatics provided a 'shield against smells', constituting what was for a long time thought to be 'the best protection against disease' (Corbin 1986: 63).

Miasma-based analyses of risk and beliefs in the permeability of the body sustained and legitimized conflicting strategies. Corbin quotes one eighteenth-century commentator who advanced the view that dirt obstructed the pores and that dirty skin, 'too often regarded as a protective coating against miasmas' in fact 'impeded the aeriform exchanges necessary for organic equilibrium' (Corbin 1986: 71). If smell spelt danger, the best indication of hygiene was the lack rather than the presence of overpowering scent. This conceptual shift justified the deodorizing of both body and environment and a new under-standing of 'natural' fragrance. Themes of freshness, spring flowers, desire and sensuality converged in what Corbin describes as a 'new calculus of olfactory pleasure' (Corbin 1986: 85). As we shall see, contemporary bathing and laundry practices continue to be informed by many of these notions despite the decline of 'aerist', or miasmic schools of thought.

In scientific terms, germ and miasma-based explanations offer competing accounts of disease and of appropriate forms of preventive action. Parasitic micro-organisms are not necessarily associated with dirt or smell, and things that look clean might yet prove dangerous. Equally, filth can be harmless. According to Tomes (1998), moralists were initially anxious that the much-vaunted relationship between cleanliness and godliness would lose its grip in the face of bacteriological explanations. In practice, and as Latour (1988) observes, contrasting theories of disease, one focused on germs, the other on miasmas, inspired remarkably similar programmes of practical action; so much so that the regimes of cleanliness that preceded the 'arrival' of the microbe arguably set the scene for its 'discovery' and swift acceptance in the popular and scientific imagination (Latour 1998). Germ-based theories have none the less provided a distinctive and more precise focus for practical action. Germs cannot be seen so there are no obvious indicators of their effective elimination. Questions about how and how much to clean consequently arise on a daily basis. Such questions carry with them a burden of responsibility. If germs cause disease and if they can be killed by scrupulous hygiene, it is reasonable to interpret the visitation of illness not as an accident of fate but an indication

of domestic failure and lax standards. Although the collective institutionalization of germ protection, the professionalization of health care, and the decline
of tuberculosis and typhoid has taken away some of its moral urgency, cleanliness is still used as an index of domestic responsibility and care (Tomes 1998:
244).

Theories of disease undoubtedly influence meanings of cleanliness, but it is
important to take note of the social and political contexts in which the categorization of dirt takes place.

Dirt and Discrimination

Describing people, things or practices as clean or dirty is not a socially neutral
enterprise. In use, such labels contribute to more elaborate classificatory
schemes built around distinctions like those of class, race, gender and age.
Representation of the working classes as the 'great unwashed' illustrates this
point, as does George Orwell's conclusion that the 'real secret' of class distinction lay in physical repulsion. In his view the perception that the 'lower classes
smell', constituted an insuperable barrier to a less divided society (Orwell 1937:
15). Classen, Howes and Synnott (1994: 165) also observe that 'olfactory
aversions' to the smell of social groups other than ones own frequently embody
what are at root racist objections to immigrants, foreigners and outsiders of
one kind or another. Exactly what counts in the ranking of smell has changed
over time – high status is now associated with no smell rather than with
elaborate and ostentatious perfume. Even so, smell undoubtedly provides 'a
potent symbolic means for creating and enforcing class and ethnic boundaries'
(Classen, Howes and Synnott 1994: 169) and for 'deepening every social
divide' (Bushman and Bushman 1988).

In theory, such rifts can be overcome (or redefined) through hygienic reform.
A number of writers have, for example, commented on the significance of soap
and water in the colonialization of the 'Empire'. Expanding on this theme,
McClintock writes that 'soap was credited not only with bringing moral and
economic salvation to the lives of Britain's "great unwashed", but also
with magically embodying the spiritual ingredient of the imperial mission
itself' (McClintock 1994: 137). Burke (1996) also describes how missionary
reformers, bent on spreading the benefits of civilization around the world, did
so through instilling the disciplines and routines of personal hygiene. In these
accounts, the management of cleanliness is represented as a means of imposing
social order and discipline, symbolic control of the body being an enterprise
in 'organizing flows of value across the self and the community, and demarcating boundaries between one community and another' (McClintock 1994: 147).

In the case of bathing, showering and laundering, the relationship between beliefs, symbolic divisions and daily practices is further mediated by an array of domestic products, technologies and infrastructures. Again by way of preparation, some comment on the commodification of cleanliness is in order.

Commodifying Cleanliness

The recent history of cleanliness is, amongst other things, a history of the successful commercialization of an idea and the skilful development and positioning of products deemed essential for its achievement and so for moral welfare and normal life. Timothy Burke's (1996) study of commodification, consumption and cleanliness in Zimbabwe tracks the role of toiletry and textiles in making markets where none existed before. He analyses the manufacturing of need in some detail, arguing that (soap) consumers emerged partly but not simply as a consequence of global capitalism and colonialism and that their needs, once established, acquired a life and a legitimacy of their own. His account of the construction of demand echoes arguments about the domestication and appropriation of products and technologies considered in the previous chapter but adds to them by demonstrating the role of things in shaping vocabularies of social distinction and order.

Put simply, discrimination of the kind outlined above literally depended upon the consumption and production of soap powders, cleaning agents and cosmetics. Echoing this view, McClintock (1994: 142) concludes that 'late Victorian advertising presented a vista of the colonies conquered by domestic commodities'. Again the argument is that products were active ingredients in the transformation of convention and practice. Key players like Lever Brothers consequently had a dual role: as well as supplying the raw materials of respectability, their ever more differentiated product ranges further specified the meaning of cleanliness itself (Wilson 1954). Hence Burke's conclusion that 'by the 1960s the hegemonic promotion of manners, hygiene and appearance was increasingly expressed in terms of products and advertising slogans' (Burke 1996: xxx).

It is important to notice the defining role of the soap and detergent industries (Hunt 1999) but these are not the only organizations with a stake in manufacturing concepts of cleanliness. Urban planners, utilities, appliance manufacturers, textile producers, plumbers, and building designers are also implicated in what proves to be an extensive canvas of commercial involvement. Moreover, concepts of cleanliness take a variety of public as well as private forms, being translated into expressions of civic pride and societal well being, justifying regulation and legitimizing investment in street cleaning, sanitation and other forms of collective 'housekeeping'. Again such arrangements embody distinctive blends of social and moral distinction variously mediated through specific technological and/or scientific instruments and rationales.

Qualifying Cleanliness

In commenting on the relation between morality, technology and practice I have tried to identify the potential for linking competing accounts of what cleaning is about and how it changes. While I acknowledge cleaning to be a process of making and reproducing division and distinction, I remain interested in how those distinctions are materialized. In appreciating that meanings of cleanliness and dirt arise and are given expression through things and practices I also recognize that things and practices have ordering and dirt-defining properties of their own.

Although it is relevant to review the changing meanings and practices of cleanliness it would be strange indeed if habits of bathing and laundering were exclusively devoted to the moral, symbolic or utilitarian of goal of purification and if they did not make sense in other ways as well. Before going further, it is important to qualify the impression the issues explored in the next four chapters are essentially *about* cleanliness. Themes of pleasure, relaxation and temporal order are, for example, at least as significant for understanding the relative decline of the bath and the growing significance of showering once if not twice a day. Likewise ritual and routine have a power of their own in compelling and structuring what people do. To make the point again, I am interested in exploring and explaining the escalation and standardization of ordinary habits that happen to have far-reaching environmental consequences. Part of the challenge is to identify discourses, rationales and routines sustaining such customs and practices, whatever those may be. Jumping ahead, and leaping to what is properly a conclusion, the following chapters suggest that concepts of cleanliness are of surprisingly limited value in understanding contemporary conventions of bathing and laundering.

I have already explained why I chose to concentrate on bathing and laundering. There are, however, other decisions to be made about *how* to investigate these practices. In designing the next few chapters I have the further ambition of developing different ways of thinking about the social organization of normality. Although Chapter 6 is ostensibly about bathing, it is also an exercise in exploring the idea that private routines and rationales represent working responses to collective concerns and societal anxieties. The technologies involved – the bath and the shower – have changed hardly at all over hundreds of years, but patterns and logics of use are continually on the move.

I therefore concentrate on the reinterpretation of purpose and what this means for practice.

The two chapters on laundering also do multiple duty. The first shows how the specification of standards relates to the positioning of tasks within and outside the home, and how developments in fashions, textiles and detergents have a bearing on the meaning of clean. More abstractly, this chapter explores the meaning of co-evolution when many systems interact. This exercise has the further effect of introducing the problem of integration: what is it that holds 'laundering' together? This is the central theme of the second chapter on laundry. In addressing this question I make use of contemporary interview material that shows what laundering is about from the point of view of those who do it. This provides another angle on the relationship between morality, technology and practice and another perspective on the construction and reconstruction of routine.

6

Behind the Bathroom Door: Revolving Rationales

Bushman and Bushman contend that people now 'experience revulsion at the thought of going for a single week without a bath' (Bushman and Bushman 1988: 1238). This has not always been the case. Describing how well she 'bore' the experience of her first shower (in 1798), Elizabeth Drinker, the wife of a well-to-do Quaker merchant, records that she had not been 'wett all over att once, for 28 years past' (Bushman and Bushman 1988: 1214). For Elizabeth and for others of her time, bathing was a novelty and certainly not needed in order to feel clean. Puzzling over the transformation of convention between 1750 and 1900, Bushman and Bushman ask themselves how, over the course of just a few generations, washing went 'from being an occasional and hap-hazard routine of a small segment of the population to a regular practice of the large bulk of the people' (Bushman and Bushman 1988: 1214). Addressing a similar set of issues, this chapter deals with the following problem: how do bathing and showering habits come to be as they are and how and why do they change?

Up to a point the history of the bathroom and of what goes on behind the bathroom door can be told in terms of the standardizing role of science and technology and the co-evolution of increasingly convergent expectations and personal practices. In certain respects, infrastructures of mains water and sewerage parallel the use of mechanical heating and cooling, both systems permitting ways of life that would be otherwise difficult to imagine. Although it also makes sense to talk about 'standards' of cleanliness, and although some would claim that such standards have 'risen' historically and converged socially, the mechanisms involved differ from those associated with the management of the indoor climate. For a start, there are no bathing equivalents of standard-setting bodies like ASHRAE. Although sometimes formalized and written down, standards of cleanliness are more commonly shared and reproduced through tacit norms and conventions. Second, although the respecification of cleanliness is of direct relevance to powerful commercial interests, these include organizations operating in such diverse arenas as plumbing, home improvement and personal care. In and amongst all this it is hard to discern the construction of a strong path-dependent trajectory affecting the basic 'technologies' of the bathroom. New bathing habits often involve making different use of the same infrastructures and devices. Other methods and ideas are therefore needed to make sense of changing interpretations of moral and social order and of pleasure and obligation important to bathing but that have no equivalent in the reconstruction of what people take to be comfortable indoor environments.

Addressed in this way, the case of bathing provides an opportunity to introduce theories of practice that emphasize the importance of rationales and ideas. Although I argue that peoples' routines are shaped and moulded by the collective conventions of the day, I do not suppose that conventions *simply* mirror theories of disease, new systems of social discrimination or the restructuring of institutions and infrastructures. Without reaching for a functional account of action and purpose, I suggest that private habits are constructed as people steer their own course through culturally and temporally specific landscapes of legitimating discourse and classifications of ordinary and extraordinary behaviour. In order to understand the dynamics of bathing it therefore makes sense to follow changing discourses and to detail those in current circulation. I take this to be a relevant exercize on the grounds that individual practices are positioned as 'normal' with reference to collective conventions *and* that such conventions are reproduced through daily routines. I therefore review rationales of bathing from two perspectives: as guides to practical action and as justifications of it.

In taking stock of historical accounts of why people wash and shower as they do I have the further ambition of isolating enduring anxieties that are, in different ways, made manifest through bathing. These correspond to the 'problems involved in regulating personal conduct and negotiating a decent life in contemporary Britain' (Warde 1997: 56) and in deciding between alternative courses of action. This exercise leads me to suggest that bathing is usefully understood as an expression and realization of symbolic and structural concerns regarding the positioning of self in society, the conceptualization of body and nature, and the relation between pleasure and duty. These themes are given different weight in different societies and by different persons within any one culture. They are none the less relevant in that people reproduce these defining concerns in distinctive ways as they take their weekly bath or when they jump into the shower each morning. I suggest that this way of thinking about the mutual constitution of order, discourse and practice is of value in understanding changing patterns of consumption and in making sense of contemporary habits and arrangements. In essence, I argue that dominant rhetorics and reasonings 'pin' practice in place, that practices move as legitimizing rationales change and that these adjust in response to the reformulation of persistent structural concerns. At the same time, I insist on the point that it is the routinization of practice that gives these reasonings their collective power.

Having developed this argument through a review of historical work on the bathroom and its uses, I consider the responses of people interviewed about their bathing habits. These narratives have the dual function of exemplifying current manifestations of what I take to be generic organising themes, and of showing how priorities cluster. As such they inform further discussion of the normalization of daily showering. Widespread adoption of this routine is responsible for increasing levels of water consumption and is a matter of some environmental concern.

In considering why it is that people now expect to get 'wett all over' on a regular basis, I take the view that discourses of bathing (that is the reasons and rationales invoked in its favour) constitute instructive but not definitive guides to action. Rationales are difficult to recover yet certain aspects are embedded in the design and style of the bathroom. I therefore follow the history of the bathroom as a means of revealing some of the ideas around which it has been constructed. In taking this route I suggest that changing practices represent new ways of 'fixing' or resolving a handful of persistent preoccupations. Such an approach helps make sense of contemporary arrangements and is of some value in explaining the distinctive appeal of resource-intensive habits like those of power showering. As is already apparent, this chapter deals with a new menu of themes and arguments. In advancing the argument of the book as a whole, its purpose is threefold: to illustrate and exemplify the intersection of morality, technology and practice (as introduced in Chapter 5); to develop an account of changing practice that does not fit the models of sociotechnical co-evolution discussed in Chapter 3, and to introduce ideas about the specification and accomplishment of service to be taken forward in chapters seven and eight.

Bathroom Consumption

With 35 per cent of American homeowners decorating or remodelling their bathrooms in the 1998 and 1999 (American Standard 2000), bathrooms continue to be big business. In the spring of 2001, 80 per cent of the million square feet of the American National Kitchen and Bathroom Association's show was devoted to the latest showering and bathing technology and in that same year British people were expected to spend £947 million on bathrooms

(Bunting 2001). New concepts in bathroom design imply new styles of bathing and although market researchers' analyses of the future are not certain to materialize, industry leaders are undoubtedly keen to influence images of what the bathroom is for and what bathing and showering are all about.

Current trends indicate an increase in the number and size of British bathrooms. One commentator, for example, claims that 'the majority of newly built homes are now fitted with equal bathroom-bedroom ratios as standard' (Knight 2001: 77). The British market for showers is also increasing, growing by more than 30 per cent between 1995 and 1998 (Market and Business Development 2001). These figures do not necessarily mean that washing habits are on the move. The construction of more and more bathrooms might indicate a preoccupation with personalizing and privatizing space within the home rather than with bathing itself. Likewise, the fact that members of a household have access to a shower or bathroom of 'their own' tells us nothing about how they wash. By comparison, data on domestic water consumption provides more tangible evidence of changing practice demonstrating, in particular, the popularity of the shower, especially of the power shower (which pumps out water at a higher rate), and the decline of traditional British bathing habits (Herrington 1996).

Low flow showerheads use fewer litres of water per minute than those they replace but other technologies are much more profligate. At the very elite end of the market some of the most powerful showers filter and recycle the water they use. Kohler's body spa system is one such device, delivering 'hydro-powered cylinders of water' through twenty-five shower heads at the rate of 320 litres per minute (Kohler 2001). This is an extreme example for more ordinary power showers pump out between twenty and fifty litres a minute. However, this is a rate at which the water and energy consumption associated with daily showering far exceeds that of a twice or thrice weekly bath, each bath consuming an average of eighty litres of water however long the bather spends (Turton 1998).

The percentage of average daily domestic water consumption per capita devoted to bathing and showering is similar in the UK and the USA, being 17 and 18 per cent respectively. However, *actual* consumption averages out at about 48 litres per capita per day in the USA, 91 per cent of which is accounted for by showering (American Water Works Association 1999). This compares with around 27 litres per capita per day in the UK, only 36 per cent of which relates to showering (Shoulder *et al.* 1997). Although fifteen minutes under a shower is said to be 'a long time', UK water conservation managers are anxious that 'the next generation will embrace this' (Turton 1998). With an average showering time of seven to eight minutes, so far true for both the UK and the USA, such a pattern is already normal for those who shower twice a day.

Regular showering, as opposed to less frequent bathing generally increases consumption of both energy and water, so how might we explain the increasing popularity of showering and especially of power showering in Britain? Where does this convention come from, how is it institutionalized and how is it restructuring what British people are doing behind their bathroom doors?

One way of addressing these questions is to reflect upon the kind of society in which such practices make sense. Reasoning along these lines, Giedion offers a typically macro view of the social import of bathing, arguing that 'The manner in which a civilization integrates bathing within its life, as well as the type of bathing it prefers, yields searching insights into the inner nature of the period' (Giedion 1948: 628). According to Giedion, the role of bathing within a particular culture reflects that 'culture's attitude towards human relaxation' and the extent to which 'individual well being is regarded as an indispensable part of community life' (Giedion 1948: 628). By implication, frequent privatized showering indicates a specific formulation of cultural value. Also talking in general terms, Mary Douglas suggests that efforts to eliminate dirt represent a process of 'making an environment conform to an idea' and of 'imposing system on an inherently untidy experience' (Douglas 1984: 4). Again by implication, definitions of dirt and dirt-removing strategies like bathing or showering change with changing concepts of social system and order and hence with new ideas about what environments should be like.

Is this enough to explain why bathing habits are as they are or to understand the detailed dynamics of their transformation? Probably not. Acknowledging the social instability of dirt does not get us very far in thinking about *how* notions of normal practice are formulated, how societies are differentiated or how they change. To go further, it is useful to investigate the terms in which bathing practices are legitimized and which define some but not other routines as 'normal'. To repeat a point made earlier, this is not to suggest that dominant ideologies simply determine what people do. The relation between private habit and social convention is complicated and is as, Giddens (1984) points out, recursive. To the extent that ideas about bathing provide a guide to practice and a justification of it, it is worth following their development. The logics of previous generations are notoriously hard to recover but some are given substance in the form of the bathroom. The next section examines this rather specialized space as a means of revealing at least some of the rationales involved.

Reasons and Rationales

In tracking features of the private bathroom I veer between the UK and the USA and between decades and generations. My purpose is to isolate themes and issues to which the practice of bathing appears to represent a response, not to offer a chronological or culturally consistent history. As well as noticing the ebb and flow of more and less dominant preoccupations, I am interested in highlighting threads of continuity and points of intersection so as to understand the reproduction and standardization of convention.

Hydrotherapy and Gentility

In the introduction to his classic design guide on the subject, Kira makes the point that 'the private bathroom as we know it today, is a very recent development' (Kira 1976: 6). The history of the bathroom as a place in its own right is strongly associated with introduction of mains water and sewerage systems. However, running water was not a prerequisite for the invention of domestic bathing technology. Consider the 'English Regency Shower' designed around 1810. 'Made of metal painted to look like bamboo', it consisted of 'a basin with a drain on the bottom and a hidden tank at the top, joined by poles about ten feet long. A pump arrangement on the lower basin forced water up to the top basin through one hollow pipe and then down over the bather's head.' A similar hand-pumped shower system produced in 1830 included such refinements as a foot pedal controlled scrubbing brush (Plumbing and Mechanical 1994). Used or not, such contraptions represent the defining features of what Maureen Ogle describes as the first period of American plumbing, a period in which technical ingenuity was applied to the production of 'modern conveniences' for an initially elite market. According to Ogle, the pursuit of convenience understood here a matter of functionality, inspired the production of ingenious washstands combining a variety of facilities and clever devices. Often elaborately ornamented, these gadgets were status symbols in their own right.

The narratives of acquisition introduced in chapter three appear to fit this case equally well. At one level, the ownership of plumbing and of novel products like the 'English Regency Shower' seems to have been propelled by mechanisms of social difference and coherence similar to those at play in the diffusion of air-conditioning. But why did these devices take the form they did and what 'problems' were they purporting to resolve?

In detailing the diffusion of ideas (but not necessarily technologies) in the 1790s, Bushman and Bushman record a process of transatlantic trend setting in which the American gentry 'who consciously gathered ideas for their homes and their clothing from observations made in England were equally intrigued with stories of bathhouses and tubs' (Bushman and Bushman 1988: 1220). These stories, also promoted in the form of widely published guides to proper behaviour, identified personal cleanliness as an essential genteel accomplishment. Wright (1960) and Bushman and Bushman (1988) consequently conclude

that it was the fashion for cleanliness and its importance in signifying respectability, rather than any explicit association between washing, health and hygiene,
that led bathing to become a 'requirement' for some sectors of society.

This fashion was nonetheless associated with a mixed bag of reasoning and
additional explanation. As well as embodying gentility, the English Regency
Shower and its plumbed in successors promised to bring the hydrotherapeutic
treatments of the spa to the home itself. One of the devices listed in Mott's 1888
catalogue is thus described as a 'most complete bath' including needle spray,
shower, adjustable liver spray and douche, all of which can be used together
or separately, and with the added protection of a thermostat (Winkler 1989:
69). Such mechanical control also constituted an impressive if small-scale
display of what de la Peña describes as a distinctively modern capacity to tame
and reproduce natural forces for human benefit (de la Peña 1999). Bathing
was, in addition, represented as an experience valued because of the curative
properties of water and justified in terms of a 'cloud of notions' about the
benefits of immersion for 'calming the nerves, promoting circulation, curing
rickets, vomiting, and want of sleep' (Bushman and Bushman 1988: 1224).

There are two points to notice here. Although cleanliness came to be associated with social status, its achievement did not depend upon the use and
acquisition of new technology. In many cases a simple bowl of water was quite
sufficient. At the same time, and following a slightly different track, the detailed
design of bathing equipment, along with instruction regarding appropriate
methods and techniques for washing, frequently embodied specific – if contradictory – understandings of bathing as a therapeutic enterprise.

Sanitation and Social Order

On their first introduction, domestic plumbing systems were not an unqualified
success. Leaks, rats, foul smells and troublesome cesspools complicated the
lives of respectable households, adding to the price of gentility. Initially viewed
as inconveniences, these difficulties acquired new and menacing meaning as
epidemiological evidence suggested that the plumbed-in rich were at greater
risk of waterborne disease than their less fortunate neighbours. In one particularly high-profile case, bad plumbing was blamed as the source of a typhoid
infection that nearly killed the Prince of Wales in 1871 (Muthesius 1982: 55).

For a brief but intriguing period, technologies of the bathroom, which had
until then been viewed as 'prized symbols of American progress', were subject
to the scrutiny of 'sanitary science' and shown to be 'dangerous, unscientific,
and potentially deadly' (Ogle 1996: 118). Fear of sewer gas and of the social
as well as epidemiological risks of interconnection inspired some of the most
affluent members of society to rip out their plumbing, disconnect from danger

and return to the safety of the stand-alone basin. This episode reveals persistent anxiety about water and its ambivalent status as a source of sanitary danger *and* as a necessary ingredient in the prevention of disease. According to Ogle, these concerns were resolved through a combination of scientific method and military experience, both contributing to the professionalization of plumbing and public health. The institutionalization of hygiene had immediate impact on the bathroom for sanitary reformers were convinced that when safely and properly constructed – equipped with effective traps, valves and so forth – bathrooms provided the facilities required to keep disease at bay. In short families needed bathrooms in the war against germs. If they were to serve in this role, however, some things had to change. With cleanliness rather than respectability as the dominant theme, elaborate furnishings, decorative wooden mouldings, carpets and fancy wallpapers went out and simple, accessible fittings came in.

Reconceptualized as a matter of public health rather than an affectation of the elite, bathing acquired a new form of social, political and symbolic significance. Following Mary Douglas's lead, Adrian Forty relates the emergence of a public discourse of hygiene to a social context marked by 'rapid social change and disintegrating social boundaries' (Forty 1986: 159). More precisely, he takes 'the increasing political power of the working class to be behind the middle-class preoccupation with bodily, domestic and public cleanliness in the early part of this century' (Forty 1986: 159). Debate about the value of providing baths (until then high-status items) for the working classes captures this unease: would they be used for other purposes – classically, as a coal store – or would the bath prove to be an important instrument in curtailing the indiscriminate spread of infectious disease across all strata of society? Defined by the social structure of the time, Bushman and Bushman conclude that 'Cleanliness had social power because it was a moral idea and thus a standard of judgement. Cleanliness values bore on all who wished to better their lives or felt the sting of invidious class comparisons' (Bushman and Bushman 1988: 1228). Distinctions between the rural and the urban, the civilized and the barbaric, the familiar and the foreign consequently condensed into a newly discriminating language of cleanliness.

Caught up in this debate and in fact defined by it, the bathroom acquired a yet another role as an index of civilization (Lupton and Miller 1992). Nations and cultures were judged accordingly with the result that wherever and whenever 'reformers took it on themselves to improve the lower classes, cleanliness was likely to play a part' (Bushman and Bushman 1988: 1230). Burke makes a similar case, arguing that zeal for washing was part of a more substantial project of cultural reform and national identity building (McClintock 1994; Burke 1996). No longer a marker of an individual's position in the social hierarchy, regular bathing was reconceptualized as an entry ticket to society itself.

In the course of all this, the commercial importance of bathing and cleaning escalated wildly. Reflecting its status as a luxury item, manufactured soap had been taxed in England since 1632 but in a move demonstrating the redefinition of cleanliness as a social and moral necessity, soap duty was abandoned in 1852 at a cost of over a million pounds in lost revenue (Hunt 1999). Consumers' 'need' for toilet soap grew in parallel with the societal 'need' for cleanliness, a trend that had obvious benefits for the companies involved. Famous for their innovative approach to advertising, soap manufacturers like Procter & Gamble and Lever Brothers invested in making markets and brands, exploiting germ-based theories of disease in an attempt to fend off competition from cosmetics. Strategies to institutionalize washing paralleled direct marketing. The Cleanliness Institute, founded by soap producers, was for instance dedicated to the public service of improving hygiene and of instilling 'good' habits like those of washing hands before eating and after using the toilet (Vinikas 1989). The notion of removing unseen bacterial enemies was critical, for it was this that justified the use of soap even when hands and bodies looked clean. Such efforts clearly paid off for a 1938 survey showed that 'soap ranked second only to bread and butter in the essentials of life' (Vinikas 1989: 623).

The institutionalization of cleanliness involved other kinds of investment. Figures quoted in Plumbing and Mechanical (1987) show that in the USA sales of plumbing products and heating equipment rose by a staggering 367 per cent between 1925 and 1954. It is difficult to follow the intersection of public and private commitment to the material transformation this represents or to isolate the multiple rationales at play, however, the 'need' for a built-in bathroom was pretty well established by the 1920s, along with a hygiene-dominated theory of what it was for. Tomes quotes a New York City Bureau of Child Hygiene booklet that captures this reasoning in no uncertain terms: with the aid of the bathroom, the 'three deadly D's of dirt, disease and death' are to be replaced by the 'three healthful C's – cleanliness, comfort, contentment' (Tomes 1998: 186).

Consistent with this logic, the 'normal' bathroom was typically small and Spartan, white enamelled fittings and tiled, easy-to-clean, surfaces being part and parcel of its functional image. While the bathroom's script was clear, cleaning was a job to be done and this was the place to do it, coexisting ambitions of removing dirt, removing germs and maintaining moral standards generated contrasting 'rules' about when and how it should be used. To give just a couple of examples, in 1914 the New York State Department of Health recommended that 'every child should have one tub bath daily' (Bushman and Bushman 1988: 1213). Meanwhile, a 1929 advertisement sponsored by the soap industry's Cleanliness Institute advocated washing hair as often as once a fortnight (Lupton and Miller 1992: 17), a frequency taken as 'normal' by French hairdressers in the 1920s (Zdatny 1999).

This somewhat compressed account highlights three developments in the discourse of bathing. First, hydrotherapeutic benefits were well and truly upstaged by theories relating dirt to death and disease. Second, the social significance of bathing was recalibrated. From being a mark of status, regular washing became a basic condition of social acceptance: 'to escape disparagement, people had to wash' (Bushman and Bushman 1988: 1232). Third, mass rather than niche markets were established around the medical, moral, and social necessity of personal hygiene. Though it entered the home on this basis, the bathroom has since acquired other meanings and functions.

The Presentation and Production of Self

Despite academic interest in the body and its respresentation (Featherstone *et al.* 1991; Twigg 1997), few writers have paid much attention to the bathroom rituals involved in the presentation and commodification of self. One exception is Bourdieu who suggests that 'cosmetic investments' in personal appearance, for instance, in the frequency of bathing and the time spent grooming, are 'proportionate to the chances of material or symbolic profit' the different social classes can expect from them. He argues that time and money invested in this way is likely to be rewarded in the labour market for those in a position to seek and benefit from jobs that expect and demand conformity to the 'dominant norms of beauty'. The relationship between economic capital and what Bourdieu refers to as 'beauty capital' is further complicated by the notion that dominant norms of beauty are, from the start, enmeshed in the class system such that women of the dominant class have the advantage of feeling 'superior both in the intrinsic natural beauty of their bodies and in the art of self-embellishment' (Bourdieu 1984: 206).

These observations point to an as yet unexplored dimension of the social import of bathing. Ogle (1996) argued that indoor plumbing systems and other 'modern' conveniences served to symbolize status and respectability. In their analysis of cleanliness, Bushman and Bushman (1988) underlined the link between elite identity and the regular application of soap and water. As described by Tomes (1998), Forty (1986) and Hoy (1995), subsequent programmes of moral and hygienic reform had the further effect of transforming the meaning of cleanliness and its significance in demarcating and reproducing social difference. The relationship between appearance and bathing constitutes one more reason for getting wet all over and when viewed as a place for investing in stocks of 'beauty capital' the bathroom acquires another form of social significance.

What does cosmetic investment actually involve? A casual look along the shelves of supermarkets and specialist stores suggests a variety of answers. The range and variety of bath oils, crystals, foams, scrubs and salts, not to mention shower and body gels, shampoos and conditioners offers consumers an extensive palate of options. Having stripped the body of its natural odours people are free to customize aspects of themselves (skin, hair and scent) in any way they want. But there is some order to this Aladdin's cave of opportunity. As product labels make clear, nature is an important point of reference. This occurs at various levels. Most immediately, gels and lotions are designed to capture or at least evoke the essence of fruits, flowers, spices and herbs along with the spirit of mountain streams, fresh spring days or sandy seashores. The subtler message is that the application of natural essences will help restore the equally natural balance of a body thrown out of kilter by the rigours of modern life.

The loop is thus one in which washing begets washing and in which sequences of products are needed to restore what others have taken away. Amongst all this imagery, references to the body as a natural organism replace or at least supplement earlier more mechanical-hygienic interpretations exemplified by the slogan 'a clean machine runs better – your body is a machine, keep it clean' (Hoy 1995: 181). Although the restoration of natural balances figures prominently in current representations of what it means to care for yourself, and of how care translates into values of appearance and image, it is not just physical order that is to be maintained.

Contemporary bathroom design guides and popular magazines are at least as concerned to detail the mental and emotional aspects of well being. Appealing to the fantasies of office workers stuck indoors on a hot August day, Repinksi suggests that the bath serves to reconnect urbanites with the natural world. It allows them to simulate 'the feel of beach sand on the skin, the smell of a lake surrounded by evergreens, and the beauty of the sea' (Repinski 2000). Under the subheading of 'lake effects', she sketches this scene:

> You've spent the morning hiking a challenging mountain trail when a crystal-clear lake comes into view. Before you know it, you've plunged headfirst into refreshingly cool water and are reveling in the heady aroma of the evergreen forest around you. To get yourself back to that place emotionally, if not physically, take a scentsationally stimulating aromatherapy bath. (Repinski 2000: 126)

Continuing in this vein, Sacks explains that time lavished on oneself in the bathroom is time well spent, the bathroom being the place where you 'sing, dream, read, write, and plan great things' (Sacks 1998: 40). While the emphasis is more on luxury than cure, reference to the pleasures of unwinding in a steaming tub and images of running water hark back to hydrotherapeutic concepts around which the first private bathrooms were built. This theme, also evident in the luxury health 'spas' that became fashionable in up-market American homes in the 1990s, takes multiple forms including the 'hot tub', imported from Japan, and the spa-whirlpool that pumps jets of air and/or water into the bath. However, the rhetoric is not simply one of hedonistic pampering and self indulgence. Now that stress is a recognized hazard, magazine writers are free to promote bathing as a form of health care.

> It's well known that a warm, soothing bath is the best antidote for stress. But what's less known is that you can enhance the already soothing effects of water by using bath products with calming essences like sandalwood, lavender, vanilla or chamomile. (Gleason 2001: 157)

Gleason goes on to prescribe the use of 'invigorating, stimulating scents and essential oils like rosemary, peppermint and citrus' for a 'sure-fire wake-up call for body and soul' (Gleason 2001: 158). As represented in this literature, showering and bathing enhance physical appearance and mental well being in distinctly different ways. Personal routines – to shower or to bathe, to pick this sort of oil or that kind of gel – can be adjusted and customized to provide whatever it is that body and soul 'require'. Ideas about bathroom décor and design reflect changing concepts of what bathing is about and what it means to care for one's body.

Comfort and Convenience

The clean white aesthetic of the bathrooms of the 1920s and 1930s mirrored their role as 'the hospital in the home' (Lupton and Miller 1992). Streamlined values of simplicity and hygiene undoubtedly echoed 'modern' concepts of design but they just as obviously conflicted with traditionally cosier images of domesticity, interior décor and taste. Lupton and Miller argue that despite being accorded a specialist function *in* the home, the white tiled bathroom was not really *of* it. The author of an article in *House and Garden* summarizes the problem thus: 'While conforming to every law of health, the place should be made as attractive in its way as any other room in the house' (LeBaron Walker 1911: 378). As a first step, coloured ceramic and enamel products helped solve the problem of drabness and introduced new opportunities for social distinction, as did a detectable relaxation of the sanitary regime. Heather George (1999) suggests that as anxiety about domestic hygiene slackened for reasons Tomes (1998) attributes to the decline of diseases like typhoid and the development of chemical disinfectant, so the bathroom was reintegrated into the home.

Stylish and beautiful bathrooms became a real possibility: books and magazines offered advice on furnishing and design and by the 1960s fluffy carpets crept back across some of Britain's cold linoleum bathroom floors.

The image of a positively luxurious bathroom beckoned and with it the explicit rediscovery of bathing as a pleasurable activity. Although Havelock Ellis (1936: 33) concludes that the 'cult of the bath was in truth the cult of the flesh', Heather George's systematic content analysis of *Better Homes and Gardens* shows that sensual pleasure and relaxation did not figure as 'two of the bathroom's chief purposes' until the 1990s (George 1999). As contemporary themes of comfort have not displaced other discourses of cleanliness, physical appearance and natural balance, the bathroom is the site of increasingly complicated narratives. It is, as Sacks explains, a haven from the hubbub (Sacks 1998) *and* a place designed to 'speed up morning routines' (George 1999).

Summarizing the market in these terms, Korejwo concludes that body sprays, massaging jets, waterfalls, electronic controls, steam generators, special lighting effects, and CD players allow even the busiest people 'to take a few minutes to relax while they groom' (Korejwo 2000: 144). Although design advisors routinely comment on the need to blend 'in-and-out convenience' with stress-relieving luxury (Hufnagel 2000), the longer term challenge is to figure out how the bathroom relates to the rest of the house. Reviewing his experience with an admittedly exclusive clientele, one American designer suggested that in recent years the living room had been swallowed by the open-plan kitchen, which had in turn become a setting for ritual and display rather than for cooking and conversation. With the bedroom defined as a place for sleeping and the home-office dedicated to work, the bathroom was where couples planned the day ahead while sharing their morning shower, and where they compared notes when showering together again in the evening. The now 'standard' provision of 'his' and 'her' showerheads (National Kitchen and Bathroom Association 2000) provides some support for this social-architectural model of the bathroom as communications centre of the home.

Whether its future is as a social space or a place of retreat, there is no doubt that the modern bathroom is depicted as a site of leisure and pleasure as well as efficiency and convenience. Justified more in terms of appearance than cleanliness, washing is represented as a generic form of preparation for social interaction. No longer strongly associated with dirt and water borne disease, the medicinal benefits of bathing and showering are currently framed in terms of stress relief and relaxation. Echoing back-to-nature movements of the nineteenth century, contemporary bathing and showering is presented as a matter of restoring and maintaining natural balances (Giedion 1948: 679).

Understanding Bathing and Showering

The private bathroom's relatively short history has been marked by a succession of contrasting rationales: issues of gentility and respectability giving way to a preoccupation with germs and disease followed by a renewed preoccupation with luxury and convenience. This is matched by the chameleon like status of individual devices. The plumbed-in bath has variously featured as a convenient (easy to use) novelty, then a weapon in the war against disease and now an instrument of relaxation, comfort and retreat. Whatever the technologies involved, the social significance of daily washing has undergone equally radical transformation, variously figuring as a curiosity, a symbol of social standing, a precondition of acceptability, a means of enhancing 'beauty capital' and a way of marking the start and end of the day. What do these erratic narratives reveal about the process of normalization and the creation of more and less resource demanding habits?

Bathroom historians have their own ideas. Maureen Ogle's work on the history of plumbing suggests that the motivations for its acquisition were bound up with social identity and comparison and with efforts to signal membership of respectable society. The widespread adoption of regular washing was, by contrast, explained in terms of the institutionalization of scientific knowledge, the professionalization of public health and concerted effort in the name of moral and social reform. Ross (1995), writing of the relation between French and American culture in the post-war period draws other more sweeping conclusions about purification and its place in national identity. Less dramatically, recent developments in bathing culture are rationalized in terms of making and meeting demand for leisure and convenience and the commodification of health and beauty.

Does this suggest that different engines of change – social, technological or commercial – have come in to play at different points in the bathroom's career? Markets, technologies and ideologies intersect to such an extent that it would be tricky to argue that bathing and showering have been propelled *more* by scientific understanding of germs than by morality or *more* by technological development than social comparison. Equally, increasing water and energy consumption is not simply a consequence of the sequential ratcheting of demand associated with the path-dependent development and diffusion of standardizing technologies. In this arena what matters is the ebb and flow of ideas and rationales and their temporally and culturally specific materialization in the hardware of the bathroom and in the routines and self-justifications of those who bathe and shower. Dobell (1996) argues that the history of the bath is cyclical, not linear, yet the catalogue of positions outlined above shows that discourses of value and purpose do not simply recur. Instead, interpretations of 'normal' practice are built around clusters of belief and convention, some of which persist while others come in and out of vogue. It is none the less possible to discern some order amongst this waxing and waning of rationale. Looking back over the histories of ideas about bathing I identify a number of recurrent tensions.

The first has to do with the relation between self and society. In Goffman's (1969) terms, washing is back-stage preparation for public, front-stage appearance. In practice, the meaning of front and back stage and the relative significance of each is of defining importance for the positioning of personal bathing and its status as an optional, normal or necessary activity. In other words, bathing conveys contextually specific messages about who you are and how you fit in society (even though the substance of those messages has changed dramatically over the last century). The issue of whether bathing is preparation for 'going out' or recuperation from social interaction is relevant in this regard. In practice, such considerations might hold in place personal routines of bathing in the evening, as a form of relaxation, or of showering in the morning in anticipation of the day ahead. Some people might fit both into their daily schedule.

The second theme concerns the extent to which bathing is positioned as a means of working with nature or keeping it at bay. At one extreme, bathing and showering are valued as forms of natural restoration in which the curative properties of water are harnessed for the benefit of mind and body. In other situations, the stated purpose of bathing is that of purification, 'civilization' and the eradication of natural elements like those of sweat and smell. The degree to which bathing is routinely understood as a preventative or a restorative enterprise is almost certainly related to prevailing theories of disease. Few now think the skin to be porous and although the saying 'too much bathing will weaken you' is still in circulation, the idea that it endangers health is nothing like as pervasive as it was a few centuries ago. However, one model does not necessarily exclude another and at the level of practice, competing concepts of nature frequently coexist. Even at their most dominant, preventative discourses of hygiene failed to displace alternative more therapeutic interpretations of what bathing is about. This is to be expected for it is the balance between theories of body and nature that gives bathing regimes their distinctive character.

The third dimension relates to the status of bathing as a personal pleasure or as a social duty. Wilkie reflects on the bath's ambivalent position in these terms: 'while tubs may have helped teach people to be productive, orderly members of society, private bathing also indulged the industrialized individual's narcissistic impulses' (Wilkie 1986: 659). Forms of luxury associated with long lingering baths contrast with accounts of rapid showering as a an obligation,

Table 6.1. Dimensions and discourses of bathing

Positioning in terms of:	Hydrotherapy and gentility	Sanitation and social order	Comfort, convenience and commodification
self and society	Bathing signals membership of an elite	Bathing signals membership of civilized society	Bathing is about image and appearance
body and nature	Focus on the curative aspects of immersion in water	Focus on preventative aspects, soap and water required	Focus on curative aspects, especially restoring natural balances
pleasure and duty	Pleasure, ease of use, the spa in the home	Duty to protect own health and that of others	Bathing and showering embody different aspects of pleasure and duty

as something that simply has to be done, like it or not. If United Utilities' advertising is anything to go by, the present trend is to differentiate between these two experiences, hence: 'Water can help you relax and forget the troubles at the end of a long day', or it can be the opposite, 'a wake up call, helping you get ready for the new day ahead' (United Utilities 2001).

Table 6.1 groups discourses of bathing together along these lines and shows how they define and legitimize different styles of bathing.

This classificatory scheme helps make sense of seemingly erratic historical and cultural trends in the rhetoric of bathing. In doing so, it suggests that conventions of bathing are informed by a combination of rationales some of which revolve around the three 'defining' themes identified above. It also suggests that change along any one of these dimensions gives new meaning to the practice of getting 'wett all over'.

How does this scheme work out today and how might it be used in analysing contemporary experience? People do not generally discuss their bathing and showering habits so they have little knowledge of what goes on behind other bathroom doors. Because these most private arrangements are none the less important social practices, individuals tend to think their washing routines are normal and that deviance from the norm is minimal or confined to rare cases of obsession or extremes of personal neglect. The following collection of bath-time stories illustrates contemporary reasonings and shows how themes of self and society, body and nature, pleasure and duty are currently positioned.

Bath-time Stories

Partly because bathing and showering is a delicate subject and one of consider-able social and moral significance it arouses curiosity: just what is it that other people do? Anonymized accounts compiled from conversations with people aged between seventy and ninety, (from the North Berkeley Senior Centre, California) and with students and staff aged between twenty and forty (from Washington State University, the University of California, Berkeley, and from Lancaster University, England) provide some insight into current bathing habits. Some of these interviews were conducted one to one but more were collective affairs involving groups who knew each other already as colleagues or friends. In this latter situation details of private routines were traded at first warily but then with growing interest. The fascination of learning what others took for granted increased as the conversations continued.

The variety, the subtlety and the precisely calibrated judgements involved in taking a shower revealed a scale of ordinary sophistication that few had appreciated before. There were other surprises in store. Lengthy discourses on the pleasures of bathing pointed to a world of leisure and luxury entirely unknown to those for whom washing was a chore. Awe and amazement were not the only responses for there were times when respondents struggled to disguise their distaste – even their disgust – on learning of habits that trans-gressed their own thresholds of decency. Although they do not reveal normal practice in any representative sense, extracts from these discussions indicate the range of experience and explanation described.

When Jane was a baby, her mother bathed her in the kitchen sink. There are pictures to prove it. However, her first real memory is of sharing the tub with her older sister, Sally. This was recalled as a daily ordeal, one that con-tinued until Sally graduated to the shower at the age of about eight or nine. Jane soon followed suit. The right to shower alone signified freedom and independence: it was a rite of passage on route to adulthood. As a teenager, Jane had lots of long, thick hair and a set of expectations that obliged her to shower for thirty minutes during an hour-and-a-half ritual of 'getting ready'. Appearance was a central concern and the nature of her unruly hair was such that it 'needed' shampoo, conditioner, detangler and more. Unnoticed until early adolescence, Jane's skin also demanded special treatment. Jane's elaborate yet necessary morning routines were thrown into disarray by a brief but significant school exchange to water-short Spain. Fearing the excesses of their

American visitor, her hosts provided clear instructions on how to kneel in the bath and make the most of just one bowl of water. To Jane's surprise she got used to this new regime. Although still committed to detangler and conditioner, she tells this story by way of explanation. She now showers just three times a week, never for longer than a few minutes, and she really can't remember when she last had a bath.

Tim's early history was much like Jane's. He has two brothers, one older, one younger. They bathed together and positively enjoyed splashing around and playing with favourite bath toys. In time the boys moved on to the shower, first at home and then at college. Showering in the morning became a routine: it was good for curing hangovers and for waking up. The pattern set and a quick shower and a cup of coffee are now so essential that Tim simply 'can't get going' without. As well as being quick and convenient, the morning shower buys Tim a private moment in which to plan the day ahead. Shampoo features but as far as he knows his hair needs no conditioning. In the last few years, and for reasons he could not exactly pin down, Tim has taken to having three, maybe four baths during the winter. More for relaxation than anything else, these are a bit of a performance. Candles and scented bath oils help create the right atmosphere and when everything is ready Tim will soak for up to half an hour.

Sarah also likes a bath. In fact it would be fair to say that bathing and showering is something of a hobby. Her bathroom shelves are crammed with oils, salts, gels, body scrubs, shampoos, conditioners and assorted additives. With all this to choose from running a bath is like preparing a cocktail. Will it be fizzy or foamy, should the flavours be fruity or herbal, is the ethos to be one of spring or summer? There are decisions to be made and reading matter to select (magazines and articles but not books). Reading and soaking are a prelude to washing and finally showering to rinse away the dirty, soapy water. Hair washing happens aside from bathing and is only sometimes part of showering. Sarah has been told she'll damage her hair if she washes it too often and, like Jane, she is concerned to treat it right. The bottles on her bathroom shelf emphasize this natural theme, their medicinal style labels promising to restore balances and provide what her body needs.

Looking back, Sarah's pattern was one of bathing as a child and of showering (but sometimes bathing) as a teenager and young adult. The selection of one or another option depended on where she'd lived and on how 'nice' the facilities were. She could recall cold bathrooms down the corridor, faltering showers, erratic thermostats and systems that simply did not work. But for now, relaxation, sensual pleasure and expert consumer knowledge dominated the discussion. Experimentation was part of the fun and with gifts and advice from her sister and guidance and specialist supplies from her hairdresser there were always new products to try. In essence, bathing represented a relatively inexpensive but deeply luxurious form of pampering and self indulgence – a film-star lifestyle for the price of a bottle of bath foam.

By contrast, David hates the whole business. His weekly shower has always been a brief affair, an optional extra tacked on to a morning ritual of washing hands, face, armpits and sometimes other parts of the body too. All he needs is a flannel, soap and water from the basin. This habit of a lifetime is enough to keep him neat and tidy and that is all there is to say. That might be fine for David but the idea of showering any less than twice a day, more in case of exercise and physical exertion, makes Angela squirm. Sweat and its removal is her main concern and it is this that determines and gives meaning to when and how she washes. She will not exercise without the prospect of a shower ahead. Likewise, only a shower will do for the purpose is to get clean and this is not, in Angela's view, something that can be done in a bath. The idea of sitting in a pool of dirty greasy water is essentially revolting and the notion of washing her hair in this liquid is quite beyond the pale.

Although all imply at least weekly washing, these bath-time narratives demonstrate an impressive variety of contemporary belief and practice. At the same time they show how deeply anchored, how naturalized and how normalized routines appear to be. Habits are sometimes related to the technology on offer – to the existence of a bath or shower, or to the availability of hot water – but partners, parents and siblings evidently use the same facilities in different ways.

Routines are, for example, organized around different understandings of pleasure and duty. For Angela, showering is a twice-daily requirement and something she must do before presenting herself to wider society. By comparison, Sarah's response is coloured by a view of bathing as a source of pleasure and by a particular concept of what her body needs by way of care and attention. Human biology is a consistently important point of reference. Time and again, sweat, hair and skin types were invoked by way of explanation. However, it is also clear that washing is not only, and perhaps not predominantly, about cleaning. Waking up, preparing for bed, reproducing routine and enhancing comfort are inseparable parts of the experience. In addition, baths and showers provide opportunities for thinking, singing and reading. Amongst much else, bathrooms are essentially private spaces.

Although my analysis of dimensions and discourses is useful in organizing accounts of past and present practice, I have yet to contend with the dynamics of change. What is the relation between the theory and practice of bathing and how do new routines arise? In constructing this chapter, I have assumed that notions of normality are held in place by practical responses to a handful of defining themes. By implication, movement on any one of these dimensions

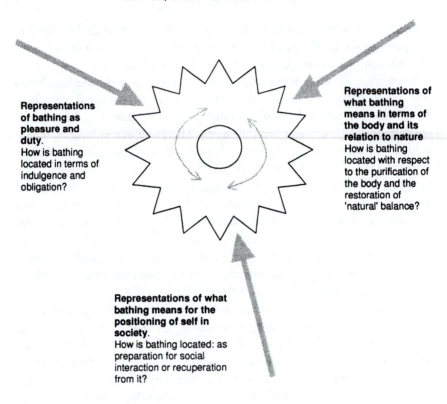

Representations of bathing as pleasure and duty.
How is bathing located in terms of indulgence and obligation?

Representations of what bathing means in terms of the body and its relation to nature
How is bathing located with respect to the purification of the body and the restoration of 'natural' balance?

Representations of what bathing means for the positioning of self in society.
How is bathing located: as preparation for social interaction or recuperation from it?

Figure 6.1. Pinning bathing in place

resets the scene and opens the way for new rationales, justifications and practices to take root. Instead of imagining a ratchet-like mechanism of uni-directional change, such as that associated with the path-dependent embedding of air-conditioning, the picture invoked is of a wheel free to move in one direction or another but momentarily pinned in place by a specific combination of legitimizing discourse. When rationales (represented by the different pins) retreat or are reconfigured, so the 'wheel' of normal practice changes position. Figure 6.1 illustrates this idea.

This figure can be used to characterize long-term transformations of practice and to represent the reorganization of individual habit. As the interview material shows, habits change over the course of a lifetime, each adjustment representing a re-configuration in the reasoning that guides and justifies what people do.

My next step is to see how this pinwheel model might be deployed in under-standing the routinization of power showering.

Power Showering in Theory and Practice

In this final section I put ideas about the collective and individual positioning of bathing routines to use in conceptualizing the relative decline of the bath and the rise of power showering in the UK. In trying to explain what prompted individuals to abandon the sponge bath in favour of a 'warm water shower', Ogle concluded that practices changed 'because of beliefs about what is right and sensible' (Ogle 1996: 7). So what it is that now makes the daily shower more 'right and sensible' in Britain than a weekly or twice weekly bath? What norms, conventions and pleasures are reproduced when knowledgeable and reflexive social agents take a shower? I begin by taking note of past and present representations of the difference between bathing and showering and the relative merits of each, describing these in terms of the three defining dimensions isolated above.

Writing from an American perspective, Kira advances a straightforwardly material explanation of why bathing remained popular in Britain up to the 1970s. He argues that the bath 'enjoys particular favor because of a generally damp raw climate and the lack of central heating' and concludes that: 'this also accounts in large measure for the general lack of showers throughout most of Europe ... to take a shower comfortably one must take it in a heated bathroom' (Kira 1976: 19). Differing histories of plumbing and infrastructure have practical consequences for domestic water pressure. According to bathroom designers like Snow and Hopwell (1976) this made it distinctly difficult to add a shower to a conventional British bathroom. In explaining why these obstacles should be overcome, they conclude that the effort is in the end worthwhile because showering is so more *hygienic* than bathing.

Showering also has a reputation for being *invigorating*. Indeed, there was a period when the force and athleticism of the rain bath or 'morning bracer' was believed 'incompatible with female grooming rituals' (Lupton and Miller 1992: 31). Now valued by both men and women, one of the more important features of showering is that it is *quick*. In practice, the total time spent bathing or showering may not vary that much: people spend, around three times as long in a bath as under a shower. Daily showering therefore takes about as much time as a twice-weekly bath (Boyd 1985). While the two forms do have distinctive temporal qualities (with a shower, there is no need to wait while the tub fills up or to get out when the water turns cold) the critical difference is that in the popular imagination showering is both rapid and effective.

Adding the proposed advantages together, frequent power showering represents a 'good' solution for those who value convenience, invigoration and speed and for whom it is socially important to wash every day. Seen in this way, power showering is dominated by, and at the same time reproduces, a distinctive preoccupation with time, stress and sensation. The result is a logic that involves and justifies the quick and convenient consumption of energy and water, that defines such consumption as normal and necessary, and that does so in ways that the infrequent, time-consuming bath cannot match. This is important in that the repositioning of showering simultaneously redefines the role of the bath. Both allow you to clean yourself, but the relative decline of this aspect as a defining purpose has allowed consumers and producers to elaborate on the distinctive qualities of each experience.

As represented here, the pinwheel of bathing is currently fixed in position by a contemporary valuing of time, duty, invigoration and personal appearance. This combination of rationale and reasoning is unlikely to last forever. Indeed, in the course of this chapter I have suggested that interpretations of bathing and showering are fundamentally unstable because they are related, if not tied, to a handful of core concerns to do with self and society, body and nature, pleasure and duty. There is therefore a sense in which 'the structural anxieties of our age are made manifest in discourses' (Warde 1997: 56) not only of food but also of bathing. This does not make it any easier to forecast the future but it does provide a framework within which to locate current trends and specify the conditions that situate regular power showering as normal practice.

Before moving on I want to underline three features of the discussion so far. The first has to do with cleanliness. It is by now obvious that bathing is not only about cleaning. Accounts that emphasize the reproduction of order (such as those of Douglas and Elias), or the relationship between cleaning, dirt and disease (for example, Tomes and Melosi) are at risk of underestimating the codetermining role of other defining themes around which rationales and practices of bathing revolve. In particular, they underplay the social construction of the experience itself. Second, this chapter has highlighted the multiple anchoring of 'the same' practice. When Sarah slips into her foam filled tub she is *simultaneously* getting ready to go out, luxuriating in the warm scented water, building up her beauty capital, restoring the natural balances of her body (if that is indeed what her bath oils do) and buying time to herself. While this overlapping makes perfect sense it presents problems still to be resolved by those interested in analysing and understanding the transformation of habit. Although I have sought to distinguish between dimensions of bathing as a means of showing how constitutent rationales have changed it is important to remember that these flow together in practice. Returning to the arguments introduced in Chapter 3, the challenge is therefore one of understanding the co-evolution and mutual positioning not of technology and practice but of relevant rationales and discourses. How do 'new' ideas about bathing fit together and how do they displace established conventions? For historians of science, the process is typically viewed as one of replacement; hence, bacterio-logical theories oust those that came before. Others argue that ideas of cleanli-ness percolate through the social structure, being adopted and appropriated like any other commodity or technology. But in reviewing the transformation of bathing habits, it is clear that processes of configuration and appropriation are themselves shaped by a complex of shared convention. In tracking the terms in which bathing has been justified, I have explored the idea that this complex is built around a number of persistent themes. I have suggested that there are, in effect, interlocking regimes not of sociotechnical systems but of ideas, arguments and rationales. As indicated above, the popularity of power shower-ing cannot be understood in terms of cleanliness, invigoration or convenience alone. What counts is the way this practice resolves and in a sense reproduces all three dimensions, all at once.

I have taken the further step of suggesting that the meaning and practice of bathing depends upon individual and collective responses to a handful of core concerns that are in turn related to persistent 'structural' anxieties. This move introduces a significantly different 'logic' of systemic change as compared to that discussed in previous chapters. Rather than thinking about how socio-technical regimes are constructed, and how one development leads to the next, this chapter implies a kind of 'external' dynamic in which bathing practices represent ways of 'fixing' or resolving 'problems' (concerning the reproduction of social order, the status of the body, and so forth) that arise elsewhere. In bathing and showering as they do, people manage these defining concerns in their own terms, tapping into a contemporary repertoire of reasons and ration-ales in support of their actions. It is, however, important to qualify this sense of 'external' pressure. After all, routines and practices are themselves construct-ive and constitutive of collective convention. Normality is made of what people normally do – hence Jane, Tim, Angela, David and Sarah convince themselves of dirt and cleanliness, of being relaxed or awake, of the rigours of the outside world and of being ready to face them, through the way they bathe.

The pinwheel image illustrates key elements of this argument, suggesting that more but also less resource-intensive conventions of normal practice may arise in the future. It acknowledges that the pursuit of cleanliness is only part of the story and allows for the fact that ideas about bathing (for example, regarding its hydrotherapeutic benefits) come and go over time. Although the practices considered here are *not* locked in to a one-way narrative of resource escalation, they are none the less subject to important forms of social standardi-zation. While respondents' bathing routines varied widely, all took for granted the 'need' to wash on a regular basis. In explaining convergence across cultures and social classes I have pointed not to the unifying effect of mains water systems or power showers, but to the representation of frequent bathing as a necessary condition of normal social acceptance. Failure to conform to such standards is consequently cast as a matter of right and wrong, not (now) of modernity, Westernization or technological advancement. In this respect, styles of bathing constitute an expression of societal propriety in a way that comfort does not.

The next two chapters on laundering also deal with an issue about which conventions of proper practice have swung this way and that, and that are again peppered with symbolic and moral significance. Unlike bathing, which has remained a privatized and relatively low-tech enterprise, these transformations are built around an elaborate network of inter-dependent yet rapidly changing technical and commercial interests.

7

Laundering: a System of Systems

It is no longer usual to sew children into their clothes for the winter, nor is it common practice to do all the laundry on just one day of the week. Despite the net drop in dirtiness and despite the popularity of regular showering and bathing, the last century has seen a shift of collective routine such that on average British washing machines are used 274 times a year. The figure is even higher for the USA where the average is 392 cycles per year. One result is that domestic laundry currently accounts for something like 21 per cent of per-capita residential indoor water use in the USA and a smaller but still significant 12 per cent in British homes. With the diffusion of the domestic washing machine at 'saturation' point in both countries (98 and 92 per cent respect-ively), the evidence is that people are washing and drying loads of clothes more frequently than ever before and in the process consuming copious quantities of energy and water. The central challenge for this chapter and the next is to explain both the engraining and the transformation of laundry-related routines.

As with bathing, it is important to appreciate the social and symbolic signifi-cance of being clean. In Douglas's (1984) terms, laundering and bathing both contribute to the reproduction of social order and in both cases, transitions are of consequence for the specification and policing of social-symbolic bound-aries (and vice versa). There are, however, a number of relevant differences. Unlike bathing, laundering is a composite and complex task and one that has been transformed almost beyond recognition by the introduction of new devices, materials and appliances. More obviously than comfort, its accom-plishment depends upon the active co-ordination of a multitude of relatively independent sociotechnical systems. In addition, and again unlike the cases and examples examined this far, laundering constitutes a form of work: some-thing that is divided, allocated and managed within and between commercial and domestic settings.

For these three reasons it is a good case with which to show how practices are formed (and how they change) around the intersection of seemingly discrete pathways of sociotechnical change. In developing this idea, I argue that innovation in the production of clean clothing depends upon the practical *integration* of a variety of relatively self-contained systems. The size and content of the laundry basket is, for instance, closely related to the textile and fashion industries and to the mass production of clothing. Meanwhile, the design of domestic washing machines reflects the range of fabrics in circulation, the availability of detergents of one kind or another and contemporary concepts of cleanliness, domesticity and propriety. The exercise of placing the production of 'appropriately' laundered clothing centre stage and of viewing this as a system or, more accurately, a system of systems introduces a new way of thinking about transitions toward sustainability.

From a policy perspective, theoretical accounts of sociotechnical regimes and landscapes are of limited value unless they can be used to identify points at which the course of path dependent development might be turned in a more sustainable direction. Government departments and research funders are increasingly interested in managing transitions in technology and practice that offer 'large potential to achieve environmental gains' (Elzen *et al.* 2002) and that promise to increase environmental efficiency by factors of five or ten. It might seem strange to apply this way of thinking to the laundry, to compare washing with automobility or to look for parallels between this practice and the development of electrical power or of telecommunications. However, scholars investigating large technical systems have written about societal transitions in ways that prove useful in understanding the laundry as an enterprise also built around intersecting interests and inter-dependent component parts (Summerton 1994).

Borrowing some of these ideas, I conceptualize the laundry as a 'systems of systems'. I argue that meanings of washing well change as a result of interaction between the various elements and components involved (for example, fabrics, washing machines, detergents, reasons for washing, stocks of clothing and so forth). In other words, I take the enterprise of laundering to be a co-production involving those who do the washing, their values and ambitions, the conventions and standards of the day and the tools and technologies they use. In figuring out how washing routines have changed and why, I examine the laundry from various angles, asking why people clean clothes, what it is they wash, when these tasks are undertaken and what they involve. In taking this route, I recognize that with laundering, more so than with bathing or comfort, the division and management of associated tasks is itself important for the meaning of the result, the appropriation of technology and the respecification of convention.

This chapter builds on those that have gone before by investigating a case in which normal practice is structured not by one but by many technical systems, by examining the materialization of moral, social and symbolic meanings of cleanliness and by looking at how divisions of labour influence the routes through which conventions and standards are established and through which they change. It begins with two introductory sections, first considering laundry as a form of work and then reflecting on the specification of standards. Consistent with my view of laundering as a composite enterprise, I go on to review a selection of historical and contemporary material in order to gain a sense of why people wash, what they wash, and when and how they do it. I use this material in developing a model of change that helps explain how and why new understandings of laundering arise as they do. This generates new questions regarding the media and mechanisms of *integration*. In exploring these issues, the chapter turns attention away from the 'vertical' integration of sociotechnical regimes and landscapes, focusing instead on the 'horizontal' co-ordination of practice within any one such system. Put simply, it combines elements of the discourse-based analysis of bathing with aspects of the more technologically oriented accounts explored in the chapters on comfort. In so doing, it develops a macro-level perspective on the relation *between* sociotechnical systems and on routines and practices as forms of integration.

Laundering as Work

The job of washing clothing and household linen can be divided and delegated. Although the task of bathing those too young or infirm to wash themselves can be similarly allocated, the business of personal hygiene is typically indivisible. But it is not just that laundry can be given to other people to do. The management of linen has long been identified with women, whether as housewives, washerwomen or dressmakers. Taking this to be a powerful relationship, Kaufmann suggests that as guardians of its linen, women are the 'guardians of the family destiny', that 'women's history is deeply inscribed in every fold of their linen' and that senses of self are very much at stake in the handling of laundry (Kaufmann 1998: 13). It is certainly the case that in contrast to personal bathing, the definition and distribution of laundry-related responsibilities is inextricably bound up with the reproduction of gendered identities and with the division and management of domestic labour. Understood as housework the details of laundering also reflect and reveal the role of the domestic sphere as a site of production and/or consumption.

As laundry is routinely positioned as women's work and since the results are constantly on show, judgements about clothing and appearance are at the same time judgements about standards of domestic performance. In the postscript to *More Work for Mother*, Ruth Schwartz Cowan reflects upon her unwillingness to let her daughter wear a stained shirt or a filthy skirt to school: 'the fact of the matter is', she says, 'that I cannot stand the sight of my children in dirty clothes. I associate dirt with poverty, with loss of control; and like a somnambulist, I am walking through the rituals and responding to the symbols that really meant something seventy years ago' (Cowan 1983: 218). As well as indicating the symbolic import of the *process*, Cowan suggests that the practices of earlier generations throw shadows of expectation that reach deep into the present. This observation reminds us to take note of the changing terms in which laundering is scrutinized and the social significance of such judgement.

In addition, and again in contrast to bathing, laundering is a typically sequential operation consisting of a series of discrete activities. These might now include sorting clothes, filling a washing machine, adding detergent, drying and ironing. In other situations, necessary steps have included lighting fires, boiling water, soaking, hand wringing, rinsing, soaping, bleaching, blueing, starching and crimping. Exactly what 'doing the laundry' means depends, in a rather immediate way, upon the technologies involved and upon contemporary understandings of what it takes to produce a pile of appropriately cleaned clothing. I have more to say about this, but for now it is enough to recognize that innovation in any one part of the system (for instance, in textiles, detergents or washing and drying technology) will have repercussions for the whole.

A related observation is that the tasks of which laundering is comprised can be organized and managed in different ways and that any one society can sustain parallel but distinct systems of laundry provision (Fine and Leopold 1993). In the 1920s, householders in the UK or the USA might send 'flatwork' like sheets and towels to a commercial laundry but deal with other fabrics themselves. Twenty years later, they might go for a partial service, doing the washing at a laundrette but drying and ironing clothes at home, or they might do everything themselves, or do it with the aid of a domestic washing machine and/or a tumble dryer. The history of options on offer mirrors wider social trends: the decline of the servant classes, the mechanization of domestic labour and the extent to which commercial interests penetrate the home. As Arwen Mohun's history of steam laundries shows so well, the relationship between commercial and domestic laundering directly affects the specification of what people think of as normal standards. Occupying what Mohun characterizes as a 'middle position on the continuum between consumption and production' commercial laundries were continually locked in competition with their own customers (Mohun 1999: 66). While commercial laundries could do washing in spotless factory-style conditions, thereby achieving 'higher' standards (here meaning a whiter wash) than would otherwise be possible, they tried to produce laundry that looked as if it had been done by hand. In the symbolic world of laundering, hand washing figured as the necessarily superior solution and commercial laundering as the necessarily inferior substitute. This particular ranking of quality is intriguing, yet the more general point is that different systems of provision generate different definitions of proper cleaning, both in terms of the process involved and the status and quality of the finished result.

The decline of the commercial laundry and the failure to sustain other forms of collective provision have been explained with reference to Marxist and/or feminist analyses of women's position within and outside the labour market. In describing collective approaches to housework and reflecting on the routes not taken, Cowan argues that peoples' enduring commitment to preserving activities deemed central to family life, and their pursuit of privacy and autonomy, are vital in understanding why laundering is now done at home (Cowan 1983: 150). Reflecting on the same question, Susan Strasser reaches a different conclusion, pointing to the complex of economic interests at stake in promoting washing as a private activity *and* in undermining other more collective arrangements. She writes as follows: 'Home laundering – which encompassed not only the washing machine industry but also those that produced detergents, textiles, electrical parts and plumbing supplies – demonstrates the interconnections between segments of the economy that facilitated its continual expansion' (Strasser 1982: 122). Sold as devices to which laundry responsibilities could be delegated, domestic washing machines have challenged and sometimes entirely eliminated other systems of provision. As the rest of this chapter demonstrates, one consequence is that fabric, detergent and appliance manufacturers have together tightened what amounts to a corporate grip on the meaning of cleaning, and have done so within the heart of the home.

To summarize, laundering has certain characteristics relevant for an understanding of how expectations and conventions change. First, it represents a form of work that can be divided and delegated in different ways. Second, it is typically viewed as women's work and is, as such, associated with notions of domestic performance. Third, the production of clean clothes depends upon the sequential accomplishment of a number of inter-dependent activities. Finally, the manner in which the laundry is organized (within or outside the home) is of immediate consequence for the definition and reproduction of cleanliness and for the sorts of skills and judgements involved. It is important to acknowledge the social status and positioning of laundering as a form of work, but what does this mean for the escalation of standards and how does it help explain patterns like those of washing every day?

Escalating Standards or Redefining Service?

In outline, it is easy to see that conventions and practices have changed over the last century. Reviewing this period, Niall FitzGerald, Chairman of Unilever PLC, summarizes his company's achievements as follows:

> Our consumers can now machine wash their clothes, with minimal effort, at much lower temperatures than ever before, using detergent powders, liquids – and now tablets. We have greatly reduced the grind and drudgery of household chores, and built a reliable and trusted range of brands. Clothes themselves can now be made out of dozens of different types of fabrics; coloured using an amazing range of some 200,000 dye combinations; and even finished with space age coatings, like Teflon. (Fitzgerald 1998)

In the course of a generation or two, washing has undoubtedly become both easier and more complex. Commenting on the latter feature, one observer notes that she is obliged to run no fewer than five separate washing programmes to clean the kit worn by her son in a single soccer game. 'Amongst other things, she has to take care that the red and white team colours do not bleed together, and she has to cope with muddy cotton socks, thin polyester jerseys, and unsoiled but sweaty undershirts' (Santiago 1977). Also reflecting on the developments of the last hundred years, Cowan (1983) concludes that many have had the ironic effect of creating 'more work for mother'. She argues that domestic technologies have been so positioned that work previously shared with men, with children or with hired labour has fallen ever more exclusively to the housewife herself. Mechanical appliances have, as Fitzgerald claims, reduced grind and drudgery and in a sense increased 'productivity' but they have not necessarily diminished the time and labour expended on domestic work. In trying to make sense of this unanticipated result, Adrian Forty agrees that 'what seems to have happened is that appliances lightened the burden and saved time in certain tasks, but also made it possible to achieve higher standards' (Forty 1986: 210).

Washing machines and detergents have evidently transformed what it means to do the laundry but is it useful to see this as a process of *escalating* standards? Have expectations steadily and sometimes rapidly advanced along a continuum of ever more exacting demands or is this a misleading model? One reason for distinguishing between *different* as opposed to *increasing* standards is that there is no obvious metric with which to evaluate such a complex and composite service as the laundry. Data on the number of washing cycles per year or the weight of the average load tell us something, but do they indicate higher standards? The types of clothes people wear, the number they own, and the fabrics of which they are made are vitally important in shaping ideas about what needs washing and when. But does the global proliferation and mass consumption of light weight clothing – a trend that is itself related to the standardization of the indoor climate – foster 'higher' or 'lower' standards? What, if anything, do volumes of laundry or rates of energy and water consumption tell us about conventions of cleanliness? In technical terms this is a tangled issue for new detergents have made it 'possible' to wash at lower temperatures and although they have become more energy efficient, washing machines have also got larger. The more one enquires the more elusive the concept of standards becomes.

Standardized tests and instruments like the 'illuminometer', a special device for measuring the whiteness of a wash, have influenced the development of new washing powders and machines from the 1930s onwards. However, scientific measures of this kind do not provide a suitable frame of reference against which to track the evolution of 'the laundry' as a whole. To the extent that it has one, the history of laundry is a history of establishing, revising and sometimes abandoning expectations about degrees of whiteness, the precision of ironing, the quality of starching and so forth. As organizational arrangements and technologies change so have the criteria invoked and the steps and stages to which judgements attach.

Rather than trying to discern and report on a narrative of rising standards, the following sections take laundering and associated definitions of cleanliness to be the outcome of situationally specific complexes of belief, practice and technology. In the real world, issues of what is to be laundered, why, when, how and by whom are bundled together in the daily routine of washing. In pulling these aspects apart and drawing upon examples from the past, I want to disentangle something of what is at stake in repositioning and redefining the theory and practice of washing. As in previous chapters, the purpose is to help understand what it means to do the laundry today and to see how current configurations of technology and convention lock people into more or less sustainable and more or less malleable patterns of consumption. The first question to explore is why wash at all?

Why Wash?

Georges Vigarello (1998) suggests that the appearance though not necessarily the cleanliness of outer clothing constituted an increasingly significant indicator of social decency during the middle ages. He relates this to the thirteenth-century practice of wearing separate layers of clothing and of distinguishing between under and outer wear, a habit that continues to structure the symbolic meaning and organization of laundering today. Back in the middle ages, shirts of fine material, often linen, constituted what was thought of as a protective second skin: a lining between the socially anonymous body and socially significant outer garments, and a line of defence against external vapours. For those convinced of the body's porosity and for those subscribing to a humour-based theory of disease, this kind of underwear had the dual function of excluding unwanted influences from the outside and of mopping up the outpourings of the body and its parasitic residents. In their role as 'boundary objects', underclothes like shirts were quite appropriately viewed as sponges and as cleaning agents in their own right. Framed by such an understanding, it might be relevant and even socially desirable to clean one's clothing but not the skin beneath.

Sensation

Although it does not seem to have been a terribly frequent event, changing the shirt reputedly took the place of refreshing and washing the body in mid-sixteenth century France (Vigarello 1998: 58). At around the same time, judgements were made about the relative whiteness of shirts and, by association, the cleanliness of the bodies they enclosed. Previously hidden by outer clothing – which was not subject to calculations of cleanliness – shirts and other linen undergarments began to peep through. In following these developments Vigarello concludes that the emergence of visible telltale indicators like collars and cuffs demonstrate a new association between fashion and an explicit valuing of cleanliness in the seventeenth century. As he explains, this was a critical move. From this point on, laundered linen was not simply associated with a private world of personal experience and sensation. Instead, 'cleanliness was expressed in a world of things' and 'what counted was to display these things' (Vigarello 1998: 77). Certain forms of clothing, including elaborate ruffs, lace collars and cuffs, maximized opportunities for an increasingly conspicuous exhibition of inner cleanliness.

These observations highlight two possible reasons for washing clothes. One has to do with pleasure and sensation. A clean shirt or a fresh towel was believed to revitalize sixteenth-century bodies. Invoking much the same idea, current television advertisements for Lenor fabric conditioner suggest that consumers will be invigorated and stimulated by their properly conditioned, freshly laundered clothing. Clothes are no longer viewed as sponges or wash cloths, yet the brand name Comfort (another fabric conditioner) provides further indication of the enduring importance of sensual values like softness and pliability. By implication, laundering is still about reproducing the sensory attributes of what we wear (Sams 2001).

The second reason relates to the social value of cleanliness and the need to give it material expression by quite literally keeping up appearances. A visibly clean shirt continues to signify propriety, decency and morality not because it is believed to clean the body beneath but because it is now simply important that clothes are clean. The terminology of 'clothing care' captures this subtle but also crucial shift of emphasis. In washing, drying and ironing as they do, people strive to keep their shirts, trousers, skirts and jackets looking and feeling as good as they did when new. As considered later, this logic sustains a repertoire of laundry practices that have relatively little to do with personal hygiene. Instead of cleaning clothes as a means of protecting the body from harm and disease, the logic is reversed. Laundry is increasingly represented as an exercise in restoring clothes contaminated through contact with the sweaty, smelly bodies of those who wear them.

Disinfection

Changing beliefs about the functions of the skin and the relationship between dirt and health have legitimized different forms of laundry. While the microbes, bacteria and invisible monsters made real by Pasteur's 'discoveries' were not thought capable of penetrating the skin, it was still necessary to defend oneself against them. As the inconspicuous came into its own in an unambiguously threatening manner, so the focus of attention shifted from cuffs and collars and from the most visible surfaces of display to those that were most hidden. Gripped by the concerns of her time, Flora Rose, a Cornell home economist, warned that 'when ever organic matter accumulates on clothing even to only a slight extent there is a possibility of the presence of bacteria' (Tomes 1998: 145). This led her to propose that underwear be boiled for at least ten minutes to 'complete the washing process by destroying germs and thus to purify clothing'. Any little microbes that might have survived a prolonged simmering were finally eliminated by the disinfecting power of the flat iron. Writing in 1928, Louise Jordan concludes that their destruction represented a social as well as a personal duty given the 'large, annual, social loss due to sickness caused by unhygienic clothing' (Jordan 1928: 333).

Although modern detergents promise to deal with bacteria as well as dirt, there is a growing literature on the problem of controlling house dust mites, especially with low temperature washing (Bischoff *et al.* 1998). The tone of urgency adopted in Katzman's article 'Scalding, dust mites and lice, and your washing machine' confirms the view that purification and the elimination of invisible sources of harm constitutes a persistently powerful reason for washing things even when they look clean (Katzman 1998).

Deodorization

Corbin's work on the sociology of smell suggests a further rationale. The association of bad odour with danger and disease, and the plague-related fear that such might penetrate the fragile boundary of the body favoured a defensive use of perfume and clothing. What Corbin describes as the 'new calculus of olfactory pleasure' had the practical effect of reversing this equation in the eighteenth century. Convinced that 'Fresh bodily odor depended even more on the quality and cleanliness of underwear than on scrupulous hygienic practices' nineteenth-century sanitary reformers instituted rigid timetables for changing and washing sheets and clothing (Corbin 1986: 180). It is perhaps no coincidence that it was in this context that a 'new appreciation of the pleasant odor of fresh linen' took root (Corbin 1986: 180). Dealing with both aspects at the same time, laundry acquired the dual role of eliminating unwanted odours and replacing them with a positively desired fragrance.

Although it is hard to figure out exactly what it involves or how one learns to apply it, clothes that fail the 'sniff test' are today bound for the wash. In so far as 'American culture associates sweat with stink', sweaty clothes, like sweaty bodies, 'need' cleaning whether they are visibly dirty or not (Lau 2001). In evaluating a range of detergents, the authors of a UK Consumers' Association *Which?* report acknowledge that cleaning is not the only consideration. As they admit, 'often the weekly wash's main purpose is to freshen up clothes which is why some brands of detergents come in a range of fragrances', and why some products contain perfume but no detergent at all (Consumers' Association 1999: 37). As this makes clear, deodorizing and 'freshening up' are now justification enough for doing the laundry.

Finally, but perhaps most relevant of all, people wash clothes because they are accustomed to doing so. Routine and a sense of appropriate performance constitutes a further motivation and for those in the way of changing their sheets every two weeks or every six months, such periodicity has a momentum of its own: they simply have to wash.

To summarize, clothing is no longer expected to require washing because of its role as a cleansing agent for the body. Having more or less broken this link, the more dominant rationale is that of clothing care. Defined in this way, laundry is about decontaminating clothes that have been in contact with the body and restoring valued attributes of style, feel and image. Smell is a persistently important consideration loosely allied to disinfection (despite the waning of miasma-based theories of disease) but strongly associated with self image and social convention. While there is no necessary link between these kinds of expert discourses and what people do in practice, what Cowan refers to as the 'senseless tyranny of spotless shirts' appears to be held in place by a contemporary blend of ideas about sensation, display, disinfection and deodorization.

There are obvious parallels between the rationales and reasonings described here and those invoked in support of different styles of bathing. Purification and decontamination are important as are changing understandings of the relation between the body and nature. Laundering also constitutes a form of preparation before appearance in public. In both cases there seems to have been a drift from previously dominant themes of health and hygiene to values of image and presentation. However, this does not in itself explain the trend towards more frequent washing. To gain a better idea of the processes involved I now review the range and types of fabric to which these laundry-related rationales are applied.

What is Washed?

Should such a thing exist, a detailed survey of the quantities of material typically owned by people from different times, cultures and social backgrounds would give some clue as to what there is to clean in any one society. The mere existence of clothing certainly does not mean it is washed, yet changes in the stocks of stuff that people own have undoubtedly transformed the character of the laundry and the lives of those who do it.

Textile Taxonomies

Outer layers of medieval clothing, often of woven wool, felt or leather were as likely to be brushed or wiped as scrubbed in water. Without going too deeply into a history of fashion, certain styles and types of garments have generated distinctive opportunities for differentiation in terms of fabric and (visible) cleanliness. From a laundry perspective, the nature of the material is vital. In the words of Matthias Bode, 'as long as linen dominated, typical washing stages included leaching (with an ash leach), brushing or beating, rinsing, blueing and bleaching (through exposure to sunlight in the fields) and treatment with starches before being mangled, ironed and put away' (Bode 2000: 29). Although the short oily fibres of cotton attract and retain dirt, cotton is 'easier' to wash than linen, the typical sequence being one of soaking, boiling and washing in soap suds and soda, followed by several stages of rinsing (Jordan 1928: 337).

The emergence of the cotton industry effectively revolutionized both the practice of washing and the content and size of the laundry basket. Sewing machines, together with the mass production of cotton fabric permitted the equally mass production of cheap ready-made garments (Fine and Leopold 1993). With more fabric around than ever before, and with more of it being of cotton, Cowan claims that the manufacturing of cloth 'served to augment women's work by increasing the amount of household laundry that had to be done' (Cowan 1983: 65). The exact nature of this burden related not only to the stock of clothing in circulation but also to issues of fashion, style and hygiene. Theories about the relation between dirt and disease made a difference to the cut of working-class and middle-class clothing, to the stuff these garments were made of and to how complicated they were to wash. As the discourse of germs took hold, simplicity gained the upper hand. Previously fashionable skirts and trailing dresses were trimmed and re-styled so as not to drag filth into the home (Berner 1998). Still full of advice in the 1920s, Jordan recommends that even 'underwear should be simple in design so as to offer no complications for laundering from this source', after all, she continues, 'when a garment is hard to handle for any reason, laundering or other cleaning is apt to be undesirably delayed' (Jordan 1928: 337). These demands reflect a reformulation of the relationship between status, fashion and hygiene. Rather than conspicuously demonstrating and displaying the care and effort invested in its upkeep, clothing and especially cotton clothing was literally made to be washed.

The development and refinement of patterned and printed cottons also generated new 'classes' of washing each demanding special treatment. By 1950 the American Institute of Laundering recommended an eleven-part categorization of laundry based on distinctions between light and dark coloured fabrics made of various types of fibre (de Armound 1950). Not long after, the requirements of nylon and other 'easy-care' synthetic textiles like tricel, viyella, clydella, courtelle, orlon and terylene extended the taxonomy still further. The evolution of international systems for fabric labelling provides a telling indicator of what there is to wash. The range of fabrics in circulation makes a difference to the meaning and practice of laundry, but so does the total quantity of stuff that people own.

Stocks of Stuff

The mass production of clothing has proceeded apace and wardrobes are now filled with things made from an immense variety of natural and man-made fibres. In her book on *Nylon*, Susanna Handley (1999) describes the proliferation of cheap synthetic fabrics and their effect on the fashion industry. One immediate consequence was to change the types of clothes produced and the perception and relative status of already established textiles, especially silk. However the indirect but arguably more important impact was to establish the possibility and the expectation that people of all social classes would amass private collections of increasingly disposable personal clothing. On this latter point, recent research from the Netherlands reveals that 'an average piece of clothing is worn for about 13 days per year, i.e. 44 days during its use-life', excluding second-hand use (Knot 2000).

Trends in the use and accumulation of personal clothing and developments in textile technology are in turn related to changes in the social and material status of what we wear. Despite the spread of 'casual' clothing, the social differentiation of activity has arguably fuelled (or been fuelled by) the development of specialized equipment and 'gear'. Separate outfits are thus required for playing football, for tramping over the fields or for going to the office (Shove and Warde 2001: 238). Meanwhile, one side effect of standardizing indoor climates has been to redefine clothing's traditional role as a means of managing the relation between the body and its immediate environment. In the UK, there is, for instance, a direct relationship between the spread of central heating and the decline of thick tweed suits, waistcoats and chunky jumpers. More generally, the global convergence of the indoor environment has correspondingly global implications for the clothes we wear.

Simply owning a lot of clothes does not necessarily entail a greater volume of laundry: after all, only a fraction will be deemed 'wearable' in any one context. Even so, the prospect and possibility of slipping into something different each day *is* likely to increase the volume of what there is to wash. This is especially so given developments in the weight and 'washability' of the garments people own. Just as clothing is designed for washing, so laundry processes are designed to cater for the racks and rows of machine washable clothing with which wardrobes are typically filled. This discussion of the relationship between textiles, hygiene and fashion goes some way towards explaining the content of the contemporary laundry basket but how often is it emptied?

When is the Laundry Done?

How is it that the number of washing cycles has increased so dramatically over the last century and what prompts people to wash when they do? One obvious answer is that they have run out of what they count as 'clean' clothing.

Running Out and Getting Ready

In eighteenth-century Germany the higher social classes expected to possess more than one outfit as well as a special suit of holiday clothing. Since the amount of clothing a person owned was an index of their social standing, infrequent 'washing cycles were expressions of the social hierarchy' (Bode 2000: 29). This is apparently not the case today for a recent survey of the

German clothing industry suggests that between twenty and forty per cent of the clothes people own are not used at all (Albaum 1997). No longer prompted by the experience of literally running out, the need to wash is more commonly related to the goal of having socially suitable items ready to wear.

The housewives whose lives are described by Cowan (1983), Strasser (1982) and Zmroczek (1992) had to start the washing cycle on Monday if they were to provide freshly laundered clothing in time for going out on Saturday night or for going to church on Sunday. In thinking about when things are washed it is important to appreciate that some items are reserved for special occasions and that others are worn every day. As detailed in the next chapter, people are now more likely to do their washing 'to order', getting 'special' clothes ready as the occasion arises. Strategies for washing 'normal' items vary. Stocks of everyday clothing are often such that it is possible to defer the laundry for quite a time. Even if one pair of jeans is dirty, there is likely to be another in the cupboard. But this is not quite how it works. Within the range available to them, people have favourite garments, things they like to wear all the time and which are therefore always in the wash. The tendency to distinguish between favourite clothes and others that are worn for short periods and washed after every use has the overall effect of increasing the throughput of laundry. Specialization also creates new pressures of laundry-related timing with the result that people who own lots of clothing may still find themselves with nothing (suitable) to wear.

Frequency and Turnover

Now built around individual rather than collective schedules, laundry routines are none the less governed by ideas about how often things like towels, underwear, shirts and trousers should be washed. Without knowing more about the exact content of those Monday morning wash baskets it is difficult to tell how long individual items were worn before they 'needed' washing. Much no doubt depended, as it still does, on the fine grain of social convention, social class, individual resources and personal histories, but in all such circumstances there are judgements to be made about the frequency with which it is necessary to rid clothing of dirt, germs, odours or compromising creases.

Household manuals were once full of advice on this matter, offering clear and often demanding guidance (Cowan 1983; Mohun 1997). Although it is now easy to find instruction on *how* to wash – fabric care labels are designed for just this purpose – it is rare to come across explicit advice about *when* to do so. Yet there are moments when collective understandings of normal practice come into view. Reporting on the practical consequences of a sudden increase in the cost of energy in San Francisco, Joe Garofoli (2001) noticed that people were 'stretching' their laundry, letting 'yesterday's skirt become tomorrow's' and 'coaxing another appearance out of their pants, jackets and other parts of their wardrobe'. The sub-text is that under normal circumstances, skirts would be worn just once. Conventions of this kind may be policed informally, especially in working environments where failure to conform is immediately evident. More ordinarily, family traditions provide taken-for-granted benchmarks and points of reference. As Kaufmann (1998) explains, parental practices are important in shaping, embedding and legitimizing habit. But as he also shows, these may figure as models to which offspring conform or against which they react – in other words, the fact that your mother washed the sheets every two weeks is no guarantee that you will do the same. However they are acquired, it seems that rules of thumb are subject to collective and systematic redefinition.

Laundry data is difficult to interpret because the practicalities and meanings of washing change all the time. Since washing machine ownership is now so widespread, estimates of the number of washing cycles per year (that is the number of times washing machines are run) and the weight of the average load, provide a reasonable indication of how much washing is done and how often. Piecing together information from different sources, American households currently wash an average of 1,332 kg of laundry a year, made up of 392 loads of 3.4 kg (Biermeyer 2001). This is nearly three times the amount recorded in 1950, when American machines ran an average of 156 times with loads of 3.6 kg (Consumers Union 1950a), and nearly twice the volume washed in the UK where 274 washing cycles are run with an average 2 kg load (DEFRA 2000). Such figures obscure relevant differences including household size, the extent of hand-washing and the use of commercial laundries yet the main message is clear: what used to be a weekly pattern has become a never-ending spiral of refreshing and revitalizing a steady stream of discarded clothing.

Although represented in separate paragraphs, questions about why people wash, what there is to clean, and when that work is done are firmly locked together in ways that also relate to the social and technical organization of the tasks involved.

What Does 'Doing the Laundry' Involve?

In my back garden I have a washhouse. This small brick building, now a shed, was where the women of the street would gather to do the washing. Whether communal or private, washing by hand is hard labour and like other kinds of labour it has been shared, bought and sold in different ways. The development of various types of washing machinery has, over the years, generated further possibilities for division and delegation to humans and non-humans alike. Drawing inspiration from the textile and agricultural industries, some of the earliest commercial machines were truly massive pieces of equipment (Giedion 1948). Other smaller scale prototypes sought to mimic the actions of hand washing and of rubbing and scrubbing (Maxwell 2002). As with so many other household technologies, the small-scale electric motor and indoor plumbing were crucial to the domestic washing machine's development and to the meaning of laundry.

Definition and Delegation

It is not necessary to follow the history of the washing machine in any detail to see that at every step along the way such devices have reconfigured the tasks involved, introduced new categories of washing and of washing well, and thereby challenged established routines and habits. Several of the Canadian housewives interviewed by Joy Parr (1999) took the investment of physical energy, time and technique to be so much part of their identity that they were reluctant to even think of delegating 'their' laundry to a man-made appliance. Such persons were 'slow' to adopt automatic machines and relinquish important role-defining abilities like those of correctly estimating quantities and qualities of soap or getting the timing of soaking and boiling exactly right. Meintjes (2001) makes a similar point, also underlining the symbolic importance of hand washing as a form of domestic care. Amongst the Soweto women she studied, the washing machine's semiotic status was ambivalent: on the one hand it signified affluence and membership of modern consumer society, on the other its use indicated indolence, laziness and lack of domestic commitment. Defined by these tensions and by the intergenerational negotiation of proper practice, washing machines were resisted and appropriated in ways that reflected (and also redefined) the structuring of domestic identities.

Domestic washing machines have none the less come to dominate the process and practice of cleaning clothes in the UK. As well as reshaping the skills involved and establishing new goals like those of minimizing ironing, fluffing towels and refreshing clothing, their widespread diffusion has the further effect of positioning the laundry as a solidly privatized practice involving the use of increasingly standardized technology. In this, washing machines have the dual function of locating clothing care firmly within the home and of rather directly scripting their users' practice. Other technologies – like those involved in drying and ironing – are also important yet it is the washing machine that sets the scene for the rest, and it is around this device that the commercial interests of appliance and detergent manufacturers and of textile and fashion industries spin. One consequence is that washing machines, in association with an array of specially formulated detergents and conditioners, have acquired a pivotal role in specifying the meaning of appropriately laundered clothing. For all practical purposes, and as detailed in the next chapter, 'clean' clothes are quite simply clothes that emerge from the machine. That is to say, through dominating and reinforcing a domestic system of provision washing machine manufacturers and other commercial interests have acquired the power to define cleanliness and laundering. Tentacles of commercial interest are consequently wrapped around what people think of as private habits and routines. This is important in that images and assumptions embedded in the modern machine position washing as something to be done more frequently than ever before, at lower temperatures than ever before, and with the aim of freshening as well as cleaning clothes.

Having commented on the why, what, when, and how of washing under separate headings the next step is to think about how they fit together.

The Laundry as a System of Systems

This final section considers ways of conceptualizing the transformation of domestic laundering. One obvious option is to reach for ideas already introduced in previous chapters. The co-evolution of air-conditioning and attendant expectations of comfort might thus be matched by an equally co-evolutionary narrative about washing machines and concepts of cleanliness. Just as the built environment has been reconfigured around air-conditioning to the point that there is 'no way back', so the washing machine has become enmeshed in daily life. Also making use of concepts like those of ratcheting and path dependency it would be possible to show that the washing machine's global diffusion has the further effect of standardizing concepts of cleanliness and freshness around the world.

In the light of the paragraphs above, device-centric analyses of this kind (including those that underline the societal embedding of technologies and their positioning within sociotechnical regimes and landscapes) are not especially well suited to the task in hand.

The detailed design of washing machines is important but so are developments in the realm of textiles and detergents, gender relations, ideologies of health and hygiene and concepts of domestic well being. In other words, washing machines contribute to a dynamic equation the outcome of which also reflects conventions of use and practice, of when the washing is done, what is washed and why. This argues for a shift of emphasis and for taking account of how technologies are domesticated and inserted into existing routines and habits. Yet the problem runs deeper than that. What is required is not simply

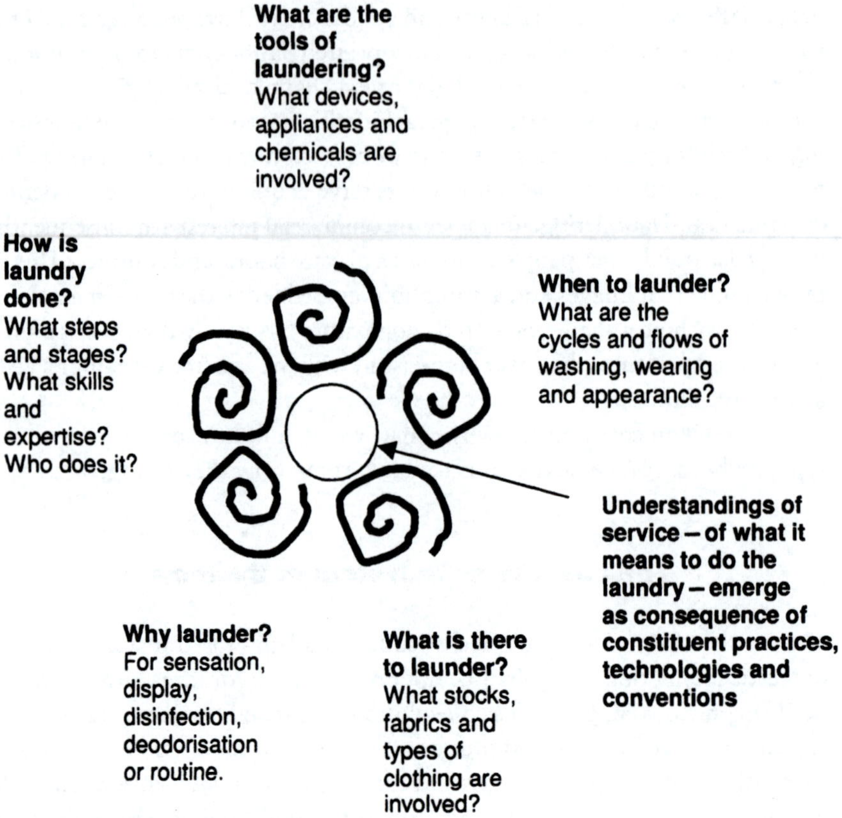

What are the tools of laundering? What devices, appliances and chemicals are involved?

How is laundry done? What steps and stages? What skills and expertise? Who does it?

When to launder? What are the cycles and flows of washing, wearing and appearance?

Understandings of service – of what it means to do the laundry – emerge as consequence of constituent practices, technologies and conventions

Why launder? For sensation, display, disinfection, deodorisation or routine.

What is there to launder? What stocks, fabrics and types of clothing are involved?

Figure 7.1. A whirlpool model of laundry

a way of tracking the influence of one or another component of the laundry system but of better understanding their *combined* effect and of thereby comprehending the transformation of the complex as a whole.

As a first step, it is useful to summarize the inter-dependent elements involved. With this in mind, Figure 7.1 represents the five core questions considered above: why wash, what is there to wash, when is washing done and what does that involve in terms of knowledge and technology? The little eddies and spirals associated with each suggest that answers to these questions develop in a relatively independent manner. Meanwhile, the circle at the centre implies that composite understandings of the service of laundry, that is of the processes and results that constitute proper laundering, emerge as a consequence of these constituent practices, technologies and concepts, whirling together and inter-acting in concert.

In many respects this figure does little more than re-describe the problem. It indicates the need for an analysis of multiple codetermination rather than mono-dimensional ratcheting but it gives a misleading impression of equivalence. Some of the constituent eddies may be spinning much faster than others. Indeed the whole model may be momentarily slewed to one side, for example, by the mass production of cotton, the development of detergent or the social significance of freshness. Although the whirlpool's implicit mechanisms of mutual adjustment suggest that equilibrium will return, that is only true to the extent that turbulence of one kind or another generates a new understanding of what it is to launder. As it stands the picture offers no clues as to where the momentum for change might lie.

Second, this model could be as readily applied to nineteenth-century France as to contemporary Japan. In this it has the perhaps unfortunate effect of disguising both the character and the combination of localized and cross-cultural ingredients. In thinking about the relative weight of the whorls and the way they interact it is important to notice that the seven largest washing machine manufacturers have over 70 per cent of global market share (Weiss and Gross 1995). While appliances may be customized and detergents coloured to suit the customs and preferences of different national markets, the mechanisms through which commercial interests colonise meanings of cleanliness are much the same. Although not everyone owns a washing machine, those who do buy into (or are bought into) an increasingly dominant technological repertoire.

Chapter 4 described an apparently similar situation in which standardized technologies, products and images flooded into culturally and climatically contained systems and societies. In that case, I homed in on the relationship between micro, meso and macro levels of sociotechnical development. By implication, new forms of house design, new ways of life and new concepts of comfort were engendered and animated through a process of vertical co-ordination between those analytic layers. Although the whirlpool model can clearly accommodate the development and worldwide diffusion of new methods of doing the washing or, for that matter, the proliferation of standardized fabrics and fashions, it offers a different interpretation of the dynamics at stake. In essence, it supposes that change is engendered by the circulation and mutual adjustment of ideas and practices not hierarchically, or between levels, as before, but across one horizontal plane.

Referring back to arguments introduced in Chapter 4, Figure 7.1 illustrates the manner in which localized and trans-national techniques and ideas are spun together. One implication is that the concepts of service that emerge from this inter-dependent whirling are forever localized. They cannot be detached from the specific conditions of their production and reproduction, not even when they depend upon ideas, methods and technologies that are widely shared.

This still leaves open the question of what is it that energizes the multiple whorls shaping the dynamics of the system as a whole. At this point it helps to refer to the work of those who have analysed large technical systems. For the most part, this literature has examined relatively bounded 'infrasystems' like those of electric power, telecommunication and automobility and has, in addition, been preoccupied with the institutional and technological phasing of their development. Effort has therefore focused on processes of system building and the sequential construction of demand (Hughes 1983; Fischer 1992). Little of this is of immediate relevance for, although I have described the laundry as a system, it is not one that has been deliberately 'built'. Laundering has *not* passed through successive stages of early development, diffusion and stabilization, there are no obvious system builders in sight, and there has been no requirement to co-ordinate, enlist, or enrol key actors, to mobilize the public or to institutionalize regulatory frameworks. While change has involved the locking-in and unlocking of expertise, this is knowledge shared across a multitude of households, not concentrated and invested in a handful of critical actors. Although the details of interdependency, that is, of what inter-depends with what, clearly differ between one large technical system and another, certain insights can be taken from this literature and applied to whirling configurations like the laundry.

One relevant observation concerns the dynamics of problem definition and problem resolution in the context of system development. In addressing this issue, Hughes (1983) appropriates the notion of 'reverse salients', borrowing this idea from military terminology. In its original use, a reverse salient is a point where there is a dip in the front line that prevents advance elsewhere. Applied to technology, 'reverse salients' constitute features, gaps, or bottlenecks thwarting further growth of the system as a whole. According to Hughes, the system builder's task is to identify these dips correctly and find ways of turning them into problems that can be fixed. In his analysis, system development is a process of spotting and resolving bottlenecks. This is a constant challenge for as soon as one is dealt with, another appears. Although it might not be possible to identify a single laundry system builder, it may be that several exist, each seeking to advance upon a particular front, fixing problems and overcoming reverse salients as they go.

To put it more concretely, in searching for new markets and market shares, detergent manufacturers address what seem to them to be blockages in 'their' system. They are constantly on the look out for features that hold back future development along the lines they would like to see. For example, how might home dry cleaning be developed or prevented? How might dust mites be killed at low temperatures? Could the smell of line-dried laundry be captured and reproduced in powdered form? Meanwhile, washing machine manufacturers

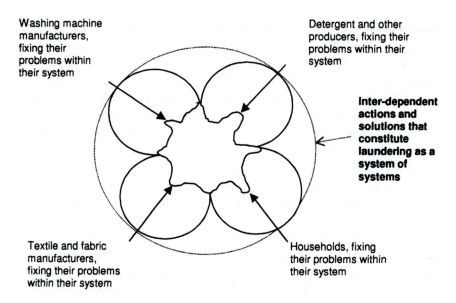

Washing machine manufacturers, fixing their problems within their system

Detergent and other producers, fixing their problems within their system

Inter-dependent actions and solutions that constitute laundering as a system of systems

Textile and fabric manufacturers, fixing their problems within their system

Households, fixing their problems within their system

Figure 7.2. Laundering as a system of systems

confront a similar though not identical set of puzzles but from behind a different 'front line'. They too face an array of system-shaping problems that would, once fixed, open the way for further development. For their part, users and consumers, viewed here as system builders in their own right, also deploy the resources around them to configure laundry routines in ways that resolve their own current concerns. The relative power of any one of these players and their capacity to shape and specify what others count as a 'problem' is critical. There are real inequalities of influence and as I have already noted, washing machine producers are now in an especially good position to structure the meaning and future of the enterprise as a whole. Important though this observation is, it does not detract from the value of seeing the laundry as a system of systems.

Figure 7.2 helps to illustrate this account. Behind each of the four 'front lines' lies a different actor trying to push forward by fixing reverse salient type problems currently impeding their advance. The fact that the problem-defining, problem-fixing actions of detergent producers, washing machine manufacturers, textile designers and householders have implications for others in this system of systems is indicated by the dotted line with which they are all encircled.

In essence, Figure 7.2 suggests that change is driven by the specification of problems and the management of reverse salients. The difference, as compared to the system building of electrification, is that with laundry there is movement on a number of fronts, all at once, and sometimes in different directions. In practice there is likely to be some overlap at the level of problem definition: in fact the extent to which problem definitions do or do not converge represents one of the more important features of meta-systemic development. But in representing the laundry as a meta-system I suggest that collective conceptualizations of normal and appropriate practice, that is, emergent definitions of service and of what it is to wash well, change as a consequence of efforts, practices, innovations and solutions initiated by multiple actors, each driven by their own system-building strategies. What goes on within this system of systems structures the detail of what is washed and when, why and how washing is done.

At the start of this chapter, I referred to policy interest in steering systems in transition. For the most part, such interest has focused on supply rather than on demand; that is, on analysing and encouraging transitions to a hydrogen economy or to a society built around micro-networks of embedded generation and electric power. This discussion highlights an important fault line in such debate. Commercial activity revolves around the construction of new concepts of *service* and the production of new ideas about hygiene, new images and sensations of 'freshly laundered clothing' and new visions of domesticity and normal practice. Meanwhile, governments and environmental groups have concentrated on only part of the equation. Although willing to advise consumers to wash a full load at a time and keen to encourage the development of more efficient machines, national policy makers rarely venture into the domains of fashion, body odour and appearance. Because they focus on *resources*, a good part of the potential for system innovation lies beyond their reach. As represented here, it is impossible to think about transitions to sustainability without also considering the redefinition of service. In this case, as in others, it is the relation between resource efficiency *and* the simultaneous respecification of demand that counts in practice.

The system of systems analysis developed here does a reasonable job of representing the co-production of laundry and of identifying the emergent properties of what it means to wash well, but as a theory of change it is not especially well developed. Amongst much else, there is more to say about the specification of system boundaries, the mechanisms of system integration and the day-to-day detail of meta-systemic change. I want to keep these questions in reserve and return to them in Chapter 9, where I shall also elaborate on the value of conceptualizing the laundry as a service. One reason for this is that the next chapter considers the reconfiguration of laundering and the construction and abandonment of habit from a different perspective, that is from the point of view of those who do the wash.

8

Laundry Habits: Integrating Practices

It is all very well to talk of whirlpools and systemic inter-dependencies but if new patterns of laundering are to take hold, peoples' habits have to change. This chapter examines the making and breaking of routines and conventions from different points of view, first looking at the role of new technologies and then at the terms in which meanings of cleanliness are expressed and reproduced. There are several reasons for analysing changing habits – specifically those relating to the decline of boiling, the valuing of freshness and the use of the tumble dryer – in this way. Returning to issues discussed in Chapter 5, one is to document the co-production of morality, technology and practice. Building on these ideas, the second is to investigate the experience of change and discover how systems of systems develop in practice. Although concepts of scripting and appropriation are useful in explaining some of the processes involved, they do not reveal much about how the steps and stages of laundering are reorganized or how multiple tools and techniques are deployed together in reconfiguring normal standards and conventions. The third goal is to show how constituent practices are packaged and to explore the idea that the process of routinization is itself instrumental in shaping the course and direction of change.

The specification of appropriately clean clothing is more obviously associated with concepts of propriety, self-respect and domestic order than is the definition and reproduction of an ideal indoor climate. Writing about the laundry, Kaufmann concludes that habits 'are a memory of the individual buried beyond the reach of memory, in daily routines, the movements of the body, the way we interact with those around us' (Kaufmann 1998: 9). This makes the analysis of change all the more intriguing. How are standards transformed given that this also requires a transformation of image and identity, not to mention knowledge, practice and performance?

This is the terrain of what Giddens refers to as practical consciousness, a terrain in which actors routinely 'and for the most part without fuss – maintain a continuing "theoretical understanding" of the grounds of their activity' (Giddens 1984: 5). The questions addressed in this chapter have to do with the reshaping of these theoretical understandings and with the reconfiguration as well as the reproduction of habit. When dealing with the laundry, activities are framed by typologies and classifications not just of dirt, but of what can be washed with what, of the necessary steps involved and the quality of the result. Such categories provide a structure with which people make sense of how, when and why they wash as they do. New habits consequently require a reshuffling of classificatory frameworks *and* of the actions and experiences associated with them. In real life, categories and practices run together but when thinking about the rewriting of routine, it helps to keep these dimensions at least provisionally apart. Such separation makes it possible to compare and track the relationship between peoples' classificatory schemes and those built into the washing machines, fabrics and detergents of different eras.

It is extraordinarily difficult to follow the reformulation of meanings and typologies that are, by definition, embedded, engrained and rarely visible. Yet there are moments when consumers' and producers' expectations are rendered explicit. Consumer associations analyse and compare domestic appliances, evaluating the latest models on behalf of potential buyers and users. It is true that these organizations and the magazines they produce exemplify a distinctively rational model of consumer choice in which function and value for money dominate (Aldridge 1994). Partly because of this, they provide a telling indicator of the historical reinterpretation of quality and performance. My analysis of the reconceptualization of laundering is therefore based on a comprehensive survey of all the reports and reviews of washing machines and dryers that have featured in the UK Consumers' Association *Which?* Magazine from 1957–2001, and in the American Consumers Union *Consumer Reports* from 1937–2001.

This trail reveals a number of environmentally important transformations in the meaning of washing well and in the technologies involved. Thanks to the generosity of Unilever's Consumer Science Insights, I have been able to explore some of the processes involved in overturning and sustaining routine and habit. Unilever allowed me to examine first-hand accounts provided by a socio-demographic cross section of people who do the washing in the UK today. Individuals were interviewed and videoed as they toured the home discussing their laundry, the frequency with which they wash specific items and their concepts of cleanliness. In showing how routines hold together *and* how they evolve, this material reveals the momentary cohesion of tradition and novelty both in the 'theoretical understandings' Giddens talks about, and in the daily reproduction of identity, pleasure and performance. The latter half of the chapter concentrates on the doing of laundry and the repertoires of meaning and experience associated with it. This shows how the declining importance of boiling and the increasing significance of freshness work out at the level of meaning and practice. In addition, the Unilever interviewees describe how the steps and stages of laundering are routinized and embedded in the taken for granted rhythms of daily life. It is, as one respondent put it, 'an on-going thing. Its like breathing really, it just, it happens'. Such observations inform the last section of this chapter in which I consider the relation between collective trends and highly personalized strategies. In conclusion, I argue that the somewhat abstract systems of systems described in Chapter 7 are held together through practice: that is through the active coordination of materials and meanings by the people who do the wash. Again this implies a reorientation of enquiry. Instead of studying the co-evolution of specific technologies and practices, or even the construction of regimes, the task is to better understand how multiple elements and components are integrated, how they come together in shaping collective conventions of service and how these composite conventions evolve.

However, I begin by showing how domestic laundering has been restructured around categories and classificatory schemes 'invented' and effectively imposed by successive generations of washing machinery.

Classifications and Categories

For Jean Claude Kaufmann, who studies the laundry as a means of revealing the dynamics of being and becoming a couple, the decision to get a washing machine is 'a major step in the process of domestic commitment' (Kaufmann 1998: 57). It symbolizes the joint organization of the home, simultaneously signalling the end of a prior era of self-sufficient provisioning and/or dependence upon other family members, typically the mother. More mundanely, this decision also restructures the process and practice of laundering. Depending upon the model selected and the range of technologies available at the time, the couple will from then on confront a more-or-less complex menu of choices. How they handle these is, as Kaufmann explains, a delicate matter and one that reflects and constitutes the character of their emerging relationship. As he documents so well, the formation of the couple involves the mutual adaptation of habit.

However, the machine is not an innocent party in the ensuing negotiation of coupledom or cleanliness. Laundry appliances have a history, so the detail of what there is to negotiate about varies over time. Not only that; routines built around one suite of material possibilities are broken, or at least bent, when new technologies are introduced. Developments in washing machine design consequently engender what amounts to a continuous dialogue between the classificatory schemes embodied in the latest models and those inscribed in previous generations both of machines and users.

Rates and patterns of diffusion differed significantly between the USA and the UK – in 1951, 76 per cent of American households had a washing machine compared with just 8 per cent in the UK (Bowden and Offer 1994) – but there is now a contemporary mono-culture of washing organized around the private use of the domestic machine. While American and British appliances are of typically different design, technical specifications reflect culturally specific assumptions about what laundering involves and what is required of an acceptable appliance (Parr 1999: 220). Being produced *for* the consumer, the tests and evaluations undertaken by the Consumers Union in the USA and the Consumers' Association in the UK provide a unique record of designers' and users' definitions and categories and of the relation between the two. Analysis of this material shows that far from simply 'doing' the washing, machines have continually changed the terms in which laundering is defined, evaluated and understood. In this role, washing machines are machines for producing (categories of) dirt.

Machine-made Typologies

There are many ways of classifying laundry: by the type of dirt to be removed – sweat, mud, oil and so forth – or by the extent of soiling and the nature of the fabric. The age and gender of the article's owner can also be important, along with its intended use. Is it, for example, a piece of household linen, is it underwear or outerwear, is it to be worn during the day or the night and is it something that deserves special care? Where washing is done by hand, such distinctions are reproduced in the way that individual items are treated. For example, his dirty socks might be washed apart from her underwear, tea towels are not put to soak in the same water as that used for bath towels, and so on.

One of the most obvious advantages but also one of the problems of a machine is that batches of laundry are washed together and therefore washed in ways that contravene conventions of cleanliness, economy, precision and care. The widespread adoption of the washing machine depended upon all sorts economic and infrastructural conditions *and* upon the normalization of a cruder typology of care. In an effort to minimize the conceptual leaps involved, the designers of the so-called 'suds-saver', produced in the USA in the early 1950s, promised to combine the benefits of machine washing without compromising concepts of cleanliness associated with washing by hand. To this end, the machine included a separate tub into which the not too dirty water from a first wash could be pumped for reuse with a second round of dirtier items, and so on. But in a report that already implies acceptance of machine-oriented typologies, the Consumers Union (1950b) criticizes this awkward hybrid. As the authors point out, the suds-saver undermines the distinctive benefits of *machine* washing, that is, the capacity to handle large quantities of laundry at the same time and with minimal human intervention.

As well as eroding existing categories, washing machines introduced new ones of their own. This is immediately revealed through an analysis of the settings, dials and programmes on offer. Some of the earliest American machines like the Bendix, reviewed in 1940, required the operator to set and reset a time switch to determine the duration of each wash, rinse and spin. With care and knowledge, users could manipulate these controls so as to mimic, if not exactly replicate, 'their' way of washing. The users of a General Electric model from 1948 had no such chance: for them, the machine took charge, putting loads of laundry through a pre-determined, pre-timed, sequence of soak, spin, wash, spin, rinse, dry off and empty off. Although manual over-riding was sometimes possible, automation promised – or threatened – to obviate the need and opportunity for user involvement. Successive moves in this direction involved continual revision of classes and categories of washing. How many types of laundry are there and how many should the machine permit? For reasons that are themselves of interest, answers have ranged from forty-eight to three.

In the UK, the number of options on offer increased during the 1960s as designers sought to extend the range of materials entrusted to the machine. At about this time, the classificatory system switched from one organized around the washing process to one defined by types of fabric. You no longer needed to know *how* to wash colourfast cotton, you just needed to know what your clothes were made of. New settings were also required to cater for 'delicate' and woollen items previously washed by hand. Meanwhile, synthetics, first featured in the reports of the early 1960s, complicated the two-part distinction between cotton and linen, a divide that had until then been 'the mainstay of most families' washing' (Consumers' Association 1960: 196). A similar trend can be observed in the USA. According to Consumers Union reports of the time, machines of the 1960s bristled with 'enough push buttons to suggest you can wash anything except your French poodle' (Consumers Union 1960: 412).

Rather than seeing this as an advantage the Consumers Union was critical of such sophistication. The report of October 1961 concludes that with the proliferation of options, the automatic washer had become 'an over compli-cated and finicky problem child' (Consumers Union 1961: 568). The ambition of reproducing the fine-grain distinctions of hand washing conflicted with other machine-oriented values of simplicity, functionality, reliability, ease of use, economy and efficiency. As these criteria took hold, the number of programmes deemed necessary declined over the next decade. In 1971, the Consumers Union declared five pre-set 'programmes' to be sufficient, revising this down to four in 1974 on the grounds that the quality of the wash was not impaired by rinsing in cold rather than hot water.

In persuading users to define cleanliness in their terms, designers freed themselves from the need to compare results with those achieved by hand or to mimic the processes involved. Although users have little knowledge of what goes on within the machine, its ability to clean is now taken for granted, so much so that Consumer Union reports omitted reference to this feature ten years ago. Meanwhile, the invention of new programmes signals the invention of a new vocabulary relating to reinvigorating, softening and refreshing (but not cleaning) clothes. This terminological switch suggests that clothes are washed in order to restore qualities of appearance, style, smell, texture and touch. As well as giving washing a new meaning, this move changes or at least adds to the terms in which performance is defined and judged (Sams 2001).

Washing machines have apparently 'demanded' that users abandon old habits and accept new typologies of cleanliness and proper practice. As described above, responsibility for deciding how different fabrics should be treated has passed from operator to designer. Designers' responses (and hence the classificatory structure of the laundry) reflect competing demands including the need to make machines that are flexible yet simple to operate; to construct and cope with the ebb and flow of performance requirements, and to produce 'the same' result while using less energy and water. As well as eliminating previously central skills like those of wringing, mangling and boiling, washing machines have 'black boxed' once important dimensions of judgement and discrimination. In the laundry, as in the kitchens de Certeau describes, the addition of 'tools and appliances, born of an intensive use of work in metals, plastic materials and electric energy, has transformed the interior landscape' of the family home (de Certeau 1998: 210). With laundering, as with cooking, the 'gestures of tradition withdraw before those imposed by new tools' and in this case too, 'the change involves not only the utensil or tool and the gesture that uses it, but the *instrumentation relationship* that is established between the user and the object used' (de Certeau 1998: 211). Interpreted negatively, washing has been so de-skilled that it involves no more than matching standardized 'care labels' with equally standardized programmes, adding a dose of detergent and pushing a button.

But in understanding the reorganization of routine and meaning, it is important to notice that this is *not* what happens in practice. A 1988 survey showed that people rarely used more than three programmes, fabrics were often mixed in a single load and users persistently disregarded or failed to read instructions.

Of the 200 questioned, 45 per cent admitted to washing items labelled 'dry-clean only', 37 per cent did not isolate woollens and 57 per cent failed to separate 'delicate' items (Anson 1988). There are different ways of interpreting this 'misbehaviour'. One is that people have so totally abandoned responsibility that machines and detergents are expected to cope even when fed the wrong materials or set to the wrong programme. Another is that users have their own ideas and that doing the washing does not necessarily mean following instructions and picking the 'right' programme.

Laundry technologies have undoubtedly rescripted the options on offer, yet trends like the decline of boiling or the establishment of laundry as an (almost) daily operation are not determined by the machine alone. The instrumentation relationship may have changed but with that, new forms of experience and skill come into play. Picking up this theme, the following sections detail the emergence of new understandings about when and how to do the wash.

The Way to Wash

Not so long ago, 'boiling was considered essential for getting the wash really clean and germ-free' (Zmroczek 1992: 176). In 1998, 64 per cent of British laundry was washed at 40 °C (DEFRA 2000) and over the last thirty years, the temperature of the washing water has dropped by half. I use this case as a means of investigating how deep-seated beliefs (in this case about the relation between heat, disinfection and cleanliness) can change so fast.

A few machines heat water to boiling point, Loehlin for instance describes one that was explicitly promoted as offering a 'new way of carrying out an old fashioned practice' (Loehlin 1999: 144), but the upper limit for most horizontal axis washers is 90 °C. For some users, this is a serious limitation. A sixty-six year old respondent interviewed in Zmroczek's study is adamant on this point. As she explains: 'just putting it in a washing machine, to me it is not clean, it wasn't the amount of lather that got things clean, it was just the boiling up of it, you know, the real boiling up' (Zmroczek 1992: 177). To succeed at all, manufacturers had to get over the rather basic problem that according to this person and others like her, washing machines could not wash. Their response was to redefine cleanliness as whiteness rather than the removal of germs. Test procedures involving the use of instruments like the illuminometer, reflectometer, spectrometer, or spetrophotometer were used to set standards in terms that automatic machines could meet. Washers that turned standardized swatches of dirty fabric suitably white – such levels of whiteness were not always visible to the naked eye, hence the need for scientific instrumentation – were, by definition, capable of producing cleanliness. With this as a benchmark, extensive boiling was no longer strictly necessary. Although critical, this move did not break the association between purification and heat. Instead, it inspired the development of revised, machine-friendly, specifications of necessary and appropriate temperatures. Consumers Union and Consumers' Association reports produced between the late 1950s and mid 1970s are full of clear, if inconsistent, recommendations about how hot the wash should really be. An American report of 1958 concludes that 'for a really clean wash, your water should be between 140 and 160° Farenheit' (Consumers Union 1958). Meanwhile, a UK Consumers' Association report of 1962 recommended that 'cottons should be washed at 180–185° Farenheit for ten minutes'. By 1967, the results of a Consumers' Association survey of twin-tub users found that although 32 per cent bemoaned their machine's inability to boil, boiling had slipped to ninth on the list of important features, gentleness with clothing having become the top priority (Consumers' Association 1967).

For reasons that are also to do with detergent design, the mix of fabrics in the wash basket and the financial and environmental cost of energy consumption, recommended temperatures have since plummeted. Although washing machines are likely to have a 'very hot' setting, the authors of a 1992 Consumers' Association report observe that 'we rarely have to deal with washing that is really dirty', and advise consumers not to 'use 95 °C unless you think you really need it' (Consumers' Association 1992). In statistical terms, the percentage of UK laundry washed at 90 °C declined by 18 per cent between 1970 and 1998, when it accounted for just 7 per cent of the total. In what is perhaps the most telling move of all, the UK Consumers' Association standard test procedures are now run on 'normal' washes of 60 and 40 °C, in line with reported practice.

The trend is clear but how is the loss of boiling understood and how have meanings and standards been revised in practice? The Unilever study suggests that there are two camps: those who have first-hand experience of the loss of boiling and those who have grown up without it. The views of the first group are especially instructive. Still convinced of an association between disinfection and heat, some do their best to reproduce 'traditional' methods and values. When asked about how she did her washing, one respondent, echoing the views quoted above, explained that she always puts 'whites' on to boil, arguing 'its just the heat of the water' that is needed, no matter whether the clothes are dirty or not. Others, reasoning that modern detergents 'don't need heat to operate', have been willing to abandon the habits of a lifetime. However, the most common response was a combination of the two: for normal purposes washing was done at lower temperatures but for special items a bit of boiling was still required. These two extracts illustrate such strategies.

If I cannot get a stain out . . . I boil, because washing machines don't always take the stains out, so I will boil, that'll lift it out.

These sorts of bits will just stand up on a quick wash because they've only sort of been worn probably for a couple of hours, they then just go through on a quick wash. But if I was doing sheets, I mean then I'd put them in a boil wash. If they've been on the children's beds for two days then they get a boil.

Now defined as a specialized activity, boiling or washing at the hottest setting the machine can manage is something to be explained and excused. Struggling to justify what she took to be deviant behaviour, one interviewee went to great lengths to detail the troublesome nature of her child's school uniform and explain that she had inherited a stock of white towels, all by way of defending the 'occasional hot wash'.

For those who have no boiling habits to lose, such discourse is entirely alien. Often recognizing that things were different in their parents' day these people viewed laundry as a process of refreshing rather than disinfecting clothing. Taken together, the Unilever interviews indicate the coexistence of multiple systems and at the conceptual level, different ways of seeing 'the same' products and technologies. While new users accept the categories inscribed in the latest devices, others accommodate them with the help of elaborate distinctions between normal and special practice. In both cases, theories and working understandings of *how* to wash are woven around the opportunities their appliances afford. The fact that nearly two thirds of UK washing is now done at 40 °C is revealing on two counts: as well as demonstrating the reduction in 'normal' washing temperatures it confirms the collapse of previously complex taxonomies of method.

Perhaps as a consequence, contemporary classifications have much more to do with *what* needs washing *when* than with the process itself. While the loss of boiling is a splendid example of the de-escalation of energy demand, changing concepts of need have the opposite effect.

The Need to Wash

When asked about what is involved in producing clean clothing, virtually all those interviewed in the Unilever study agreed: anything that had been through the washing machine was, by definition, clean. Items emerging still stained or marked might be discoloured or disfigured but they were not dirty. When asked 'what has to be done in order for it to be clean . . . what actually has to happen, for you, for it to be clean?' respondents had no hesitation. This reply is typical: 'For it to be fed through that washing machine, that is it.' With the process more-or-less out of the frame, the meaning and symbolic significance of laundering now revolves around the specification of when things should be cleaned and why.

Cleanliness is, as Kaufmann acknowledges, an unquestionable principle: 'to be oneself, to be a self-respecting individual, is to be clean' (Kaufmann 1998: 16). While personal definitions of cleanliness vary and change over time, failure to comply signifies failure to sustain a central part of one's self image. In practice this means that everyone has his or her 'own' system for defining dirt and so for determining the need to wash. Going around their home with an interviewer in tow, the Unilever respondents explained that they washed their curtains once, twice or four times a year. Towels were variously laundered after every use, after every three baths or after a couple of days. Some distinguished between jeans and other trousers. Pyjamas were, or were not, viewed as underwear and therefore changed (or not) on a daily basis. Beds were often, but not always, stripped each week. Meanwhile cushion covers deserved a wash 'every so often', or every other Thursday. Taken as a whole, this material reveals an array of distinct if not unique bundles of practice held together, case by case, by coherent – if usually tacit – classifications of need.

When asked to explain why things needed washing when they did, respondents justified their actions in terms of one or another of three dominant rationales. Two relate to the nature of the 'dirt' in question: does it come from the inside, that is from the body, or is it external? The outside world is a source of judgement as well as filth hence the third rationale relates not to cleaning per se but to the maintenance of a neat, tidy or smart appearance. How do these three types of reasoning relate to the increasing frequency with which people wash? Are sensitivities to body odour increasing? Are sources of external contamination on the rise, or is it that conventions of image and style are more exacting than before? The following paragraphs consider each possibility in turn.

Because the body is a reliably constant source of pollution, the elimination of sweat and smell has its own temporal rhythm. Most of the Unilever interviewees were convinced of the need to change underwear every day. The importance of this convention is made explicit in this case, where a mother complains that her teenage sons have yet to realize (or agree) that T-shirts are underwear and should be treated as such. She explains: 'they have to sort of be reminded [about the T-shirts] but they do change their socks every day, and they're quite good with their pants but, um, they'd wear a T-shirt all week'.

Another tries to persuade her son that it is *not* necessary to 'chuck something down on the floor which he's only worn for a few hours'. In this instance his 'excessive' understanding of contamination conflicts with her interpretation of need. In both instances, the ensuing negotiations are about where the margins of acceptability really lie. It is relevant to notice that these order-maintaining discussions are generally couched in terms of smell, not dirt or disinfection, a theme echoed by another of the Unilever interviewees: 'a lot of things that I wear next to the skin, really I only like to wear once because they do tend to get body odours no matter whatever you put on'.

Not everyone agreed that all contact with the body was contaminating, yet the preoccupation with smell has obvious implications for the 'need' to wash.

What of external sources of contamination? Quite other criteria, and quite other temporal frames, come in to play when estimating the 'need' to wash things like jackets, trousers and skirts, these being items that become dirty from the outside in, rather than from the inside out. Rules and conventions are most obvious when people reflect on the significance of wearing things that are technically clean, having just been through the wash, but still visibly stained. Much depends upon social context and the status of the item in question, as this respondent explains: 'If I'm in the house, and I'll slob around, and I'm really dirty by the end of the evening anyway. But I wouldn't wear anything with a stain on for going out, I would chuck it out and buy something new'.

So have expectations of appearance developed in ways that generate more washing? Is there a total increase in the number of occasions on which people need to look smart? Is the meaning of 'smart' becoming more demanding? Although concerned about the whiteness of their children's socks and the colour of collars, the Unilever interviewees talked about other aspects of appearance. As they explained, simply wearing things degraded the way they looked.

> when you get like a T-shirt and it's either been folded up or it's been hung up, it's all nice and crispy and perfectly in shape, and then when it's worn it's got your shape and body in it and it sort of looks messy and untidy . . . you can tell that it has been worn. It was fine, and it didn't smell and it wasn't dirty.

But it still needed washing. The same logic is here applied to a pair of jeans: 'the jeans, he usually puts them in because when you've worn them for a little while, I don't know if you've noticed, you can see the knee, you can see where you've worn them so he'll put them in the wash to be washed'.

In both cases, clean items were headed for the wash in order to restore the feeling of crispness and the sense of being freshly laundered. The valuing of 'freshly laundered' as a quality in its own right generates a more exacting, more unending sense of need than that associated with merely removing dirt. The concept of freshness also complicates the so far useful distinction between sources of contamination arising from the inside, where odour is of defining importance, and from the outside, where visible appearance is key. In practice, looking good, on the outside, is also associated with feeling good, on the inside.

It is in this marginal realm somewhere between the inner and outer 'skin' that more laundry-intensive expectations of freshness are arising. This extract captures the reasoning involved.

> sometimes I pull out a shirt from the wardrobe that I know I washed and put away and didn't wear, literally for about three or four months but I wash it. Even though it's not done anything . . . because I just smell it and I just think because it's been hanging round in the wardrobe for a bit it's gone a bit musty so technically it's clean but it's just not been used for a long time. That's why I just wash it.

Time and again, people acknowledged the need to wash already clean clothing so as to freshen it up. These examples are typical:

> I don't think half of my washing's dirty. I just think that it needs freshening up.

> I can put it on a low wash, even lower than that, and sometimes things aren't very dirty, they just need freshening up. I don't know so long as it looks fresh – I like it.

Never mind bacteria, dirt and sweat; washing is also, and increasingly, about turning items that are fusty, musty or tired into things that are fresh, scented, fluffy and 'ready' to wear. Smell and texture are relevant but as the following exchange indicates, freshness is in essence a state of mind: knowing things are clean, people feel good about wearing them.

> I   So do things feel different as well when you haven't washed them?
> R   I feel different –
> I   Right.
> R   I know I'm clean – I know I've put all clean clothes on – so I'm alright – do you know what I mean? . . . it wasn't dirty, it wasn't smelly or anything, it just really wanted freshening in my mind

The need to wear fresh as opposed to simply clean clothing is especially demanding for those who don several outfits during the course of the day. It is difficult to unscramble what is going on in this arena: are dress codes becoming more or less stringent, is the variety of social contexts increasing or decreasing, or is it that people are moving from one situation to another more often than before? Whatever the overall picture, the experiences of selected individuals show just how much laundry a complicated social life can generate. As one respondent recounts, she goes to a gym four times a week for two to three hours at a time. When she gets there she changes out of her normal clothes into a tracksuit, then into her gym kit, then back into her tracksuit, before changing to go home and maybe changing again if she goes out to the shops or to visit friends. While the tracksuit is washed weekly, everything else is laundered after use. The net result is that few items are worn for long but an increasing number come into contact with the skin and so require washing.

The ready availability of washing machines evidently contributed to the redefinition of a proper wash and the decline of boiling. Although washing machines have also influenced the specification of need (Forty 1986), other dynamics are at stake. The material presented here points to two forms of social change. In the last example, demand for freshly laundered clothing increases as people switch between social contexts each of which has a dress code of its own. In addition, frequent reference to the importance of wearing recently laundered clothing and to the relation between freshness and self-respect suggests the emergence of new and distinctly demanding criteria. It is instructive to follow the revision and redefinition of what washing involves and of when and why it should be done. But in real life, routines have to do with action as well as classification. The next section looks at what the respecification of need means for the (re)organization of practice and the reconstruction of routine.

Innovation and Tradition

Innovation and tradition are in constant tension as people appropriate new styles of laundering, all the time subscribing to what they take to be non-negotiable injunctions and standards of performance. As the collective creep of convention is in part a result of these adjustments, further examination of *practice* shows how new systems of meaning come into being.

Appropriating Appliances

An historical catalogue of laundry-related equipment would reveal a patchy and inconsistent picture of acquisition and innovation. The electric iron was, for example, in common use long before the washing machine and while 92 per cent of UK households now have a washing machine, only 50 per cent also have a dryer (DEFRA 1999). Because laundering is a composite enterprise it is important to know how new devices are incorporated into existing systems of meaning and habit. A discussion of the relationship between dryers and clotheslines helps to illustrate how elements of laundering fit together and what this means for the emergence of new routines.

When mechanical dryers were first introduced Consumers Union and Consumers' Association reports weighed up their pros and cons as compared with line or 'sun' drying. Dryers were manufactured in the USA in 1939 but not sold on any scale until the 1950s (Ryan 1999). In the USA and Canada, machine-dried clothes 'were said to last longer, smell sweeter, and require less care' (Parr 1999: 259). In addition, dryers allowed people to complete the laundry cycle whatever the weather outside. A Consumers Union report of 1954 details their multiple benefits as follows:

> with a clothes dryer placed beside her washing machine, the housewife need no longer lug heavy baskets of clothes outdoors or down to the basement for line hanging . . . drying clothes are free from exposure to soot, dirt, smoke, insects, pets and children, and no unsightly space consuming clothes line need mar the beauty of the back yard. (Consumers Union 1954)

By contrast, the UK Consumers' Association's special issue on 'Drying the Family Wash' found in favour of the line, concluding that: 'the best method of drying the family wash is a country garden, a stiff breeze and a sunny day'. With line drying set as the 'gold standard', mechanical dryers were positioned as inferior substitutes only of value to working wives and those not 'lucky enough to have a clothesline in the garden' (Consumers' Association 1959). Although reaching opposing conclusions these 'expert' reports are framed in similar terms, both dealing with issues of performance, convenience and care.

So how do dryers and lines actually fit into peoples' lives? The following observations suggest that the acquisition of a dryer and the consequent adjustment of habit is a complicated and symbolically sensitive process. In the course of her research Joy Parr found that 'many who owned dryers continued to use their lines regularly even after they had invested in a machine' (Parr 1999: 264). As she explains, the availability of both line and dryer set the scene for inventing new 'rules' and sometimes idiosyncratic practices. The women she spoke with might put cotton and linens outside to dry but run children's clothing through the machine, or they might partially dry sheets and towels on the line outside and bring them in for a final finishing in the machine. Rather than simply replacing the line, the dryer offered distinctive, sometimes complementary, sometimes contradictory qualities. But it was not just a matter of trading between convenience, speed, fragrance, texture and ease of ironing for users' rationales and actions show that both devices (and attendant practices) are positioned within highly elaborate systems of personal and domestic *propriety*. Pure white sheets flapping on the line epitomize a romanticized vision of domesticity still powerful enough to make this Unilever respondent feel guilty when using the dryer: 'I do use it yes, but when people have got all their washing blowing on the line and I'm using the tumble dryer I feel naughty'.

As this extract indicates, dryers and other laundry-related technologies challenge routines already laden with symbolic and moral significance. The experiences described above suggest that conventions are reworked as individuals reinvent what they believe to be personal styles and strategies: using the dryer for this but the line for that, and so on. Yet the transformation of habit involves more than the reinterpretation of *purpose* and *propriety*. New ways washing also generate new sensations and in this regard it is important to appreciate the feelings involved. For many of the Unilever interviewees pegging washing out to dry is a real source of pleasure, sometimes because it signals a job well done:

> It's the satisfaction of having new stuff again, seeing it fresh on the line, I don't use tumble dryer other than to fluff the towels sometimes

because the experience is enjoyable in itself,

> I think actually there's nothing nicer than pegging washing on a line. And I must say that if someone else pegs my washing out, ...I don't know about you, ...but I never, ever think it's quite the way I'd do it.

Or because they value the result, and especially the smell:

> This sounds stupid, but you know when you go for a nice walk, and the wind is blowing through and you just feel fresh. I just think the washing smells like that when it's been outside.

> when I do sheets, I love the smell of sheets on the line. I like to see things drying, I'll have a look and see if it smells nice.

Although the loss of the line brings all this to an end, new sensations and concepts of propriety are constructed around the tumble dryer:

> If you put them [towels] in the tumble dryer with a couple of those tissues, they come out and they feel really soft.

As these examples demonstrate, values and purposes are actively constructed through use with the result that there is no simple continuum between tradition and innovation. Meanwhile, the practice-based rationales that people weave around their actions have the effect of reconstituting the bedrock of normality against which future alternatives are judged. Whether localized transformations of this kind add up to a collective shift of convention depends on the relation between one step of the laundry process and another and on the routinization of the operation as a whole.

Scheduling and Order

Laundering is a sequential enterprise in which washing comes before drying and drying before ironing. In analysing the making and breaking of habit I take note of one last aspect, that is the *scheduling*, as well as the meaning, purpose and experience of doing the wash. There are two dimensions to this: one relates to the management of the steps involved. The second concerns the positioning of laundry-related activity within the flow of everyday life.

Compared with twin-tubs and semi-automatic models, modern washing machines 'create' time that can be put to other uses while the programme runs its course. The dryer has the further effect of separating the washing from the weather and although combined washer-dryers do not always permit a perfect flow (these machines wash a greater weight of laundry than they can dry), the synchronization of washing and drying is generally becoming easier. New technologies have changed the temporal properties of certain aspects of the process but the question remains: how do the component parts fit together, and how do they fit into domestic routines? In addition, how do other aspects of daily life turn around the time and work required to produce a clean, dry and ironed shirt for tomorrow, a supply of fresh bed linen every two weeks, and a weekly replenishment of all the towels in the house?

The Unilever interviewees report on a variety of personalized strategies for 'keeping on top' of the laundry. Whether ironing is done for twenty minutes a day between six and seven in the morning, whether it is reserved for Sunday evening or completed 'on demand' depends, above all, on the timetabling of the household as a whole. Details of order and organization are continually adjusted when children reach school age, when people take on a new job or when they work different hours. This rejigging is informed by an enduring sense of necessity. The need to cope with an unending stream of washing is unavoidable but the fine-grain of when and how this happens varies depending upon the precise configuration of other demands and timetables. In effect, the minutiae of domestic management constitutes another kind of glue, holding expectation and action together in unique routines that are none the less built around collective conventions and shared sociotemporal rhythms.

It is this combination of case-by-case coping within a network of social and domestic obligation that explains the relationship between individuals' accounts of their own routines – perfectly represented in the much repeated phrase 'I do it my way' – and the forceful yet largely invisible coordination of separate, seemingly privatized 'ways'. 'Doing it my way' is an encompassing notion having to do with scheduling, with the details of practice (are trousers turned inside out or not, are towels given special treatment and so forth) and with specifications of minimally acceptable performance. In the real world, all dimensions roll into one 'way' of doing things. In some respects this means that the laundry – here understood as a practically and theoretically coherent enterprise – is resistant to change. No aspect can evolve without consequence for the system as a whole. At the same time levels of interdependence are such that purpose, practice and experience are constantly being adjusted and recalibrated.

The very complexity of the system – what is to be washed, when and why – permits extensive customization around a range of increasingly standardized products and appliances. People represent their way of washing as a unique solution – that is, as the solution that fits their circumstances and the tools and materials available to them – to the problem of maintaining and reproducing order and self respect. The process of appropriation is therefore one in which people actively and more or less continually redefine both the meaning and the process of washing well. Although Silverstone (1993) and Lie and Sorensen (1996) make similar points, they do not take the discussion on to the next stage, which is to think about the units of practice and convention into which things and ideas are appropriated or to document the day-to-day dynamics of (re) integration.

Millers of Meaning and Practice

Looking back, the positioning of laundry as a task to be done within the home, and the development and marketing of a range of devices and products designed for this purpose proves crucial for the specification and production of appropriately clean clothing. Over the last 100 years, there have been a number of environmentally significant developments in when and how people wash: the decline of boiling and the expectation of washing 274 rather than fifty-two times a year being two of the most important. In following these changes I have made use of different types of explanation starting with the notion that washing technologies have rescripted practice. In the first part of the chapter I argued that domestic washing machines transformed not just the doing but also the meaning of laundry. In this capacity they modified the moral and symbolic landscape, redefining concepts of cleanliness and introducing new categories of their own. This takes the concept of 'scripting' further, implying that (some) technologies change both the way things are done *and* the frameworks of meaning and of right and wrong in which such doings (and related activities) make sense.

I then turned the argument around in order to see how machines were actually used and how established classifications and habits were overturned in practice. Rather than overhauling a lifetime of value and meaning all at once, those who had habits to lose developed elaborate and sometimes idiosyncratic conceptual schemes in which it was legitimate to use new technologies for some purposes but not for all. Others simply accepted that what came out of the washing machine was, by definition, clean. In other words, machine-made typologies are mediated by the contexts in which they have effect. In addition, and in thinking about this relationship, it is important to appreciate peoples' capacity to add new layers of symbolic meaning on to existing senses of how things should be.

In investigating why people wash as often as the do and how this changes, I have taken an approach much like that adopted in Chapter 6. In other words I have reviewed rationales invoked in support of current practice. From this point of view, the contemporary valuing of freshness is especially significant. The concept of freshness extends already naturalized notions of dirt (especially sweat) but with the important difference that anxiety about smell and appearance justifies washing things even when they are clean. But this has not only been a history of ideas. In the real world, narratives of reinvigoration and freshness are enmeshed in the doing of washing. This is another important conclusion. In organizing and managing the production of clean and dry clothing day in, day out, people are engaged in a complex process not of incorporating one appliance or another but of *integrating* all into a seamless and to them coherent 'way' of doing the washing. In considering the socio-temporal structure of washing routines I changed perspective, analysing laundering as an accomplishment requiring the effective co-ordination of multiple steps and stages and of equally elaborate complexes of tools, meanings and experiences. In describing how they did the laundry 'their way', people described much more than the co-production of discrete technologies and consumer practices. Instead, their accounts took the form of epic narratives in which a variety of elements including fabrics, detergents, conditioners, concepts of freshness and senses of domestic obligation were woven together. There are two conclusions to draw from this. First, the language of appropriation does not do justice to the processes of continual adjustment involved in maintaining and reproducing self-respect and self-defining standards of 'cleanliness'. Second, an appreciation of the practicalities of integration puts the conclusions of the previous chapter in a new light.

In the latter half of this chapter I have taken the people who do the wash to be central to the reproduction and revision of normal standards. As represented here, it is they who 'make' systems of laundry through the day to day 'milling' together of meaning and practice. Looking first at changing classifications and then at changing habits, I have documented the fluidity of acceptable practice. Reflecting on the rapid and recent loss of boiling one might come to the view that people (and their typologies of propriety) are endlessly accommodating and that the meanings of washing well can be radically reformulated without fear of failure. Accordingly, the future of the laundry would seem to be infinitely malleable. Anything might happen and just about anything could be incorporated into new systems of meaning and into new versions of 'my way'. However, the ingredients – the fabric, the detergents, the conditioners and the machines – with which people work and around which they make 'their ways' of washing are not innocent materials. To return to the whirlpool image with which the last chapter concluded, producers and manufacturers are together involved in pushing notions of sensation and smell in one direction, coping with anxieties about allergies in another, and constructing new concepts of what washing is all about. At this level, the possibilities for change are not open for they depend on the dynamics of mutual adaptation and adjustment. This suggests the existence of two parallel forms of integration: one associated with the whirling together of the laundry as a system of systems and one that happens on the ground as people construct their own ways of doing things.

In considering the relation between these two forms, it is possible to discern dominant conduits of change. The washing machine and the dryer have, for example, permitted and sometimes required particular forms of de- and re-scheduling, de- and re-skilling and de- and re-meaning. In so far as the work of laundering has been delegated to these technologies, they have become especially effective pathways for the transformation of habit, the reconfiguration of meaning and the temporal organization of the process as a whole. The next chapter elaborates on these ideas and on the relationship between socio-technical systems and taken-for-granted concepts of service.

9

System and Service

In Chapter 4, 'Regimes of Comfort: Systems in Transition', I concentrated on 'vertical' relationships between key technologies and sociotechnical regimes and landscapes in an effort to understand the escalation and convergence of convention and expectation. This analysis missed elements important in the discussion of cleanliness. Critically, it overlooked the moral and symbolic structuring of practice and the positioning of new and established technologies within systems of meaning and order. In focusing on the unfolding of socio-technical trajectories relating to lighting, heating and cooling, I took relatively little account of how these systems affected either the experience or the socio-temporal organization of everyday life. By comparison, the chapters on bathing and laundering have been preoccupied with the 'horizontal' dynamics of change: that is with relations *between* the component parts (be they appliances, ideas, beliefs and values) of contemporary practice.

This chapter has two purposes: one is to take stock of what has already been said about how routines hang together and about the mechanisms of integration. The second is to set the scene for the final part of the book, which is explicitly concerned with co-ordinating and scheduling obligations and activities essential for the reproduction and maintenance of 'normal' ways of life. In considering the temporal dimension of sociotechnical change, I argue that the day-to-day business of 'horizontal' integration – that is the fitting together of symbolically and technically coherent packages of practice – has implications for the respecification of what people take for granted and for the 'vertical' ratcheting of demand.

At first sight, it is difficult to maintain a clear distinction between the 'vertical' configuration of regimes and the 'horizontal' structuring of service, that is of understandings about what it means to wash well or what constitutes a normal bathing routine. Notions of regime and landscape are of value precisely because they highlight the extent to which sociotechnical trajectories are shaped and formed by codetermining aspects of the social, moral, economic and material contexts in which they develop. On the other hand, figuring out how the 'horizontal' relations of codetermination actually operate demands a different kind of analysis. In reviewing the last few chapters on 'cleanliness', I want to develop this idea and in the process make the case for studying the transformation not of specific routines and technologies but of composite suites of convention that I shall refer to as 'services'. This leads me to conclude that there *are* relevant and important differences in the conceptualization of regime and service.

In working towards this conclusion, I begin by reconsidering theories of cleanliness in the light of the last three chapters. In so doing, I develop the idea of 'service' in an effort to accommodate some of the conclusions drawn along the way. My next step is to relate the transformation of service to the co-evolution of sociotechnical systems *and* to the work that people do, day in day out, in making, reproducing and revising normal ways of life.

Reconsidering Cleanliness

Accounts of cleanliness and of how routines have changed tend to focus on selected aspects of what I take to be a more wide-ranging, more complex enterprise. For example, Hoy (1995) and Tomes (1998) organize their histories around the specification and revision of medical knowledge. Tomes is explicit: what interests her most is 'how scientific precepts become a part of the working hypotheses of everyday life' (Tomes 1998: 14). If dangers are believed to emanate from the body, it makes sense to view the shirt as a sponge. If disease is transmitted from hand to mouth, it makes sense to advocate regular scrubbing, and so on. While theories about bodies, smells, germs and disease have filtered into the discourse and practice of bathing and laundry, ideas of cleanliness continue to develop in ways that are unrelated to scientific or medical knowledge (see, for instance, the increasing importance of freshness). As Douglas argues, cleaning is important in making social distinctions and reproducing order. By implication practices change as new boundaries are drawn. But again there is more to it than that. As the previous chapters have demonstrated, material objects and technologies construct, stabilize and respecify the categories involved. The evolution of the washing machine has, for example, required continual reinterpretation of what constitutes cleanliness and how it is to be achieved. In other words, changing concepts of cleanliness reflect changes in the actions, tools and techniques deployed when people do what they think of as 'cleaning'. The status of such action also relates to experience and expectation. That the feeling of pounding water on skin is now something to be appreciated, not feared, as would have been the case in the sixteenth century, indicates that the social construction of the *process*, the very doing of washing, is as important as the specification and interpretation of the outcome. Related to this, the reinvention of normal practice has to do with the systems of provision involved. The dominance of a privatized system of laundry provision has, for instance, structured the very landscape in which change takes place. In this regard it is important to notice that washing is done at home and with the aid of machines the designers of which set standards of their own making.

It is also clear that routines fit together within a more encompassing framework of sociotemporal order. Some people shower twice a day, others bathe a couple of times a week; some wash shirts after every use while others expect them to last for days on end, but from the perspective of any one individual, his or her strategy constitutes *the* way of doing things. Habits give shape to what people do and to when and how they do it. In this they have the dual effect of reproducing judgements about how things should be and of structuring the day.

If it is to be of use in understanding changing practice, the concept of cleanliness has to be stretched to accommodate all these dimensions and dynamics. One way of achieving this is to think of cleanliness as a composite service, formed and given meaning by the activities undertaken in its name. Again we confront what is becoming a familiar question: if composite notions of service are made up of so many elements (for example: scientific rationales, signifiers of difference and order, sociotechnical configurations, sociotemporal structures, systems of provision, experience and expectation), how do they evolve?

Reconfiguring Routine

I have argued that personal senses of necessity and pleasure and working concepts of service are constructed through the active stitching together of routines and through their daily reproduction within families, social contexts and networks. The resulting ensemble is powerful in its effects. Kaufmann talks about it in terms of injunctions. For him, an injunction is 'a social construction (historical, family based, personal) which has produced the framework of assumptions triggering the action – the thing that simply has to be done' (Kaufmann 1998: 21). The perfect injunction, that is the perfect trigger to action, is silent, invisible, and buried deep in the layer of what Giddens describes as practical consciousness. While some actions seem optional and some figure on mental lists of things to do, many others – like showering, ironing, or washing hair – are accomplished without further thought or reflection. Social norms and conventions are, Giddens argues, sustained and recreated through practices like these. It is all very well to appreciate this 'duality of structure'

(Giddens 1984: 19) but how do new injunctions arise and how do new patterns of cleanliness and new concepts of service break through the sedimented bedrock of engrained habit?

Sources of change often lie beyond the boundaries of the practices in question. Since bathing and laundering are embedded in the flow of everyday life, shifts in the hours people work or the time it takes for the washing machine to run its course have a bearing on how these activities are defined, positioned and organized. Likewise, bathing and laundry represent just two arenas in which contemporary preoccupations with smell and fragrance are worked out. These and other trends are in turn related to the construction and management of commercial opportunity. As we have seen, new products and technologies simultaneously create and resolve novel problems like those of achieving softness, freshness and comfort. In other words, both the respecification of issues to be dealt with and the contexts in which people respond have the potential to engender change. But this still does not tell us *how* routines are reconfigured.

Rick Wilk (1999) draws on Bourdieu (1977) in offering one possible explanation. This account depends upon the notion that there is an unconscious (doxic) realm of taken-for-granted common sense and habitual practice, on the one hand, and a (heterodox) realm in which rules and norms of conduct are explicit, contested and manipulated, on the other. The proposition is that 'social limits and standards are taken for granted, and only change through being brought out of the doxic realm of the unconscious habitus, into the discursive sphere of heterodoxy' (Wilk 1999: 6.2). Having been reconfigured in this sphere of explicit discourse, new arrangements 'eventually sink back into the accepted daily practice of the habitus' (Wilk 1999: 6.2). Wilk describes the two processes involved as those of cultivation, in which wants arise and are made explicit, and of naturalization, through which wants are turned into taken for granted needs. Figure 9.1 illustrates this idea.

This is an immediately attractive scheme that makes good sense of certain forms of change and that has much in common with theories of reversal and abstraction explored in Chapter 4. However, the terminology of needs and wants and the necessary cycling between the realms of explicit discourse and taken-for-granted habit does not capture the kinds of dynamics observed with bathing and laundry. It would be easy to describe the introduction of specific laundry products in this way and instructive to follow the mechanisms of cultivation and naturalization involved. However, such an exercise would not reveal the inter-dependence of apparently discrete products and practices, the sideways creep of mutual adaptation or the reformulation of entire complexes of convention and service. It would not tell us how the laundry has come to be as it is or why people shower as they do.

Habitus   Need   Taken-for-granted

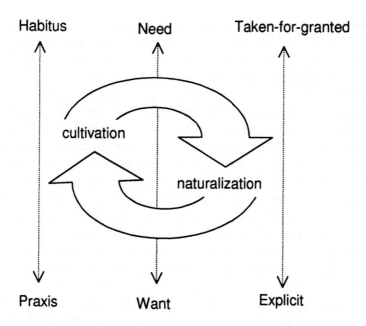

Praxis   Want   Explicit

Figure 9.1. The cultivation of want and the naturalization of need

In highlighting the importance of problematization Wilk introduces an ingredient largely missing in Giddens' account of the relation between agency and structure, namely the specification of challenges around which rules and resources are mobilized. However, Wilk's interpretation of the cycling of needs and wants is too narrowly focused on consumption (and by implication the consumption of things) to cope with the transformation of multi-dimensional enterprises like those of bathing and laundry. But can we adapt this model and use it to think about the cultivation and naturalization of composite services, rather than of more narrowly specified needs or wants? Such an approach has several advantages.

First, it serves to relax the implied relation between means and ends and allows that there may be different ways of reproducing what are none the less shared conventions. In this it makes it easier to acknowledge that individual habits vary despite being held in place by what are experienced as collective injunctions. Second, by casting the frame of reference wider – by talking about styles of laundering and bathing rather than specific needs and wants – it is easier to imagine the creep of convention *within* the realm of the taken for granted. While new practices *sometimes* arise as a consequence of explicit challenges to routine, as when innovative technologies are launched and adopted, they also emerge through barely visible adaptations and adjustments within and across existing frameworks of order. Kaufmann's descriptions of how habits erode as couples slip into new routines illustrates this process perfectly. As he explains, habits take root and accumulate imperceptibly. Without notice, they 'become part of the couple's joint heritage, buried all the more deeply in the silence of interaction for never having been challenged' (Kaufmann 1998: 75). Third, it allows for quite explicit recognition of inter-dependency within what amount to systems of need, here termed services. It is not just that the dynamics of cultivation and naturalization have to be understood in terms of 'interconnected chains of provision linking production, distribution, marketing, advertising and consumption' (Fine and Leopold 1993: 24), though that is important. If services are built of what I described in Chapter 7 as systems of systems, and if they are also configured through the milling of meaning and practice (as described in Chapter 8) it is impossible to understand how routines change without also understanding how compo-nent ideas, practices and sociotechnical systems are integrated.

In some situations it seems that consumers do much of the integrative work themselves, picking one but not another from a multitude of shower gels and washing powders and constructing what is for them a coherent way of life. In other cases the functioning and value of one element literally depends on the coexistence of another. For example, washing machines require detergents just as detergents now require washing machines. More broadly what washing means today is powerfully shaped by the mutually determining activities of textile manufacturers, detergent designers and appliance producers. Not only that but the details of temporal co-ordination, for example the management and scheduling washing, drying and ironing, also contribute to the shaping of habit. In short we can discern different modes of integration. It is important to think about what these are and how they change over time. But what is the package that is thereby held together? What does this notion of service really mean?

Redefining Service

Much of the literature on consumption focuses on the acquisition of things. Although there is increasing interest in how these things are used, customized and appropriated, relatively little notice has been taken of how families of consumer goods are deployed together in the achievement of 'higher level' enterprises like those of constructing a cosy home or a welcoming environment. Addressing this theme but in the context of energy policy, Hal Wilhite has persistently argued that in focusing on the consumption of resources, analysts overlook the simple point that people do not in any meaningful sense 'consume' electricity. Although they pay for electricity, householders in fact consume cultural energy services like lighting, heating and cooling (Wilhite *et al.*1996).

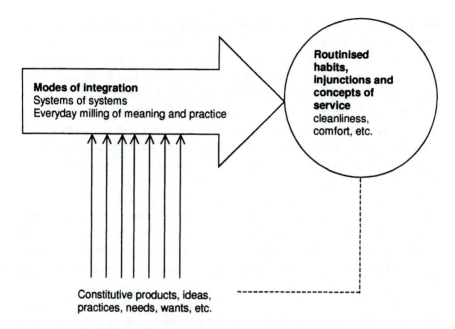

Figure 9.2. Integrating routines

What does it mean to consume services defined in this way and how are concepts of service related to the repertoire of ingredients involved in their provision and/or to the details of their integration? Typically defined as those not providing goods, the so-called service industries constitute a major part of the economy and include such areas as telecommunications, finance, insurance, education, health and leisure. Yet there are other ways of thinking about services, not as industrial groupings but as composite accomplishments generating and sustaining certain conditions and experiences.

Conceptualized this way, services have to do with the orchestration of devices, systems, expectations and conventions. What counts as appropriately laundered clothing depends, in this analysis, on the co-ordination of otherwise bounded sociotechnical arrangements and on their integration in terms of an also co-ordinative framework of meaning and rationale. Figure 9.2 illustrates some of these features. It shows how products and practices are combined in the course of everyday life and through the configuration of systems of systems, and it positions concepts of service – including those of comfort and cleanliness – as the outcome of these integrative processes.

In figuring out how *services* change the key questions have to do with integration. How do suites of technology interact, how are they deployed together and with what consequence for expectations and specifications of normal practice? What are the modes of integration involved and are these also subject to change? Though only now made explicit, these have been consistent concerns running through the previous chapters. In discussing laundry as a system of systems, Chapter 7 took note of the multiple adaptation of textiles, detergents, and washing machines. In this context, collective specifications of service had to do with mechanisms of integration associated with systemic and device-specific narratives of sociotechnical change. Looking at the same territory but from a different perspective, Chapter 8 detailed the co-ordinative work involved in constructing what people described as 'their way' of doing the laundry.

As I noted at the start of this chapter, there are similarities between the notion of regime, as used in Chapter 4, and the concept of service as developed here. Regimes of comfort, like those of cleanliness, are made up of rules, 'ways of handling relevant artifacts and persons, ways of defining problems' (Rip and Kemp 1998: 338), technologies, skills and procedures. Concepts of service depend on much the same blend of method, meaning and hardware. The difference is that the analysis of regime-formation is, at heart, an analysis of the more or less path dependent 'outcomes of earlier changes' (Rip and Kemp 1998: 338). Understanding regime transformation is a matter of understanding the relation between micro and macro-level processes of sociotechnical change. By comparison, analysis of service formation requires analysis of contemporary processes of integration and co-ordination. Understanding the evolution of service therefore depends on understanding the 'horizontal' dynamics of integration and the range and variety of modes and methods involved.

The terminology of service has the further effect of drawing attention to the working units of sociotechnical change and the bounding of co-evolutionary processes. In this it helps to define the larger packages of habit and convention into which new arrangements and technologies are incorporated. In other words, specific devices and appliances like air-conditioning systems and washing machines have to be examined and understood with reference to the achievement of more encompassing services like those of comfort and cleanliness. What matters is not just their appropriation, or even their co-evolution, but the consequences of such for the rest of the service-related system as a whole. This implies a shift of emphasis. Instead of concentrating on the result, that is on what changes when new technologies are 'domesticated', the focus is much more on the process itself: on how change comes about and what the necessary integrative work involves. Finally, and again in distinction to the earlier discussion of regimes, analysis of the specification and reproduction of service forces us to attend to the day-to-day management of normal practice. This means thinking not only about what is done but also about how those doings are organized and scheduled. The next chapter on convenience, convention and co-ordination investigates the temporal structuring of everyday life in order to better understand how this affects (and is affected by) the definition and management of normal and necessary service and with what consequence for the standardization and escalation of demand.

10

Convenience, Co-ordination and Convention

In Chapter 9, I made the case for analysing forms of integration, arguing that this was important in understanding how composite services like those of comfort and cleanliness evolve. Building on these ideas, and taking the practice-based approach a stage further, this chapter considers the temporal co-ordination and scheduling of activity. I have already commented on a number of time-related features. The standardization of the indoor environment has, for instance, freed people from a shared regime of diurnal and seasonal change. The waning of the siesta and the development of a twenty-four hour society rely, in different ways, on the technologies of heating, cooling and lighting. The polarization of leisurely bathing and rapid showering reveals something about contemporary distinctions between rush and slow. Meanwhile, launder-ing, an enterprise that used to occupy a day or more, has been fragmented into a sequence of discrete tasks each requiring moments of attention. Although I have made these points in passing, I have not considered how the activities involved in maintaining contemporary standards of comfort and cleanliness fit into the stream of daily life. Doing so draws attention to an as yet unex-plored mechanism of change.

Whereas the chapters on comfort emphasized the 'vertical' ordering of sociotechnical change, those on cleanliness concentrated on the 'horizontal' integration of practice. Linking these themes together, the following discussion suggests that forms of co-ordination and integration themselves engender path dependent patterns of demand, responses to which create new specifications of service. In developing this argument I examine the relation between practice, time and technology.

Up to now I have chosen to investigate practices currently evolving in ways that require greater consumption of energy or water. In this chapter I take a different approach, focusing on issues of convenience and temporal co-ordination not because they are environmentally problematic in their own right (though some may be so) but because it is important to understand the personal and collective scheduling of practice in order to understand the transformation of convention. I concentrate on the notion of convenience because the changing meaning and value of this idea is especially useful in illuminating developments in the sociotemporal order. More than that, the term is frequently applied to material objects and systems that purport to ease problems of co-ordination and integration and which are therefore implicated in the achievement of socially important injunctions and hence in the reproduction of normal standards of service.

I suggest that the diffusion and appropriation of things like freezers, washing machines and answerphones paradoxically increases problems of scheduling and co-ordination and inspires the search for new, yet more convenient arrangements. In addition, and just as relevant for the present argument, reliance on convenient solutions has the cumulative effect of redefining what people take for granted. Put simply, how socially necessary activities are fitted together, and how the dynamics of integration are managed in space and time, is itself significant for the (re)specification of normal and necessary ways of life.

Initially referring to ease of use, then to saving time, convenience is now associated with the capacity to shift, juggle and reorder episodes and events. In this environment, things that are 'convenient' are those that enhance peoples' control over the scheduling of activity. Studies of how such technologies are actually used reveal a variety of unexpected but important relationships between domestic time management and the specification and accomplishment of socially necessary practice. Recent research into household scheduling (Southerton 2001), together with material from the Unilever study, suggests that people structure and manage their time around core, non-negotiable activities or injunctions. In other words, it is the ambition of maintaining standards in the context of an increasingly fragmented temporal environment that drives the pursuit of convenience.

In analysing this interaction I argue that new routines and habits arise not as a result of path dependent ratcheting, not because of shifting rationales and not because of the mutual determination of complex systems of systems. Instead, concepts of service are revised and redefined as a consequence of the measures people take in coping with the ever increasing challenge of 'keeping on top of things' and 'holding it all together'. Going full circle, this challenge is ever increasing *because* problems of co-ordination are exacerbated by the means taken to resolve them.

In concentrating on the temporal patterning of practice and the fracturing of activity, this chapter offers another way of thinking about the relation between individual habits and the transformation of collective convention. In this it shows how people are drawn into new ways of life whether they like it or not. It would be possible to see the demands of sociotemporal co-ordination as yet another force for change, merely adding to those already considered. Taking a different approach, I conclude that the spiralling dynamic examined in this chapter constitutes a centrifugal force energizing the development of new reasonings, rationales and sociotechnical arrangements. In other words it is through processes like those described below that the dynamics of integration fuel processes of escalation and standardization. Before getting into these more abstract debates, I start by introducing the idea of convenience and reviewing arguments about the sociotemporal structure of society.

Convenience and the Pace of Life

In its earliest formulation, convenience had little to do with the management of time. Initially defined in terms of functionality and ease of use, the term justified the acquisition of a range of consumer goods including furniture and clothing. As Crowley explains, it was used in the eighteenth century to describe the layout of rooms within a home and when listing places where one might buy wine, hire carriages or borrow books. In this role, convenience had two advantages: 'it measured usefulness according to "any purpose" and it left the purposes themselves morally neutral' (Crowley 1999: 10). The terminology of convenience, like that of comfort, legitimized new forms of consumption and located them as self evident and sensible. Exemplifying this approach a 1918 advertisement runs all three Cs together, promoting the merits of 'Challenge cleanable collars' that 'save money and ensure cleanliness, comfort, and convenience' (Handley 1999: 24). Although items are still marketed in this way, other interpretations are in circulation.

'Modern' conveniences like indoor plumbing and hot and cold running water saved time as well as reducing toil and trouble. Domestic appliances were therefore classed as convenient when they reduced (or were expected to reduce) the hours spent on domestic chores (Forty 1986). A third more contemporary usage relates convenience to the scheduling and co-ordination of people and objects in time and space. Understood in this way convenience is about *timing*, that is, the ability to shift and juggle obligations and to construct and determine personal schedules. From this point of view, the really important benefit of convenience food is not that it saves time but that it makes it possible to prepare and eat a meal at very short notice. Technologies and devices offering this form of 'hypermodern' convenience include microwave cookers, freezers, answerphones and text messaging facilities, to name but a few (Warde *et al.* 1998). The valuing of speed and of instant response is sometimes relevant but the more important issue is usually that of control. In allowing users to 'store' time, defer activity or manage and minimize interruption, tools of this kind enhance capacity for autonomous organization.

The increasing significance of convenience appears to relate to a contemporary sense of always being short of time. A respondent interviewed as part of a UK study of traffic and congestion puts it this way:

> Everybody's in so much of a rush nowadays, now everybody's trying to make money, trying to get to places, they've got to get here, they've got to get there, they've got to do their shopping – this, that and the other, I think there's a lot more pressure, you haven't got the time to do as much as what you want in a day nowadays. (Hedges 2001 part 4: 14)

Authors who have written about the time squeeze tend to focus on the loss of 'free' time, that is time people can arrange themselves and spend as they like. Addressing this issue, Juliet Schor's (1992) unambiguously escalatory thesis is that Americans work more to spend more with the result that the time they have to share with family and friends is doubly pressed. Time not spent at work is consumed by the very activity of consumption: meanwhile, the more people shop, the more they need to earn, and so the cycle continues.

Buying into this kind of analysis, critics of consumer culture and advocates of downshifting and voluntary simplicity emphasize the environmental importance of simple living. Driven by such ambitions, the Centre for a New American Dream is one amongst a number of organizations seeking to change attitudes and help people wean themselves off an unsatisfying treadmill in which consumption breeds consumption (Bell 1998: 63). This is not a programme everyone finds attractive or to which – given the configuration of capitalist society – everyone could subscribe. To outsiders, voluntary simplicity sounds suspiciously like cutting back, yet its proponents argue that far from sacrificing a high standard of living, this is precisely the prospect on offer. Though not environmentally inspired, the development of the 'slow food' movement (Slow Food 2001) reflects a more diffuse sense that important qualities of life are threatened by too much rushing about. Addressing similar issues, Darier appeals for a resurgence of laziness, arguing that something of the kind is needed to overcome the 'busy self', that is a self who has come to interpret a constant increase in activity as a valued life purpose.

Whatever the proposed solution, the common theme is that spirals of work and spend lead, inexorably, to a faster pace of (lower quality?) life for the cash-rich, time-poor 'rats' caught up in the race. But not everyone falls into this category. Already moving away from Schor's work-spend equation, Shaw argues that 'while neo-classical economics may explain the increasing harriedness of mens' lives through a progressive shifting from unproductive into productive activities, for women it is more often the inability to shift out of unproductive activities which is the cause of their ever increasing pace of life' (Shaw 1998: 384). The suggestion here is that harriedness is not simply associated with work as a source of income and identity, but with the allocation of activity, paid or not. This is also of interest to Hochschild (1997) whose analysis of the management of time at work and at home is built around a particular vision of family life and how it might be organized. The vicious circle she describes is not so much an economic relation between work and spend as an emotional 'bind' in which the more time people spend at work the more stressful their family life becomes and so the more attractive it is to be at work. In the 'reversed' worlds that Hochschild documents, home lives are managed along Tayoristic lines in an effort to cope with the demands of time-squeezed domesticity. Meanwhile work environments exhibit more and more of the characteristics expected of home, complete with family-like relationships and opportunities to relax and chat.

Although studies like these seek to explain why people work the hours they do, the time budget evidence is inconclusive. Some suggest that whatever it feels like, free time has *not* in fact declined (Robinson and Godbey 1997), others show that working hours have increased (Leete and Schor 1994). Such data are important for Schor and Hochschild but not necessarily central to the present discussion of convenience. In practice, the value attached to convenience depends upon peoples' *perceptions* of being busy, hurried and harried, not upon the number of hours they spend at home, at work or in the shops. So why might the sense of pressure have increased?

Co-ordination and Fragmentation

Efforts to quantify the total number of hours spent doing this or that tell us little about the meanings of the activities so described, their timing, duration or sequential ordering. Yet these are the aspects that matter when thinking about how the social challenge of co-ordination is managed and hence about the valuing of convenience.

In writing about the social institutionalization of time, Eviatar Zerubavel describes the importance of the week, the weekend and the working day. He argues that these elements define a taken for granted framework within which the 'rhythmic structure of social life' is played out. Being shared, the socio-temporal order constitutes a 'social fact' that exists beyond the individuals whose lives are organized and whose experiences are recalled and calibrated around it (Zerubavel 1979: 107). More ordinarily, the day and the week are of value because they reduce the resources and energy otherwise required to arrange even the simplest social encounter. Where temporal regimes are very highly structured, as in prisons or schools, there is virtually no scope for personal time management. In concluding that 'the obsession with convenience is a hallmark of the society of the schedule', Warde *et al.* (1998) suggest that convenience is important and relevant where individuals are obliged, and have scope, to construct schedules of their own. Such situations are associated with a loosening of formalized, collectively shared, temporal structures.

By implication, the social significance of convenience reflects the erosion of shared temporal order and increasing reliance on 'do-it-yourself' forms of scheduling. Symes's (1999) research on the rise of the appointments diary is relevant in this regard for it suggests a loss of collective co-ordination *within* the frame of the normal working day. In documenting the growing importance of diaries and, as they are so aptly named, 'personal organizers', Symes concludes that this trend indicates a shift from highly structured 'industrial time' to a more contingent form of 'professional time'. He associates industrial time with a period when 'most work was prescribed, continuous and unremitting, and workers had little in the way of chronological latitude', contrasting this with a new order in which work is 'discontinuous and contingent' and where workers have 'more autonomy to construct their own timetables' (Symes 1999: 372). The observation that there is no need to keep a diary on an assembly line and that office life is almost impossible without one indicates the dominance of different modes of co-ordination in each context.

Although household appliances may not have reduced the number of hours spent on housework, they have undoubtedly changed the way that time is allocated and managed. As noted above, doing the washing now requires short bursts of activity (sorting the clothes, filling and unloading the machine, putting clothes in the dryer, taking them out again and so forth) punctuated by periods of inattention during which other tasks can be accomplished. In combination, things like food mixers, microwaves and electric kettles generate semi-self-managing processes each calling for moments of necessary intervention. As in the working environments that Symes describes, new strategies are required to manage what is becoming a distinctively fractured timescape.

Various writers have described how people, and especially women, cope. One of Hochschild's busy respondents explains that she 'regularly squeezed one activity between two others, narrowing the "time frame" around each' (Hochschild 1997: 49). Only by doing several things at once, by checking her e-mail and telephone messages while the dishwasher ran its course, or by making (mobile) phone calls while bathing her child could she hope to keep on top of it all (Hochschild 1997: 49). Such techniques are familiar to those who live what Craig Thompson (1996) describes as a 'juggling lifestyle' associated with a continual struggle to 'stay on schedule'. He documents some of the methods professional working mothers used in trying to fit all that needed doing into the day, one day after the next. Multi-tasking was one strategy, careful planning another. Reflecting on the latter, Shaw observes that the value of list-making depends upon one's ability to control events and fit them into a preferred sequence. This is not always possible for those at the mercy of other peoples' timetables. In such situations, techniques like those of shifting and storing time offer some relief, making it possible to do things in a different order and thereby increasing the flexibility of the system as a whole.

As Thompson explains, the continual challenge of keeping on schedule and of 'holding it together' influenced his respondents' perceptions of consumer products and services. Valued commodities were those that helped 'effectively juggle schedules, adapt to unplanned occurrences and overcome time constraints' (Thompson 1996: 402). Although understandable, enthusiasm for tools and techniques of this kind may be misplaced. As the next section shows, products and systems that help people manage their own schedules have unexpected and sometimes perverse implications for the sociotemporal ordering of society as whole.

Convenience Devices

Technologies bring with them all kinds of temporal 'scripts'. Some have to do with speed. It is, for instance, quicker to whip cream with a food mixer than with a fork. Others cut out previously necessary activities. For example, there is no need to physically refuel an electric fire and now no reason to put wet clothing through a mangle. Possibilities for intervention are similarly structured. While users of vertical axis washing machines can add extra garments mid-way through the washing cycle, this is just not an option for those whose appliances spin around a horizontal axis for a full ninety minutes. At the other extreme, microwave ovens deal in seconds, not hours, and are infinitely stoppable.

As noted above, the capacity to protect oneself from interruption by others is important in maintaining a schedule of one's own choosing. Answerphones and e-mail allow people to respond when it suits them. Being always to hand, mobile phones combine this facility with the prospect of making adjustments and rescheduling arrangements in real time and while on the move, so helping people cope with unforeseen events.

Alone and in combination, domestic technologies modify the range and duration of events to be accommodated during the course of a daily schedule. They also influence the ability to plan ahead. Clothes generally dry faster in a machine than on a line, but the real benefit of a tumble dryer is that the laundry cycle is unaffected by the weather. In affording greater control over the timing of events, tumble dryers have something in common with cars. Cars generally enhance the driver's capacity to determine a trajectory through space and time. Drivers can leave and arrive more or less when they want, they have no connections to miss and can travel along routes of their own choosing, stopping *en route* more or less where and for as long as they want (Sheller and Urry 2000). By comparison, those who depend on public transport are constrained by timetables that are not of their own making.

As this brief catalogue suggests, some technologies modify the allocation of time, others permit new forms of scheduling and co-ordination and a few do both. But in thinking about the relation between technology and time, it is important to appreciate the worlds and contexts in which such products are situated. Silverstone, for example, notes that the 'answerphone, fax, electronic mail as well as the video and microwave are often celebrated as offering greater flexibility for the household or for individuals within the household to define their own temporalities' (Silverstone 1993: 304). However, he goes on to argue that whether this happens or not, to what extent, and in what form, depends upon the temporal culture of the family in question. Developing this point he identifies distinctive styles of 'clocking', by which he means the regulation, sequence, frequency and pace of immediately experienced events (Silverstone 1993: 296). Such styles are not entirely idiosyncratic for although families can decide to slow down or build up the pace of life they may also find new paces forced upon them.

Exactly how technologies affect domestic scheduling clearly depends on how they are used and how they fit into established rhythms and patterns of life. It is none the less important to acknowledge that people live with cars, and with tumble dryers, mobile phones and so forth, and that the temporal qualities of different devices intersect in practice. In addition, and as the following example illustrates, the time-related significance of any one technology is in turn related to its positioning within a wider sociotemporal, sociotechnical context. Now used in alliance with the microwave and an array of pre-prepared foods, the freezer affords control over the timing of shopping, cooking and eating. As such it figures as an important and widely used convenience device of the hypermodern variety. But this has not always been so.

Initially marketed as means of managing seasonal problems of over production, the first domestic freezers helped households cope with batches of home baking and with gluts of fruit and vegetables from the garden. They made it possible to beat the seasons and to 'freeze summer fruits and eat them in winter' (Norwak 1969), but that was about it. The transition from a niche to a mass market came later and came with a reinterpretation of what the freezer was for. With the development of supermarkets and the establishment of a frozen food industry, the freezers of the mid-1970s 'allowed the competent housewife to order her daily routine; to cook at her convenience; to plan trips to the supermarket; and to maintain and manage a much greater variety of meals or ingredients ready and available for consumption all year round' (Shove and Southerton 2000: 308).

As well as providing a convenient, close-to-hand, means of maintaining supplies of pizzas, burgers and ice-cream, the freezers of the 1970s allowed consumers to buy in bulk. They created new opportunities for scheduling, but imposed a temporal logic of their own: users had to think ahead and take items out in time for them to thaw. It was not until the early 1980s that microwave ovens became popular in the UK (McMeekin and Tomlinson 1998) but when they did so one effect was to redefine the freezer's role and status. With a microwave to hand, effective use of the freezer no longer required planning in advance: quite the opposite. This association of appliances dramatically increased the potential for flexibility, for leaving meals to the last minute, for *not* thinking ahead and for being able to produce dinner at short notice. The benefits mentioned above (beating the seasons, cooking in advance, storing shop-bought food and facilitating instant meals) are cumulative, so contemporary freezers do multiple duty. Nicola, one of the respondents interviewed by Shove and Southerton explains that her freezer is for

> things like bread . . . well I buy that . . . it's good to have them for reserve and that, [it] saves having to nip out at times when you haven't really got the time. We put the other usual things in there, you know some ready-meals and frozen veg for when we're caught short. (Shove and Southerton 2000: 313)

As described, Nicola's freezer is an instrument useful in the management of her daily schedule and in coping with the unexpected.

This potted history suggests that the freezer's place in the sociotemporal order of the home has continued to evolve. There are different ways of interpreting time-related trajectories of this kind. One is to hold the freezer, the answerphone or the car constant and argue that interpretations of role and purpose reflect the changing contexts in which they are deployed. In other words, what freezers are for depends upon developments in kitchen design, in the world of supermarket retailing and the structure of the food supply chain. As values of timing, scheduling and co-ordination evolve, so the freezer slips into a new role. Exactly how this works out is likely to vary from one household to the next, depending upon their style of 'clocking' and the temporal order of the home (Silverstone 1993).

An alternative approach is to view the freezers as a conceptually unstable device. Rather than being a passive bystander, it is directly implicated in the co-ordination and management of both food and time. Seen in this way, freezers help households cope with the compression and fragmentation of events: they save people from 'having to nip out' and they minimize the risk of being 'caught short'. However, the compression and fragmentation of time is itself a consequence of the development and use of technologies that bind their users into wider regimes in this case populated by out-of-town super-markets, frozen food producers, global transport systems and agricultural practices.

The proposition here is that devices like freezers have the 'unintended consequence of tying people into an ever denser network of inter-dependent, perhaps even dependent, relationships with the very things designed to free them from just such obligations.' (Shove and Southerton 2000: 315). Those who have a freezer have to shop for it, cook for it, keep it stocked and take note of its preferences (it likes ice-cream but not strawberries, peas but not potatoes) all of which implies a certain way of life and a certain infrastructure beyond the home itself. Going full circle, the freezer helps redistribute time and labour within the household and so alleviates some of the pressures of modern life. Yet those pressures are in part a consequence of just such redistributions of time and labour.

This suggests that qualities of 'convenience' should not be attributed to specific items in that this value depends upon how technologies are articulated together and used in practice. I have so far considered the role of convenience devices in structuring time and in creating (but also helping people cope with) the demands of keeping on schedule while co-ordinating an increasing number of increasingly fragmented activities. But how are hurried lives actually man-aged and when do convenience devices come into their own?

Rush and Calm

Suburban households interviewed as part of a UK study of domestic scheduling made good use of freezers, cars, mobile phones, videos and answerphones, but *not* in order spread sociotemporal demands more evenly through the day. Instead, these people deliberately created periods of intense busyness in order to generate protected pockets of what they referred to as 'quality time'; 'potter time', 'chill time', or 'bonding time' (Southerton 2001).

Southerton's research shows how domestic technologies were used to pre-serve and manage distinctions between rush and calm. Certain times of day were predictably frantic: the mornings, meal times or the last hour of the working day. This was occasionally because of an unavoidable density of events but often the result of a more or less explicit strategy. Mary, for example, explains that: 'it is one of the house rules to have everything cleared away by 7 p.m. even if that means somebody has to rush to do their job. So we have eaten, washed up, put away, and then we are free. Then it is our potter time.' Steven describes a similar strategy: 'we keep Sundays free as like our quality time but it does make Saturdays a bit hectic . . . we try and get everything done so that Sunday is free, so we can spend proper time together' (Southerton 2001: 22). In other words, multi-tasking and detailed planning go on at some times of the day and week, but not at others.

Countering the image of a fluid state of constant pressure, these accounts point to a daily, weekly and even seasonal structuring of busyness. They suggest that experiences of harriedness are generated as a consequence of individual efforts to schedule and manage daily life and that they result from the deliberate bunching of activity. This is not to deny the importance of a wider socio-temporal order: after all personal strategies are clearly devised in response to a generalized feeling of pressure. It is because quieter moments do not arise in the normal course of events that people exploit time-management techniques and convenient solutions in order to create them. Of course not everyone is able to stretch and squeeze time in this way. Unlike her friends who live 'just at such a fast pace' one of the Unilever respondents explains that she is at least able to 'choose when my life's going to be busy'. How she chooses, and whether families bunch time on Saturdays or get up early to keep the evenings free varies from case to case, as do views about what corners can be cut and which obligations simply have to be met, however long that takes. Silverstone's observation that 'the management of time in everyday life, by and on behalf of the household or family, signals its own sense of priorities' (Silverstone 1993: 304) is of central importance when thinking about the use of convenient products and the definition and management of service. As Kaufmann also indicates, certain activities are engrained, obligatory, routinized and invisible. They feature in the domestic schedule as immovable landmarks around which all else must fit. Such practices might now include showering daily, vacuuming the house and ironing every other day, or spending a whole morning cleaning one room. Exactly what needs to be done has further consequences for the management of rush and calm. As one of Southerton's respondents explains, 'she [the respondent's wife] will spend half the day cleaning one room . . . I am sure that other people don't clean to that extreme' but that is how she uses her time and that, he says, is what makes her rushed (Southerton 2001: 17).

While convenient solutions 'create' time for valued purposes the risk is that they do so at an unacceptable cost to other equally important concepts of care and proper performance (Warde 1999). When is it legitimate to rely on convenience food and when not, what practical concessions have to be made to cherished ideals and how does all this play out in the juggling lifestyle (Thompson 1996)? It is a complicated equation. On the one hand it is important that care is not compromised by too much convenience. At the same time it is important to embrace convenience in order to create periods of quality time, or to achieve other co-ordination intensive ambitions like those of eating together (Southerton 2001).

Convenience and Convention

Taking a longer term perspective, it is clear that conventions and standards move and that what might once have been defined as a short-cut or an unacceptable form of outsourcing may, in due course, become perfectly normal. Hochschild describes this process as follows: 'Over time, store bought goods have replaced homespun cloth, homemade soap and candles, home-cured meats and home-baked foods. Instant mixes, frozen dinners and take-out meals have replaced Mother's recipes' (Hochschild 1997: 209).

Senses of obligation and of what is necessary and normal creep as individuals seek ways of coping with temporal pressures of co-ordination and as they look for convenient solutions to otherwise intractable problems of scheduling and order. This search for acceptable compromise is itself a mechanism for change, drawing in new products and requiring the redefinition of standards. Though it is not the whole story, traditions of boiling clothes in order to get them 'really clean' have, for example, been eroded and new qualities invented in the course of establishing a more convenient way of doing the washing. Such moves do not imply an overall decline of social and domestic obligation: not at all. As previous chapters have shown, the importance of wearing freshly laundered clothing generates powerful compulsions with unavoidable consequences for the structuring of the day. Innumerable little events simply *must* be fitted in. Ironically, and as already indicated, many of the products and technologies enlisted in response to the ensuing challenge of keeping on schedule fragment activities still further.

To summarize, the contemporary valuing of convenience relates to an increasing intensity of small tasks and to a reliance on individualized modes of co-ordination. This goes hand-in-hand with the weakening of a shared sociotemporal order. As Figure 10.1 illustrates, there is a rather direct relation between individual and collective modes of co-ordination, a decline in one almost always leading to an increase in the other. The challenge of organizing ever more complex diaries is made more complex *because* other peoples' time is also fragmented and less formally controlled. Similarly, devices that promise

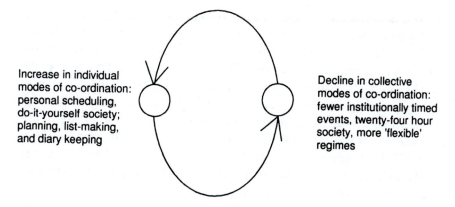

Increase in individual modes of co-ordination: personal scheduling, do-it-yourself society; planning, list-making, and diary keeping

Decline in collective modes of co-ordination: fewer institutionally timed events, twenty-four hour society, more 'flexible' regimes

Figure 10.1. Collective and individual modes of co-ordination

to increase autonomy and allow individuals greater discretion over the timing and scheduling of activity will, if successful, generate multiply idiosyncratic schedules that in turn increase the problem of co-ordination.

The personalization of scheduling has long-term and cumulative consequences for the social as well as the temporal order of society. Effective planning depends on being able to modify and co-ordinate what other people do and it is as well to notice that the powerful generally have 'greater capacity to exert autonomous control over their own trajectories through time and space, and to subordinate the schedules of others to their own' (Warde *et al.* 1998). What Breedveld (1998) refers to as 'time sovereignty' is of particular importance in a 'do-it-yourself' society, that is, one in which social interaction is co-ordinated and organized case by case. In such situations, power is exemplified not so much by the presence or absence of 'free' time, as by the capacity to respond flexibly and change plans at short notice.

Douglas and Isherwood (1996) touch upon similar issues in their discussion of the relation between status and periodicity and the association between high-frequency non-postponable tasks and low status and rank. These authors argue that social groups responsible for high-frequency activities are tied down temporally and spatially and have limited ability to participate in low-frequency but highly valued consumption events. Having described the social hierarchy in these terms, they go on to show how this patterning drives particular forms of demand. In their words, 'future necessities in the present luxuries class will be sets of goods with effective periodicity-relieving properties' (Douglas and Isherwood 1996: 88). They conclude that certain classes of goods, of which convenience devices are a prime example, are valued because they help people escape periodicity related inflexibilities and so step up the social ladder.

This supposes a strong and rather unambiguous relationship between technology, time and social order. By comparison, Silverstone is much more cautious. Will time shifting and time saving appliances provide release from the status-related periodicities to which Douglas and Isherwood refer? Does the proliferation of convenience devices imply an uncoupling of individual time-tables, resulting in a world of 'non-coincidence and non-meeting', or will they be used as instruments of temporal integration? For Silverstone, these are open questions (Silverstone 1993: 306). Looking back, often nostalgically, several of the Unilever respondents and some of those interviewed by Southerton were none the less convinced that certain technologies had restructured the socio-temporal order of everyday life. One put it this way:

> if you go back to out parents' generation, like Monday was washing day, and they had to do it all by hand, and we have all these gadgets of convenience . . . and we're still like we have our cars and that, and like neither my parents drove and they couldn't go to these places and take me wherever and life was like a lot more, well I don't know, a lot more sedate.

In this account, 'gadgets of convenience' have changed the relationship between individual and collective modes of co-ordination and it is this that turns the screw. It is tempting to conclude that more gadgets generate more rush. However, the previous discussion supports Silverstone's view that techniques and products are actively used in an effort to manage and cope with multiple obligations like those of spending unstructured time with friends and family, of showering every day and of always wearing freshly laundered clothing. It is through being drawn into this equation that the tools of convenience have escalatory consequences not just for the fragmentation and co-ordination of time but for the redefinition of convention, obligation and normal practice. Bringing these features together, Figure 10.2 depicts the relation between convenience, co-ordination and convention.

The spiralling figure shows how the introduction of new, more convenient solutions to problems of scheduling and co-ordination (at 1) exacerbates problems of scheduling and co-ordination (at 2), creating demand for new, more convenient solutions (at 1), and so on. The thick arrow through the centre represents the consequent respecification of normal and ordinary practice. Meanwhile the thin arrow at the top reminds us that strategies for shifting and saving time are especially important in societies that rely upon on individual modes of co-ordination.

The form of escalation described here is not underpinned by a professionalized or scientifically grounded concept of how things should be, nor does it relate to the reconfiguration of a singular sociotechnical regime or even to

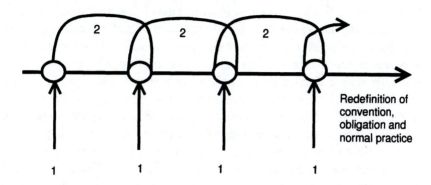

Increasing reliance on individual modes of co-ordination
Increasing importance of personal mobility, convenience and flexibility

Redefinition of convention, obligation and normal practice

1   Use of convenience devices to ease problems of coordination and create periods of 'quality' time

2   Convenience devices engender new divisions of time and labour, create more fragmented episodes, exacerbate problems of co-ordination and so increase reliance on (new) convenience devices to create periods of 'quality' time

Figure 10.2. Convenience, co-ordination and convention

a mutually determining system of systems. Instead, demand for convenience (and its continual respecification) arises as individuals struggle to cope with the contemporary challenge of allocating activities and co-ordinating them and other people in time and space. The resulting dynamic has a life of its own: each solution adding to the menu of problems that future solutions seek to resolve. The practical consequence of all of this, and the consequent valuing of convenience, differs for those who have the power to control their own schedules and those who do not. But in general, the cumulative effect is to engender and legitimize new, typically more resource-intensive, conventions and expectations built around the successive appropriation of convenient solutions, these representing a self-evidently sensible response to the unending problems of organizing life in a 'do-it-yourself' society of the schedule.

This discussion of convenience, convention and co-ordination introduces a temporal dimension strangely absent from theories about the co-evolution of sociotechnical systems. Most obviously, this has the benefit of reminding us that things like microwaves, freezers and mobile phones co-exist and that this is of consequence for the selective development of each. More than that, it serves to highlight an aspect of scripting typically missing from analyses of the relation between technologies and their users. This has to do with how new appliances and devices restructure and reorder domestic schedules and with how they reconfigure the timescapes into which they are incorporated.

In examining this process I have identified a one-directional mechanism of change, ratchet like in the sense that there is no way back from the pursuit of convenience. However, the model developed here differs from the ratcheting explored in the chapters on comfort on two important counts. While the normalization of air-conditioning and the consequent respecification of comfort advanced along a path-dependent trajectory this was a course set by a distinctive combination of commercial and scientific interests. By comparison, the spiral of convenience is quite literally self-propelling. Second, Figure 10.2 characterizes a process involving not one but a range of material systems, objects, technologies and services. In this it represents the changing status of complete families of things: things that are used *together* in managing and co-ordinating everyday life. In emphasizing this co-ordinative aspect, this model captures the coalescing of reasons and rationales and as such has something in common with the image of the pinwheel developed in Chapter 6, and in another way with the systems of systems described in Chapter 7. The difference is that the spiralling of convenience and convention is unambiguously escalatory.

In paying attention to these features I have sought to elaborate on the relationship between sociotechnical regimes and the reinterpretation of normal and necessary service. In Chapter 9 I emphasized the importance of 'horizontal' processes of integration, arguing that these were central to the making of convention. Concentrating on the routine co-ordination of people and activity, this chapter considered the practicalities of integration, looking at how people fit everything in (meaning everything that is socially and symbolically necessary for the reproduction of a normal life), how they keep on schedule and how they keep on top of things. New tools and methods have been developed and appropriated in response to the challenge of achieving and maintaining 'normal' service under conditions of increasing time-related pressure. I suggested that this pressure is increasing partly because of the development of a society characterized by the fragmenting of activity and the personalization of scheduling. Such trends are in turn related to the use of time-shifting technologies, reliance on which has the further effect of reconfiguring the meaning and social significance of normal practice. New concepts of service and new formulations of personal and societal 'injunction' – new senses of what simply must be done – arise as a result.

While this does represent a one-way process, one step leading to the next, the trajectory is not inherently irreversible. It is consequently possible to imagine an unwinding of the spiral and a reinterpretation of normal and

necessary service, the accomplishment of which demands the deliberate dedica-
tion of longer periods of unbroken time. In thinking along these lines, it is
tempting to contrast images of social integration and collective co-ordination
with those of fracture, alienation and individualized isolation (Sennett 1998).
However, this would be to miss the rather important point that people are
(within limits) actively involved in creating periods of rush in order to generate
calm. In other words certain socially important activities *currently* require high
levels of care and commitment. Indeed the sense of time-pressure is partly
related to the need to maintain and preserve opportunities for valued collective
interaction. While the fragmenting of events, the multiplication of 'choice', the
importance of flexibility and the personalization of schedules has cumulative
consequences for the sociotemporal order, the structuring and sequencing
of activity could take a different form. Although present arrangements are
sustained by a raft of technological systems, these systems do not literally determine the practices of those who use them. After all, it is the detail of appropriation and integration that counts.

This suggests that there might be political, social and technological scope
for intervention with respect to the temporal organization of society. In addition to advocating the development of 'slow' cities, or the introduction of
technical systems that promise to restructure the use of time, environmental
policy makers could take steps to fix working hours, holidays and sociotemporal rhythms so as to cut down the personalized fine-tuning of social co-
ordination. Moves to counter trends like those of spatial dispersal and
temporal fragmentation are likely to run into trouble in that they threaten to
restrict what looks like choice. It is therefore important to appreciate that the
reason for introducing measures of this kind is not because speed, flexibility
and do-it-yourself scheduling is in itself bad. In terms of the argument developed here, efforts to increase collective co-ordination are significant not in their
own right but because the higher goal is that of reversing the arrow at the centre
of Figure 10.2 and changing the direction in which conventions of normal and
necessary service are respecified.

11

Ratchets, Pinwheels, Cogs and Spirals

In Western societies, conventions of comfort and cleanliness are on the move. In looking at how related practices and concepts of service evolve and how they hold together, I have exploited and developed theories drawn from a variety of intellectual traditions. In this last chapter I show how these have been used in constructing the models of change around which the book is built. I have not been working towards one over-arching theory capable of encompassing all aspects of the social organization of normality in one go yet there is some order to the story and there are a number of conclusions to be drawn.

Each chapter investigated an aspect of everyday life that is changing and changing in ways that require greater consumption of environmentally significant resources. Each has also provided an opportunity to develop or elaborate on the conceptualization of consumption, technology and practice. With each switch of orientation I have drawn upon different kinds of material, using technical literature, historical accounts, consumer reports, advertisements and interviews to advance the argument or to illustrate specific points. By picking on the cases that I do, and treating them in this way, I set limits to my own account. For example, I have largely overlooked important and environmentally significant forms of consumption that go on outside the home and I have taken little note of key actors like the state. I have not tried to situate the material I use or to document events in any one social or historical context. Had I done so I would have undoubtedly confronted relevant differences and inequalities within and between the societies to which I refer. Partly because of these omissions I have been able to develop ways of thinking about change that engage with issues that lie at the margins of mainstream debate within environmental policy, the sociology of consumption and science and technology studies.

As I observed in Chapter 1, environmental discourse is dominated by theories of resource economics, by assumptions about lifestyle and choice and by efforts to model and forecast future trends. As a result normal and socially necessary standards of comfort and cleanliness are simply taken for granted, maybe factored in but not subject to detailed scrutiny in their own right. In bringing these themes out of the shadows I have had to hunt around for relevant ideas with which to capture the creep of convention and the escalation of ordinary consumption. While there are plenty of candidates to choose from, each carries with it a particular history. Theories of the relation between consumption and production provide plausible accounts of the 'need' for escalation, but have little to say about the direction that change might take. The literature on consumption tends to focus on the acquisition of discrete, culturally significant objects with the result that less has been said about use in practice or the demand for invisible services. Although studies of innovation and sociotechnical change detail relevant mechanisms of path dependency and irreversibility they are hazy about the transformation of composite services. Meanwhile, those who emphasize the social and symbolic knitting together of society only sometimes describe mechanisms of change, and when they do they rarely take account of the material and infrastructural anchoring of habit and practice or of the temporal integration of daily life.

Dominant agendas have skewed debate around tangible objects and moments of acquisition and development, and away from questions about how systems and services evolve or how products are used together and in practice. The realm of the inconspicuous is relatively uncharted territory and in picking my way through it I have borrowed, bent and sometimes criticized concepts designed with other purposes in mind. In the rest of the chapter I reflect on what this study has revealed about comfort, cleanliness, convenience and the social organization of normality. One reason for concentrating on comfort and cleanliness was that both have generated escalating and still increasing demand for key resources like those of energy and water. A further task is to take stock of what the arguments and models developed in this book mean for environmental policy and for the emergence of more-or-less sustainable patterns of consumption.

Regimes, Services and the Reorganization of Normality

In explaining how taken-for-granted conventions of comfort and cleanliness change and why they have become so resource intensive I began by reaching for a simple but serviceable account of the co-evolution of technology and practice. It was relatively easy to describe and represent the specification of comfort and the diffusion of air-conditioning in these terms. Taking this route, I showed how thermal comfort research, the interests of few dominant providers and the path dependent properties of the built environment have contributed to the construction and reproduction of comfort, narrowly defined.

In trying to capture the dynamics of consumption or, to be more precise, in trying to explain why air-conditioning was bought and installed, I drew a different set of conceptual tools into the frame. Having elaborated on the notion of co-evolution and distinguished between two usually tacit theories of change I reorganized and regrouped ideas abstracted from different traditions, specifically from the sociologies of innovation and of consumption. In working with these resources I argued that processes of escalation and standardization could be described in terms of a dynamic of difference and value, and/or in terms of a dynamic of coherence and stabilization. I used this scheme to show that the two traditions have more in common than might be expected and to refine the conceptualization of novelty, acquisition and normalization.

But acquisition is not the same as use. In considering how air-conditioning systems transformed experiences and expectations of comfort, I widened the field of view. Rather than following the trajectory of one or another socio-technical configuration the task was to understand the complexes of technology, meaning and practice that together constitute regimes of comfort, and to explain their convergence. At this point, distinctions between micro, meso and macro levels of change came in handy but also came in for some criticism.

The problem was to account for the circulation of standardizing concepts and technologies *between* societies whilst allowing for the fact that regimes of comfort are necessarily localized. My solution was to import yet more ideas, this time about appropriation and reversal, and patch these into an otherwise mono-cultural discussion of regimes and macro level change. By merging concepts from anthropology and the sociology of transition, I constructed a model capable of accommodating the dual processes of standardization (indicated by converging concepts of comfort) and of path dependent ratcheting (indicated by the micro, meso and macro level locking in of mechanical heating and cooling and of the ways of life associated with it).

This far, the sequence is one in which each chapter adds to the next, incorporating different materials in order to cope with a progressive redefinition of the problem. The first chapter is therefore about scientific and technological development and the construction of need. The second builds on this, looking at how scientifically determined 'needs' are made real and reviewing accounts of the introduction and appropriation of new technologies (in this case, technologies for managing and controlling the indoor climate). In concentrating on use and therefore on the more encompassing theme of comfort, the third chapter addresses the transformation of the indoor environment, viewing this as a matter of regime level transition on a global scale.

These chapters move from technical specification to the reconfiguration of social convention, from the study of one technology to the analysis of socio-technical landscapes, and from the habits of a few to debate about global convergence. In the process they make a number of specific contributions to the sociologies of consumption and technology. For example, the effort to relate theories of innovation to those of consumption gave a material grounding to otherwise abstract debates about novelty and escalating demand. In trying to understand the standardization of comfort, I was obliged to think about how (implicitly national) sociotechnical regimes intersect. This pointed to a range of questions about the global circulation of technological systems and about mechanisms of 'meso level' appropriation. Both themes are important for 'transition theory' but have yet to be developed within it. Despite making various detours, these chapters work together to show how a scientifically defined, technologically embodied concept (comfort) came to be taken for granted. In this they develop but also exemplify what I have since referred to as a 'vertical' approach to the social organization of normality. By this I mean that the hierarchical relation between micro, meso and macro 'levels' of change takes priority.

The chapters on cleanliness mark a significant break in the narrative, effectively starting the discussion all over again. While the first part of the book highlights the importance of thinking about technologies in use, in practice and in context, the second explores quite other explanations of the rate and direction of change. As introduced in Chapter 5, conventions of normality are shot through with social and moral significance. In reconsidering the relation between order, propriety and materiality, Chapters 5 to 8 work with theories that emphasize the importance of ideas (for example, ideas about disease but also about right and wrong); of policing and maintaining social and cultural boundaries and of the practical and symbolic restructuring of domestic labour. Rather than siding with one or another of these positions, I take a different tack, examining practices and legitimizing discourses as if they constituted responses and 'working' solutions to an array of collective concerns. This justified my emphasis on reasonings and rationales, and my interest in how people make sense of their actions and how the actions of others make sense to them.

In bathing and showering as they do, I suggested that people routinize finely calibrated responses to the daily problem of managing shared structural anxieties. By implication, new interpretations of normality arise as these anxieties shift. This approach positions people as 'problem solvers' and as the negotiators and managers of what are none the less collective concerns: it is they who glue coherent packages of normal practice together. By implication new technologies only make a difference when they influence the coalescing of convention and routine. Even so, it is misleading to equate bathing and laundering with cleanliness, or to assume that these are (only) acts of purification implicated in the reproduction of social order. All manner of other ingredients are involved including experiences of pleasure, the power of routine as a force in its own right, and the tools and technologies of the day. Such an approach highlights the integrative work – both practical and symbolic – involved in shaping and reconfiguring normal ways of life.

Taking this theme further, the chapters on laundering examine different modes of integration. In some respects, the representation of laundering as a system of systems harks back to earlier debate about regimes and regime formation. However, the purpose here is to show how sociotechnical systems intersect rather than how they co-evolve. Switching tack and looking at changing habits, I made much of the point that people have their own 'ways' of doing the wash and that these ways embody specific combinations of meaning, moral and symbolic significance, technology, experience and injunction. By emphasizing these aspects, I developed an account of sociotechnical integration that is not incompatible with more 'vertical' explanations of change and transition, but that draws attention to the specification and reproduction of what I refer to as services. These are composite accomplishments achievement of which involves the orchestration of devices, systems, expectations and conventions.

In thinking about how services evolve I consider processes central to the reproduction of 'normality', but so far missing from the discussion of regimes. Although they do more than this, the chapters on cleanliness identify and elaborate on some of the 'horizontal' processes of integration circulating within the different levels of the three-tiered model of change and holding patchworks of regimes together. Figure 11.1 highlights two mechanisms of integration, one having to do with the relationship between sociotechnical systems, the other grounded in the co-ordinative work that people do when constructing and reproducing what are to them coherent packages of normal and proper practice.

In reaching this position a handful of other points become clear. First, and in contrast to many historical and anthropological accounts of cleanliness, I have shown that there is much more to washing and bathing than purification and boundary making, let alone the elimination or even the reinterpretation of dirt. These are activities in their own right, and ones that involve the simultaneous reproduction of all kinds of values, experiences and sociotechnical systems. In taking this route I fold questions of scripting and technological appropriation back into a discussion that might otherwise deal with abstracted notions of propriety, culture and convention. Second, I argue that meanings of service, that is, of what it is to bathe and wash appropriately, emerge from what people do. Meanings are milled in practice, not imposed from the outside. This take on the relation between agency and structure is

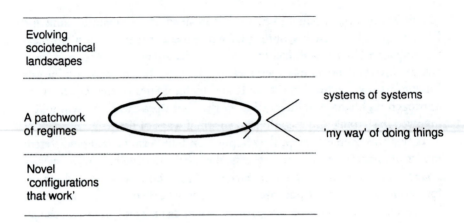

Figure 11.1. Horizontal modes of integration

not new but when used in this way it gives a sharper, practice-oriented edge to the study of material culture.

To put it very simply, the chapters on comfort emphasize the 'vertical' structuring of normal practice while those on cleanliness investigate its 'horizontal' ordering. The last chapter, on convenience and co-ordination, can be read as an elaboration of the temporal dimension of integration, as compared with integration in terms of experience, expectation, technological, moral or symbolic coherence. However, it also develops an account of how the horizontal and vertical dimensions intersect, and how their intersection is itself an engine of change. By looking at the way routines and injunctions are positioned in the flow of everyday life, and thinking about this in terms of the development of individualized rather than collective scheduling, I discerned a spiralling process underpinning the redefinition of convention, obligation and normal practice and fuelling the development and appropriation of new products and technologies.

Figure 11.2 represents this spiralling in a slightly different way, but in a way that shows how the sociotemporal ordering of society connects with vertically and horizontally oriented accounts of what holds notions of normal and necessary practice together and how they evolve. This highly stylized image is designed to make the point that the co-ordinative demands of temporal integration have escalatory qualities, energizing and in effect fuelling the development of novel configurations, new regimes and with them new understandings of service. The dark circles indicate this intersection and correspond to the turns of the simpler, two-dimensional coil represented in Figure 10.2.

It would be easy to overstate the theoretical implications of this figure and to conclude that modes of sociotemporal co-ordination somehow drive every-

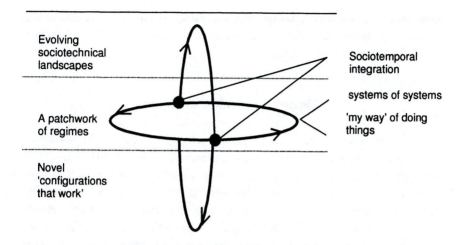

Figure 11.2. 'Vertical' and 'horizontal' theories combined

thing else. That is clearly not the case. Many other considerations and qualities are at stake and in any event, the transformation of normal practice and the respecification of service is not of a piece. As the book also demonstrates, the processes involved in standardizing concepts of comfort are not the same as those that sustain the practice of showering every day. To make the point again, I have not sought to develop one all encompassing theory of the social organization of normality. In designing the structure of the book as a whole, my more limited ambition has been to assemble a framework of ideas useful in understanding the sociotechnical, social-symbolic and sociotemporal configuration of habits that people take for granted but that are changing all the time.

In putting these pieces together I have arrived at a number of general conclusions. First, that it is important to examine the relation between co-existing technical systems and to think about how 'families' of sociotechnical arrangements interact in practice. Second, in looking at how suites of things and products are used and in studying the reshaping of composite services, it is important to appreciate the co-existence of different modes of ordering and integration. Third, senses of obligation and injunction constitute the building blocks of routines that are in turn constructed in the context of a wider sociotemporal order. Though rarely included in discussions of technology or consumption, the temporal dimension proves pivotal in understanding the social organization of normal practice.

In the next section, I adopt a different approach. Rather than showing how parts of the book fit together, I take the four main models of change (the ratchet, the pinwheel, the systems of systems and the spiral) out of context and comment on the generic qualities of each. This helps in detailing differences between the dynamics of cleanliness and comfort and in specifying what these mean for environmental policy.

Models and Mechanisms

A ratchet is 'a set of teeth on the edge of a bar or wheel in which a device engages to ensure motion in one direction only' (Allen 1990). I used this metaphor to represent the locking in of technologies and practices as they move along a path-dependent trajectory. By redesigning homes *for* air-conditioning, American house builders condemned homeowners to an air-conditioned life. There was no way back. By building this expectation into the fabric of the property itself, consumption of energy was inevitably ratcheted up. The image is easily over stretched for it is hard to specify either the size or the number of 'teeth' involved but in terms of consumption, the ratchet does a good job of graphically representing the impossibility of backward movement. It is difficult to change the course of path dependent ratcheting once such a process is under way. There are, however, two policy responses. One is to set in motion uni-directional transitions that are environmentally benign. Another is to foster variety and in that way limit and perhaps obstruct the diffusion of environmentally problematic conventions and expectations.

Unlike the ratchet, the pinwheel can move in different directions but is momentarily held in place by a particular configuration of sociotechnical considerations. I used this figure when talking about the shifting discourses of bathing, and when locating daily power showering as an activity sustained by a specific combination of ideas and practices. As the image suggests, patterns of consumption and demand can go either way. Which way depends upon the relative 'weight' of the pins holding convention in place, and their relative positioning with respect to the wheel: are they jamming it solid or do they permit it to turn? The message here is that the reshaping of practice depends on the conjunction of multiple ingredients. Mono-dimensional efforts to persuade people to use less water or to take fewer, shorter showers are unlikely to succeed. More positively, this model reminds us of the underlying fragility of what seem like basic needs. The contemporary valuing of daily showering has increased demand for energy and water, but if the social construction of pleasure or the significance of body odour were to be revised, or if regular immersion was to be seen as a source of danger, patterns of consumption would presumably change.

Systems of systems – a term I used when describing the inter-dependent relation between fabrics, washing machinery, and concepts of cleanliness – can

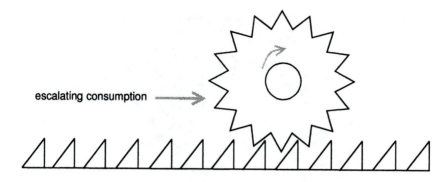

escalating consumption

Figure 11.3. The ratchet

Rationale 1
(dominant)

Rationale 2

Rationale 3

Rationale 4

Figure 11.4. The pinwheel

be represented as a series of ratchet-like cogs fitted together in such a way that the overall outcome of their operation is, as with the pin wheel, uncertain. The total assembly will move in one direction or another depending upon how the cogs mesh together. In some respects the complexity of this arrangement limits the potential for policy intervention, in other ways it enhances them. If the 'right' cog can be turned in the 'right way', the entire system may be transformed. Key devices can and do shape the direction in which whole systems evolve, but is it possible to spot these turning points as they arise? If so, what would it mean to intervene? These queries raise others about the relation between commercial and political interests and the relative influence of each in shaping what people take for granted.

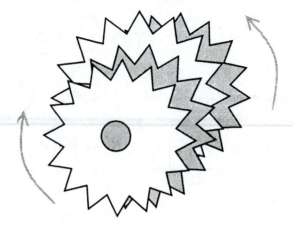

Figure 11.5. Cogs in a system of systems

The final image, that of the self-propelling spiral is like the ratchet in that again there is no way back. The difference is that the spiral has its own momentum: hence, convenient solutions generate demand for more convenience. As described in Chapter 10, rewinding the spiral implies restructuring the socio-temporal order of society.

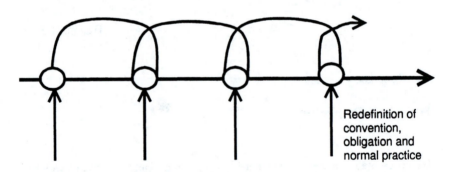

Redefinition of convention, obligation and normal practice

Figure 11.6. The spiral

These mechanical models describe characteristically different pathways of change, two of which are inherently escalatory. In the first case the route of the ratchet is stepwise: periods of stability are followed by periods of forward movement. In the second and third cases, the trajectory can go either way, backwards or forwards, and at any point in time. Finally, the spiral, like the ratchet, defines an implicitly steady path of advance. Figure 11.7 illustrates these possibilities.

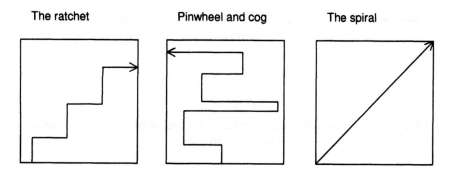

Figure 11.7. Pathways of change

Abstract figures of this kind generate a menu of questions important for environmental policy. Exactly which pathways are being followed, at what rate and in which direction and why? Some of the standardizing tendencies and pathways described in this book are quite clearly associated with the development of global markets and with them the diffusion of specific images and visions of what constitutes a normal way of life. The weight and power of distinctively American interests and ideals is evident, either directly or as embedded in forms of scientific enquiry, in codes and standards and in the design of products and appliances. Certain types of knowledge, especially those associated with universalizing forms of science and human biology have a similarly convergent effect, as illustrated by the case of thermal comfort and by rationales of hygiene and well being, still important in giving meaning and order to bathing and laundering. Although it makes sense to follow processes of standardization and resistance to it, product by product and practice by practice, this is not enough. The more demanding task is to track convergence at a higher level, that is, at the level of regime and service. In other words, it is the specification and reproduction of service that counts when considering the escalation and standardization of demand.

When analysing the dynamics of standardization it is important to acknowledge processes of domestication and reversal and to appreciate that technologies and practices are bundled together in the doing of daily life. In other words, mechanisms and processes of *integration* determine how meanings, expectations and technologies fit together in practice. At first sight there is little that policy makers can do to influence 'my way' of, for example, doing the wash. On the other hand, there are some cases in which widespread reliance on certain technologies (like the freezer and the washing machine) is doubly important. Not only do they reconfigure the meaning of service; they also restructure the modes of integration involved. The observation that convenient solutions have changed what people take to be the basic injunctions of domestic life whilst also modifying the temporal ordering of the day illustrates this point. By thinking systematically about *how* expectations are formed as well as about what they are, policy analysts might stand a better chance of influencing the character of collective convention.

Resetting the Agenda: Consumption, Everyday Life and Sustainability

In the first chapter, I took issue with environmentalists' tendency to focus on consumers' choices and to worry about the relationship between green commitments and the adoption of more sustainable products and practices. In response, I made the case for studying the reformulation of collective conventions, ordinary routines and routinely invisible habits. These last few paragraphs set out the implications of such an approach for environmental research and for the sociology of consumption and technology.

My central claim is that relevant patterns of consumption follow from efforts to provide and sustain what people take to be normal services like those of comfort and cleanliness. As I use the term, 'service' encompasses and holds together complexes of sociotechnical arrangements. It stands for the bunching of imperatives and injunctions that inform senses of what simply has to be done in order to be appropriately clean or comfortable. What this means, and how services are defined and reproduced, depends partly on the co-evolution but also on the integration and co-ordination of suites of technologies and practices and their positioning in the flow of everyday life. There are, I suggest, different modes and forms of integration and these, in turn, relate to the operation of different systems of symbolic coherence, social differentiation and sociotechnical interdependence. Completing the loop, and as illustrated in Chapter 10, methods and forms of integration are themselves relevant for the specification of service and for the development and appropriation of new technologies and new ways of doing things.

This line of reasoning resets a number of research agendas. The proposition that levels of energy and water consumption are a consequence of the way we define and achieve services suggests that effort should focus on what it means to be clean and comfortable. These are central issues, but ones that rarely figure on environmental research agendas. It is by now obvious that meanings of comfort and cleanliness do not represent free-floating expressions of personal preference. Again this implies a refocusing of enquiry. The vast majority of environmentally significant consumption is just not a matter of individual choice, green or otherwise. It is instead bound up with, and constitutive of, irredeemably social practices 'governed by norms like respectability, appropriateness, competence and excellence' (Harvey *et al.* 2001). In understanding how patterns of consumption change and why demand for energy and water is increasing it is necessary to understand the collective dynamics of normalization. How do new ways of life, new concepts of service, take root?

This means thinking about consumption in a different light. Theories of innovation and acquisition are germane, yet the arguably more important issue – but one that is much less well understood – is how commodities, products and services are *used* through and in the course of sustaining and reproducing conventions of normal practice. Just as the literature on consumption tends to focus on the acquisition of objects, so scholars of science and technology have had more to say about innovation and diffusion than the subsequent uses of things in everyday life. Where efforts have been made in this direction, notably through work on scripting and co-evolution, the tendency has been to track the development of specific devices, showing how they fit into an existing sociotechnical complex, but saying less about how more encompassing concepts of service evolve. In short, modes of integration have yet to get the attention they deserve.

A revised agenda of consumption, everyday life and sustainability needs to encompass all these issues, concentrating on the processes through which habits are acquired and jettisoned, and on the relation *between* consumption and convention, technology and practice. Looking ahead, what people take to be normal is immensely malleable. There are no fixed measures of comfort and cleanliness and it is perfectly possible that future concepts will be less resource intensive than those of today. The real environmental risk is not that services will be redefined (this happens all the time), but that there will be sweeping, cross cultural convergence in what people take to be normal ways of life, and a consequent locking in of demand for the resources on which these ways depend. This brings me to a practical conclusion. Rather than promoting energy and resource-efficient versions of products and technologies that inadvertently sustain unsustainable concepts of service, environmentalists should argue for social and cultural diversity. They should do all that can be done to engender multiple meanings of comfort, diverse conventions of cleanliness and forms of social order less reliant on individual modes of co-ordination.

Bibliography

Abernathy, W. and Clark, K. (1985), 'Innovation: mapping the winds of creative destruction' *Research Policy*, 14: 3–22.

Ackerman, M. (2002), *Cool Comfort: America's romance with air-conditioning*, Washington DC: Smithsonian Institution Press.

Akrich, M. (1992), 'The de-scription of technical objects', in Bijker, W. and Law, J. (eds) *Shaping Technology/Building Society*, Cambridge MA: MIT Press.

Albaum, M. (1997), Das Kundenbuch. Menschen und ihr Einkaufsverhalten bei Bekleidung, Frankfurt/Main: Deutscher Fachverlag.

Aldridge, A. (1994), 'The social construction of rational consumption in Which? Magazines: the more blobs the better?', *Sociology*, 28: 899–912.

Allen, R. (ed.) (1990), *Concise Oxford Dictionary*, Oxford: Clarendon Press.

American Water Works Association (1999), *Residential End Uses of Water*, Denver: American Water Works Association. Extracts available at http: //www.waterwiser. org/template.cfm?page1=awwarf/wateruse&page2=books_menu2 (21.3.01).

American Standard (2000) 'Bathroom habits survey', available at: http: //www.kitchen-bath-design.com (27.3.01).

Anson, R. (1988), 'Know your labels', *Manufacturing Clothier*, 69(11): 47–52.

Appadurai, A. (ed.) (1986), *The Social Life of Things*, Cambridge: Cambridge University Press.

Appadurai, A. (1990), 'Disjuncture and difference in the global cultural economy', *Theory, Culture and Society*, 7: 295-310.

Armstrong, D. (1983), *Political Anatomy of the Body: Medical knowledge in Britain in the 20th century*, Cambridge: Cambridge University Press.

ASHRAE (1992), Thermal Environmental Conditions for Human Occupancy, ASHRAE Standard 55, Atlanta: ASHRAE.

ASHRAE (2001), Thermal Environmental Conditions for Human Occupancy: Public Review Draft, ANSI/ASHRAE Standard 55-192 R, Atlanta: ASHRAE.

Baker, N. (1993), 'Thermal comfort evaluation for passive cooling' in Palz, W. (ed.), *Solar Energy in Architecture and Urban Planning*, Bedford: H. Stephens Associates.

Baker, N., and Standeven, M. (1995), 'A behavioural approach to thermal comfort assessment in naturally ventilated buildings', *Proceedings, CIBSE National Conference*, Eastbourne: 76–84.

Bardwick, J. (1995), *Danger in the Comfort Zone: From boardroom to mailroom – how to break the entitlement habit that's killing American business*, New York: AMACOM.

Beck, U. (1992), *Risk Society*, London: Sage.

Becker, H. (1963), *Outsiders*, New York: Free Press.

Beckman, S. (1994), 'On systemic technology' in Summerton, J. (ed.), *Changing Large Technical Systems*, Boulde CO: Westview Press.

Bell, M. (1998), *An Invitation to Environmental Sociology*, Thousand Oaks: Pine Forge Press.

Berner, B. (1998), 'The meaning of cleaning: the creation of harmony and hygiene in the home', *History and Technology*, 14(4): 313–52.

Biermeyer, P. (2001), 'Coming Changes in the US Clothes Washer Market', unpublished paper, Lawrence Berkeley National Laboratory, Berkeley, California, USA.

Bijker, W. (1992), 'The social construction of fluorescent lighting, or how an artifact was invented in its diffusion stage', in Bijker, W. and Law, J. (eds) *Shaping Technology, Building Society*, Cambridge MA, MIT Press.

Bijker, W. (1997), *Of Bicycles, Bakelites and Bulbs*, Cambridge MA: MIT Press.

Bischoff, E., Fischer, A., Liebenberg, B., Kniest, F. (1998), 'Mite control with low temperature washing – II. Elimination of living mites on clothing', *Clinical and Experimental Allergy*, 28(1): 60–5.

Boardman, B. (1991), *Fuel Poverty: From Cold Homes to Affordable Warmth*, London: Bellhaven Press.

Bode, M. (2000), *Clothing Care Function: Germany, SusHouse Project final report*, Delft: Faculty of Technology Policy and Management, Delft University of Technology.

Bourdieu, P. (1977), *Outline of a Theory of Practice*, Cambridge: Cambridge University Press.

Bourdieu, P. (1984), *Distinction: A social critique of judgement and taste*, London: Routledge.

Bowden, S. and Offer, A. (1994), 'Household appliances and the use of time: the USA and Britain since the 1920s', *Economic History Society*, 47(4): 725–48.

Bowker, G. and Star, S. (2000), *Sorting Things Out: Classification and its consequences*, Cambridge MA: MIT Press.

Boyd, L. (1985), 'The body' in Roddick, A. (ed.), *The Body Shop Book*, London: Guild Publishing.

Brager, G. and de Dear, R. (1998), 'Thermal adaptation in the built environment: a literature review', *Energy and Buildings*, 27: 83–96.

Brager, G. and de Dear, R. (2000), 'A standard for natural ventilation', *ASHRAE Journal*, October: 21–27.

Breedveld, K. (1998), 'The double myth of flexibilisation: trends in scattered work hours, and differences in time-sovereignty', *Time and Society*, 7(1): 129–43.

Bunting, M. (2001), 'Clean up', *Guardian Weekend*, 6 October: 40–7.

Burke, T. (1996), *Lifebuoy Men, Lux Women: Commodification, consumption and cleanliness in modern Zimbabwe*, London: Leicester University Press.

Bushman, R. and Bushman, C. (1988), 'The early history of cleanliness in America', *Journal of American History*, 74(4): 1213–38.

Campbell, C. (1992), 'The desire for the new: its nature and social location as presented in theories of fashion and modern consumption', in Silverstone, R. and Hirsch, E. (eds), *Consuming Technologies*, London: Routledge.

Centre for Alternative Technology (1997), 'Come Clean: A guide to green washing machines', Tipsheet 15, http: //www.cat.org.uk/catpubs/tipsheet.tmpl?cart=325196 8291341981subdir=information&sku=15&title=Come%20Clean%20&subtitle= A%20guide%20to%20green%20washing%20machines (19.01.03).

Classen, C., Howes, D., and Synnott, A. (1994), *Aroma: The cultural history of smell*, London: Routledge.

Cole, R. (2000), 'Fuel Poverty: A costly lesson', *Building Research and Information*, 28(5/6): 419–25.

Consumers' Association (1959), 'Drying the family wash', *Which?*, August: 83–7.

Consumers' Association (1960), 'Washing machines', *Which?*, September: 196–9.

Consumers' Association (1967), 'Twin-tubs', *Which?*, October: 294–6.

Consumers' Association (1992), 'Washing Machines', *Which?*, January: 44–8.

Consumers' Association (1999), 'Washing machines', *Which?*, September: 37–40.

Consumers Union (1950a), 'Washing machines', *Consumer Reports*, June: 258–63.

Consumers Union (1950b), 'Automatic washing machines', *Consumer Reports*, November: 502–7.

Consumers Union (1954), 'Automatic washers and clothes dryers' *Consumer Reports*, February: 56–69.

Consumers Union (1958), 'Automatic washing machines ' *Consumer Reports*, August: 402–10.

Consumers Union (1960), 'Washing machines', *Consumer Reports*, August: 412–20.

Consumers Union (1961), 'Life and hard times of the automatic washing machine', *Consumer Reports*, October: 568–73.

Cooper, G. (1998), *Air Conditioning America: Engineers and the controlled environment, 1900–1960*, Baltimore: Johns Hopkins University Press.

Corbin, A. (1986), *The Foul and the Fragrant*, Leamington Spa: Berg.

Cowan, R. S. (1976), 'Two washes in the morning and a bridge party at night: the American housewife between the wars', *Women's Studies*, 3: 147–72.

Cowan, R. S. (1983), *More Work for Mother: The ironies of household technology from the open hearth to the microwave*, New York: Basic Books.

Cranz, G. (1998), *The Chair: Rethinking culture, body and design*, New York: W W Norton.

Crowley, J. (1999), 'The sensibility of comfort', *The American Historical Review*, 104(3): 749–83.

Crowley, J. (2001), *The Invention of Comfort*, Baltimore: Johns Hopkins University Press.

Darier, E. (1998), 'Time to be lazy: work, the environment and subjectivities', *Time and Society*, 7(2): 193–208.

David, P. (1985), 'Clio and the economics of QWERTY', *American Economic Review*, 75(2): 332–7.

de Armound, F. (1950), *The Laundry Industry*, New York: Harper & Brothers.

de Certeau, M. (1998), *The Practice of Everyday Life Volume 2*, Minneapolis: University of Minnesota Press.

de Dear, R. (1994), 'Outdoor climatic influences on indoor thermal comfort require-ments', in Oseland, N. and Humphreys M. (eds), *Thermal Comfort: Past, present and future*, Watford: Building Research Establishment.

DEFRA (1999), 'Tumble dryers in the United Kingdom', Consultation paper: reference wttd4031, 11 November 1999, http: //www.mtprog.com/wet/tumble/index.html (15.4.02).

DEFRA (2000), 'Washing machines in the United Kingdom: a sector review paper on projected energy consumption for the Department of the Environment, Transport and the Regions', WTWM4031, October 2000, http: //www.mtprog.com/wet/wash_mach/wtwmdown4031.pdf (14.4.02).

de la Peña, C. (1999), 'Recharging at the Fordyce: confronting the machine and nature in the modern bath', *Technology and Culture*, 40(4): 746–69.

Disco, C. and van der Meulen, B. (eds) (1998), *Getting New Technologies Together: Studies in making new sociotechnical order*, Berlin: Walter der Gruyter.

Dobell, S. (1996), *Down the Plughole: An irreverent history of the bath*, London: Pavillion Books.

Douglas, M. (1984), *Purity and Danger: An analysis of the concepts of pollution and taboo*, London: Routledge.

Douglas, M. and Isherwood, B. (1996), *The World of Goods: Towards an anthrop-ology of consumption*, London: Routledge.

Elias, N. (1979), *The Civilizing Process*, Oxford: Blackwell.

Ellis, H. (1936), *Studies in the Psychology of Sex Volume 1*, New York: Random House.

Elzen, B., Geels, F., Hofman, P., and Green, K. (2002), 'Socio-technical scenarios as a tool for transition policy: an example from the traffic and transport domain', Paper for workshop on 'Transitions to Sustainability through System Innovations', Enschede, University of Twente, 4–6 July 2002.

Environment Agency (2001), 'Environment Information': http: //www.environment-agency.tv/nwdmc/being_water_wise_home/index.htm (14.04.02).

Factor 10 Club (1997), 'Carnoules statement to government and business leaders', Carnoules, France: Factor 10 Institute, La Rabassiere, F-83660. Available at: http: //www.factor10-institute.org/Publications.htm (18.4.02).

Fanger, O. (1970), *Thermal Comfort – Analysis and applications in environmental engineering*, Copenhagen: Danish Technical Press.

Fanger, O. (2001), 'Human requirements in future air-conditioned environments', *International Journal of Refrigeration*, 24(2): 148–53.

Featherstone, M. (ed.) (1990), *Global Cultures*, London: Sage.

Featherstone, M., Hepworth, M., and Turner, B. (eds) (1991), *The Body: Social Process and Cultural Theory*, London: Sage

Fine, B. and Leopold, E. (1993), *The World of Consumption*, London: Routledge.

Fischer, C. (1992), *America Calling: A social history of the telephone*, Berkeley: University of California Press.

Fitzgerald, N. (1998), 'Tomorrow's wash: challenges and opportunities for the deter-gents industry in the 21st century', World Conference on Detergents, Montreux, 5 October 1998, available at http: //www.unilever.com/ne/ut_rs/wash.html (11.10.01).

Flandrin, J. (1979), *Families in Former Times: Kinship, household and sexuality*, Cambridge: Cambridge University Press.

Forty, A. (1986), *Objects of Desire: Design and Society since 1750*, London: Thames & Hudson.

Garofoli, J. (2001), 'Laundromat blues', *San Francisco Chronicle*, 19 June: A13 and A16.

George, H. (1999), 'Bathroom Semioptics', available at: http: //www.chass.utoronto.ca/ ~hgeorge/semiopticstable.htm (14.04.02).

Gershuny, J. and Sullivan, O. (1998), 'The sociological uses of time-use diary analysis', *European Sociological Review* 14(1): 69–85.

Giddens, A. (1984), *The Constitution of Society*, Cambridge: Polity Press.

Giedion S. (1948), *Mechanisation Takes Command: A contribution to anonymous history*, New York: W W Norton.

Giovannini, B., and Baranzini, A. (eds) (1998), *Energy Modelling: Beyond Economics and Technology*, Geneva: Centre for Energy Studies, University of Geneva.

Gleason, S. (2001), 'Beauty and the bath', *Joe Weider's Shape*, 20(8): 156–9.

Goffman, E. (1969), *The Presentation of Self in Everyday Life*, Harmondsworth: Penguin.

Goldsmith, R. (1960), 'Use of clothing records to demonstrate acclimatisation to cold in man', *Journal of Applied Physiology* 15(5): 776–80.

Golton, B. (1994), 'Affluence and the ecological footprint of dwelling in time – a Cyprus perspective', Paper presented to the First World Conference on Sustainable Construction of the CIB TG16 Group at Tampa, Florida, USA, 7–9 November 1994.

Graham, S. and Marvin, S. (2001), *Splintering Urbanism*, London: Routledge.

Guy, S. and Shove, E. (2000), *A Sociology of Energy, Buildings and Environment: Constructing knowledge, designing practice*, London: Routledge.

Hackett, B. (1993), 'Clotheslines: assessing the "instrumental" character of everyday practical conduct', unpublished paper, Department of Sociology, University of California, Davis.

Handley, S. (1999), *Nylon: The manmade fashion revolution*, London: Bloomsbury.

Hannerz, U. (1996), *Transnational Connections*, London: Routledge.

Harvey, M., McMeekin, A., Randalls, S., Southerton, D., Tether, B., and Warde, A. (2001), *Between Demand and Consumption: A framework for research*, CRIC Discussion Paper No. 40, The University of Manchester and UMIST.

Hedges, A. (2001), *Perceptions of Congestion: Report on qualitative research findings*, (part 4) Department for Transport, available at: http: //www.dft.gov.uk/itwp/ congestion/04.htm (30.9.02).

Heijs, W. (1994), 'The dependent variable in thermal comfort research: some psychological considerations', in Oseland, N. and Humphreys, M. (eds), *Thermal Comfort: Past, present and future*, Watford: Building Research Establishment.

Herrington, P. (1996), *Climate Change and the Demand for Water*, London: HMSO.

Heschong L. (1979), *Thermal Delight in Architecture*, Cambridge MA: MIT Press.

Hinchliffe, S. (1996), 'Helping the Earth begins at home: the social construction of social environmental responsibilities', *Global Environmental Change*, 6: 53–62.

Hobson, K. (2001), 'Sustainable lifestyles: rethinking barriers and behaviour change', in Cohen, M. and Murphy, J (eds), *Exploring Sustainable Consumption: Environmental Policy and the Social Sciences*, Amsterdam: Pergamon.

Hochschild, A. (1997), *The Time Bind: When Work Becomes Home and Home Becomes Work*, New York: Metropolitan Books.

Houghton, F. and Yaglou, C. (1923), 'Determination of the comfort zone', *ASHVE Journal*, 29: 515-36.

Howes, D. (1996), *Cross-Cultural Consumption*, London: Routledge.

Hoy, S. (1995), Chasing Dirt: The American Pursuit of Cleanliness, New York: Oxford University Press.

Hufnagel, J. (2000), 'Tubs vs showers', *Better Homes and Gardens*, 78(2): 42–52.

Hughes, T. P. (1983), *Networks of Power: Electrification in Western society, 1880–1930*, Baltimore: Johns Hopkins University Press.

Humphreys, M. (1976), 'Field studies of thermal comfort compared and applied', *Building Services Engineering*, 44: 5–27.

Humphreys, M. (1995), 'Thermal comfort temperatures and the habits of Hobbits', in Nicol, F., Humphreys, M., Sykes, O. and Roaf, S (eds), *Standards for Thermal Comfort*, London: E & F N Spon.

Humphreys, M. and Nichol, F. (1998), 'Understanding the adaptive approach to thermal comfort', *ASHRAE Transactions – Symposia*: 991–1004.

Hunt, J. (1999), 'A short history of soap', *The Pharmaceutical Journal*, 263(7076): 985–9

Huntington, E. (1924), *Civilization and Climate*, 3rd ed., New Haven: Yale University Press.

Janda K, and Busch J. (1994), 'Worldwide status of energy standards for building', *Energy*, 19(1): 27–44.

Jelsma, J. (1999), 'Toward a sustainable society: the moralising of machines?', paper presented at 4S annual conference, San Diego, 27–30 October 1999.

Jordan, L. (1928), *Clothing: Fundamental problems – a practical discussion in regard to the selection, construction and use of clothing*, Boston: M. Barrows & Co.

Katzman, G., (1998), 'Scalding, dust mites and lice, and your washing machine', *Paediatrics*, 101(6): 1094.

Kaufmann, J. C. (1998), *Dirty Linen: Couples and their laundry*, London: Middlesex University Press.

Keillor, G. (1985), *Lake Wobegon Days*, New York: Viking.

Kemp, R., Schot, J. and Hoogma, R. (1998), 'Regime shifts to sustainability through processes of niche formation: the approach of strategic niche management', *Technology Analysis and Strategic Management*, 10(2): 175–95.

Kempton, W. and Lutzenhiser, L. (1992), 'Introduction', *Energy and Buildings*, 18: 171–6.

Kempton, W. and Montgomery, L. (1982), 'Folk quantification of energy' *Energy*, 7: 817–27.

Kessler, D. (2000), *The Needs of the Dying: A Guide for Bringing Hope, Comfort, and Love to Life's Final Chapter*, New York: HarperCollins.

Kerr, P. (1995), *Gridiron*, London: Chatto & Windus.

King, A. (1990), 'Architecture, Capital and the Globalization of Culture' in Feather-stone, M. (ed), *Global Culture*, London: Sage.

Kira, A. (1976), *The Bathroom*, New York: Viking Press.

Knight, J. (2001), 'Privies on parade', *Guardian Weekend*, 12 May: 77.

Knot, M. (2000), *Sustainable Clothing Use and Care in 2050 Clothing Care Function: The Netherlands, SusHouse Project Final Report*, Delft: Faculty of Technology Policy and Management, Delft University of Technology.

Kohler (2001), 'Kohler body spa systems' http: //www.us.kohler.com/tech/products/why_spas.jsp (14.04.02).

Kopytoff, I. (1986), 'The Cultural Biography of Things: Commoditization as Process', in Appadurai, A. (ed.), *The Social Life of Things*, Cambridge: Cambridge University Press.

Korejwo, P. (2000), *Complete Construction: Bathroom design, installation and re-modelling*, New York: McGraw Hill.

Krislov, S. (1997), *How Nations Choose Product Standards and Standards Change Nations*, Pittsburgh: University of Pittsburgh Press.

Kuhn, T. (1970), *The Structure of Scientific Revolutions*, Chicago: Chicago University Press.

Laitner, J., De Canio, S., and Peters, I. (2000), 'Incorporating behavioural, social, and organizational phenomena in the assessment of climate change mitigation options', in Jochem, E., Sathaye, J., and Bouille, D. (eds), *Society, Behaviour and Climate Change Mitigation*, Dordrecht: Kluwer.

Lambton, L. (1997), *Temples of Convenience and Chambers of Delight*, London: Pavillion Books.

Latour, B. (1988), *The Pasteurization of France*, Cambridge MA: Harvard University Press.

Latour, B. (1992), 'Where are the missing masses? The sociology of a few mundane artifacts', in Bijker, W. and Law, J. (eds), *Shaping Technology/Building Society*, Cambridge MA: MIT Press.

Lau, E. (2001), 'Sweating is just nature's way of helping humans chill out', *Sacramento Bee*, 28 May 2001: A1.

Law, J. (1987), 'Technology and heterogenous engineering: the case of Portuguese expansion' in Bijker, W., Hughes, T., and Pinch, T. (eds), *The Social Construction of Technological Systems*, Cambridge MA: MIT Press.

Leaman, A. and Bordass, W. (1995), 'Comfort and complexity: unmanageable bed-fellows?', in RIBA (ed.), *Workplace Comfort Forum, 18–19 May 1995*, London: Royal Institute of British Architects.

LeBaron Walker, L. (1911), 'Beautifying the bathroom', *House and Garden*, December XX(6): 378.

Leete, L. and Schor, J. (1994), 'Assessing the time squeeze hypothesis: Estimates of market and non-market hours in the United States, 1969–1989', *Industrial Relations*, 33(1): 25–43.

Levy, N. (1999), *To Begin Again: The journey toward comfort, strength, and faith in difficult times*, New York: Ballantine Books.

Lie, M. and Sorensen, K. (1996), *Making Technology our Own? Domesticating Technology into Everyday Life,* Oslo: Scandinavian University Press.

Loe, D. (2000), 'Daylighting design in architecture', *Caddett Newsletter 4*, Gothenburg: Chalmers Institute of Technology.

Loehlin, J. (1999), *From Rugs to Riches: Housework, consumption and modernity in Germany,* Oxford: Berg.

Los Angeles Times (2000), 'Wake up call for Spaniards: new corporate culture does not recognise the siesta', 28 March 2000, A1: A10.

Lupton, E. and Miller, J. (1992), *The Bathroom, the Kitchen and the Aesthetics of Waste: A process of elimination,* New York: Kiosk.

Lutzenhiser, L. (1993), 'Social and behavioural aspects of energy use', *Annual Review of Energy,* 18: 247–89.

Lutzenhiser, L., and Gossard, M. (2000), 'Lifestyle, status and energy consumption' in *Efficiency and Sustainability 2000 Summer Study on Energy Efficiency in Buildings,* Washington DC: American Council for an Energy-Efficient Economy.

Lutzenhiser, L., Hackett, B., Hall, D., and Hungerford, D. (1994), 'Alternative cooling technologies for California: social barriers, opportunities and design issues', University Wide Energy Research Group, UER289, Berkeley: University of California.

MacAndrew, C. and Edgerton, R. (1969), *Drunken Comportment,* London: Nelson.

MacKenzie, D. (1990), *Inventing Accuracy: A historical sociology of nuclear missile guidance,* Cambridge MA: MIT Press.

Market and Business Development (2001), 'BD2601Q and BD2601A MBD bathroom equipment development: 2001 Quarter Four', executive summary available at: http://www.the-list.co.uk/acatalog/bd2601q.html (14.04.02).

Maxwell, L. (2002), 'Lee Maxwell's antique washing machines', available at: http://www.oldewash.com (14.04.02).

McClintock, A. (1994), 'Soft-Soaping empire: commodity racism and imperial advertising' in Robertson, G. (ed.), *Travellers Tales,* London: Routledge.

McCracken, G. (1998), *Culture and Consumption: New approaches to the symbolic character of consumer goods and activities,* Bloomington: Indiana University Press.

McMeekin A. and Tomlinson, M. (1998), 'Diffusion with distinction: the diffusion of household durables in the UK', *Futures,* 30(9): 873–86.

Meintjes, H. (2001), 'Washing machines make lazy women: domestic appliances and the negotiation of women's propriety in Soweto', *Journal of Material Culture,* 6(3): 345–63

Melosi, M. (2000), *The Sanitary City: Urban infrastructure in America from colonial times to the present,* Baltimore: Johns Hopkins University Press.

Miller, D. (1992), 'The young and the restless in Trinidad: a case of the local and the global in mass consumption' in Silverstone, R. and Hirsch, E. (eds), *Consuming Technologies,* London: Routledge.

Miller, D. (1998a), 'Coca-Cola: a black sweet drink from Trinidad' in Miller, D. (ed.) *Material Cultures: Why some things matter,* London: UCL Press

Miller, D. (ed.) (1998b), *Material Cultures: Why some things matter,* London: UCL Press.

Miller, D. (ed.) (2001), *Car Cultures,* Oxford: Berg.

Mills, E. and Borg, N. (1999), 'Trends in recommended illuminance levels: an international comparison', *Journal of the Illuminating Engineering Society*, Winter, 155–63.

Moezzi, M. (1998), 'Social meanings of electric light: a different history of the United States', *1998 Summer Study Proceedings, American Council for an Energy Efficient Economy*, Washington DC: ACEEE.

Mohun, A. (1999), *Steam Laundries*, Baltimore: Johns Hopkins University Press.

Mohun, A. (1997), 'Laundrymen construct their world: gender and the transformation of a domestic task to an industrial process', *Technology and Culture*, 38(1): 97-121.

Moisander, J. (2000), 'Group Identity, Personal Ethics and Sustainable Development Suggesting New Directions for Social Marketing Research', in Jochem, E., Sathaye, J., and Bouille, D. (eds), *Society, Behaviour and Climate Change Mitigation*, Dordrecht: Kluwer.

Moore, M. (1999), 'Mexicans must say adios to the 3-hour siesta', Washington Post, 23 March.

Muthesius, S. (1982), *The English Terraced House*, New Haven: Yale University Press.

National Building Museum (2000), 'Stay Cool!', available at: http: //www.nbm.org/Exhibits/Stay_Cool!.html (12.04.02).

National Kitchen and Bathroom Association (2000), 'Pleasant dreams', http: //www.nkba.org and http: //129.41.56.41/Industry-trends-bathrooms/consumer-buying-trends-baths/2000/082000_Consumer-Buying-Trends_Misc.htm.asp (14.4.02).

Nicol, F. and Humphreys, M. (2001), 'Adaptive thermal comfort and sustainable thermal standards for buildings', in *Moving Thermal Comfort Standards into the 21st Century: Conference Proceedings*, Windsor, UK 5–8 April 2001, Oxford: Oxford Centre for Sustainable Development.

Nicol, F., Raja, I., Allaudin, A., Jamy, G. (1999), 'Climatic variations in comfortable temperatures: the Pakistan projects', *Energy and Buildings*, 30: 261–79.

Nicol, F. and Roaf, S. (1996), 'Pioneering new indoor temperature standards: the Pakistan project', *Energy and Buildings*, 23: 169–74.

Noorman, K. J. and Uitkeramp, T. S. (eds) (1998), *Green Households? Domestic Consumers, Environment and Sustainability*, London: Earthscan.

Norwak, M. (1969), *Deep Freezing: a New and Comprehensive Guide to Deep Freezing*, London: Sphere.

OECD (2001), 'Information and consumer decision-making for sustainable consumption', Report of the OECD workshop on information and consumer decision-making for sustainable consumption, 16–17 January 2001, Paris: OECD, available at: http: //www.oecd.org/env/consumption (10.4.02).

Ogle, M. (1996), *All the Modern Conveniences: American household plumbing 1840–1890*, Baltimore: Johns Hopkins University Press.

Orwell, G. (1937), *The Road to Wigan Pier*, London: Victor Gollancz.

Oseland, N. and Humphreys, M. (1993), *Trends in Thermal Comfort Research*, Watford: Building Research Establishment.

O'Toole, J. (1995), *Leading Change: Overcoming the ideology of comfort and the tyranny of custom*, San Francisco; Jossey-Bass.

Pantzar, M. (1997), 'Domestication of everyday life technology: dynamic views on the social histories of artifacts', *Design Issues*, 13(3): 52–65.

Parr, J. (1999), *Domestic Goods: The material, the moral, and the economic in the postwar years*, Toronto: University of Toronto Press.

Plumbing and Mechanical (1987), 'History of plumbing in America', available at: http://www.theplumber.com/usa.html (12.04.02).

Plumbing and Mechanical (1994), 'The stand-up bath', available at: http://www.theplumber.com/standup.html (12.04.02).

Redclift, M. (1996), *Wasted: Counting the Costs of Global Consumption*, London: Earthscan.

Repinski, K. (2000), 'Waterworks' *Joe Weider's Shape*, 19(12): 126–31.

Reynolds, R. (1943), *Cleanliness and Godliness*, London: George Allen and Unwin.

Rip, A. (2002), *Co-evolution of Science, Technology and Society*, Expert review for the Bundesministerim Bildung und Forschung's Föderinitiative Politik, Wissenschaft und Gesellschaft (Science Policy Studies), managed by the Berlin-Brandenburgische Akademie der Wissenschaften.

Rip, A. and Groen, A. (2001), 'Many visible hands' in Coombs, R., Green, K., Walsh, V. and Richards, A. (eds), *Technology and the Market: Demands, users and innovation*, Cheltenham: Edward Elgar.

Rip, A. and Kemp, R. (1998), 'Technological change' in Rayner, S. and Malone, E. (eds), *Human Choice and Climate Change: Resources and Technology, Volume 2*, Columbus, Ohio: Battelle Press.

Roberts, B. (1997), *The Quest for Comfort*, London: Chartered Institute of Building Services Engineers.

Robinson, J. and Godbey, G. (1997), *Time for Life: The surprising ways Americans use their time*, University Park PA: Pennsylvania State University Press.

Rogers, E. M. (1983), *The Diffusion of Innovation: 3rd Edition*, New York: Free Press.

Romm, J. and Rosenfeld, A. (2000), 'The impact of the market economy on energy intensity' in *Efficiency and Sustainability 2000 Summer Study on Energy Efficiency in Buildings*, Washington DC: American Council for an Energy-Efficient Economy.

Røpke, I. (2001), 'New technology in everyday life – social processes and environmental impact', *Ecological Economics*, 38(3): 403–22.

Ross, K. (1995), *Fast Cars, Clean Bodies: Decolonisation and the reordering of French culture*, Cambridge MA: MIT Press.

Ryan, J. (1999), *Seven Wonders: Everyday things for a healthier planet*, San Francisco: Sierra Club.

Rybczynski, W. (1987), *Home: A short history of an idea*, Harmondsworth: Penguin.

Sacks, D. (1998), *Bathrooms*, San Francisco: Chronicle Books.

Salisbury, D. and Robinson, M. (2001), *Managing Money in Retirement: Get the Most Out of Your Comfort Years (Essential Finance)*, London: Dorling Kindersley.

Sams, P. (2001), 'Clothes care – sending the right signals', International Appliance Technical Conference, Columbus, Ohio, 27 March 2001.

Santiago, C. (1977), 'It all comes out in the wash', *Smithsonian*, 28(6): 84–92.

Schmidt, S. and Werle, R. (1998), *Coordinating Technology: Studies in the International Standardization of Telecommunications*, Cambridge MA: MIT Press.

Schor, J. (1991) 'Towards a new politics of consumption' in Schor, J. and Holt, D. (eds) (2000) *The Consumer Society Reader*, New York: The New Press.

Schor, J. (1992), *The Overworked American: The unexpected decline of leisure*, New York: Basic Books.

Schot, J., Hoogma R. and Elzen, B. (1994), 'Strategies for shifting technological systems: the case of the automobile system', *Futures*, 26(10): 1060–76.

Sennett, R. (1998), *The Corrosion of Character: The personal consequences of work in the new capitalism*, New York: W.W. Norton.

Shaw, J. (1998), 'Research note: "feeling a list coming on" gender and the pace of life', *Time and Society*, 7(2): 383–96.

Sheller, M. and Urry, J. (2000), 'The city and the car', *International Journal of Urban and Regional Research*, 24: 737–57.

Shoulder, M., Pitts, N., Thomas, F., and Hall, J. (1997), *Water Conservation: Shower evaluation*, BRE Report No CR 164/97, Watford: Building Research Establishment.

Shove, E., Lutzenhiser, L., Guy, S., Hackett, B. and Wilhite, H. (1998), 'Energy and social systems', in Rayner, S. and Malone, E. (eds), *Human Choice and Climate Change: Resources and Technology, Volume 2*, Columbus, Ohio: Battelle Press.

Shove, E. and Southerton, D. (2000), 'Defrosting the freezer: from novelty to convenience', *Material Culture*, 5(3): 301–19.

Shove, E. and Warde, A. (2001), 'Inconspicuous consumption: the sociology of consumption, lifestyles, and the environment', in Dunlap, R., Buttel, F., Dickens, P. and A. Gijswijt (eds), *Sociological Theory and the Environment: Classical Foundations, Contemporary Insights*, Lanham, Maryland: Rowman & Littlefield.

Silverstone, R. (1993), 'Time, information and communication technologies and the household', *Time and Society* 2(3): 283–311.

Silverstone, R., Hirsch, E., and Morley, D. (1992), 'Introduction' in Silverstone, R. and Hirsch, E. (eds), *Consuming Technologies*, London: Routledge.

Slater, D., (1997), *Consumer Culture and Modernity*, Cambridge: Polity Press.

Slow Food Movement (2001), 'All About Slow Food', available at: http: //www.slow food.com (19.01.03).

Snow, A. and Hopewell, G. (1976), *Planning your Bathroom*, London: Design Council.

Sontag, S. (1991), *Illness as Metaphor/Aids and its Metaphors*, London: Penguin.

Southerton, D. (2001), 'Squeezing time: allocating practices, co-ordinating networks and scheduling society', paper presented to the International Conference on 'Spacing and Timing', Palermo, Italy, 1–3 November 2001.

Southerton, D., Shove, E. and Warde, A. (2001), 'Harried and hurried: time shortage and co-ordination of everyday life', CRIC Discussion Paper No 47, The University of Manchester and UMIST.

Spaargaren, G. (1997), *The Ecological Modernisation of Production and Consumption: Essays in Environmental Sociology*, Wageningen: Landbouw Universitiet, Wageningen.

Stern, P., Dietz, T., Ruttan, V., Socolow, R., and Sweeny, J. (eds) (1997), *Environmentally Significant Consumption*, Washington DC: National Academy Press.

Stoops, J. (2001), *The Physical Environment and Occupant Thermal Perceptions in Office Buildings*, Department of Building Services Engineering, Gothenburg: Chalmers University of Technology.

Strasser, S. (1982), *Never Done*, New York: Pantheon.

Summerton J. (1995), 'Representing users or on opening the black box and painting it green, red, blue, and white', Working paper, Department of Technology and Social Change, Linkoping University.

Summerton, J. (1994), *Changing Large Technical Systems*, Boulder CO: Westview Press.

Symes, C. (1999), 'Chronicles of Labour: a discourse analysis of diaries', *Time and Society*, 8(2): 357–80.

Thomas, P. (2001), *Cleaning Yourself to Death: How safe is your home?*, Dublin: Newleaf.

Thompson, C. (1996), 'Caring consumers: gendered consumption meanings and the juggling lifestyle', *Journal of Consumer Research*, 22: 388–407.

Tomes, N. (1998), *The Gospel of Germs: Men, women, and the microbe in American life*, Cambridge MA: Harvard University Press.

Turton, P. (1998), 'The UK Experience', presentation at CIWEM Water Conservation and Re-use Seminar, February 1998, CIWEM.

Twigg, J. (1997), 'Deconstructing the "social bath": help with bathing at home for older and disabled people', *Journal of Social Policy*, 26(2): 211–32.

United Utilities (2001), available at: http: //www.unitedutilities.co.uk/for_your_information/society/advert.htm (28.10.01).

Vigarello, G. (1998), *Concepts of Cleanliness: Changing attitudes in France since the Middle Ages*, Cambridge: Cambridge University Press.

Vinikas, V. (1989), 'Lustrum of the Cleanliness Institute, 1927–1932', *Journal of Social History*, 22(4): 613–29.

von Weizsäcker, E., Lovins, A. and Lovins, H. (1997), *Factor Four: Doubling wealth, halving resource use, the new report to the Club of Rome*, London: Earthscan Publications.

Wackernagel, M. and Rees, W. (1995), *Our Ecological Footprint*, Gabriola Island, BC: New Society Publishers.

Warde, A. (1997), *Consumption, Food and Taste*, London: Sage.

Warde, A. (1999), 'Convenient food: space and timing' *British Food Journal*, 101(7): 518–27.

Warde, A., Shove, E. and Southerton, D. (1998), 'Convenience, schedules and sustainability', European Science Foundation Workshop on Consumption, Everyday Life and Sustainability, Lancaster University, 27–29 March 1998. Available at http: //www.comp.lancs.ac.uk/sociology/esf/convenience.htm.

Weingarten, L. and Weingarten, S. (1998), 'The history of domestic water heating', *PM Engineer*, October: 72–7.

Weiss, D. and Gross, A. (1995), 'Industry corner: major household appliances in Western Europe', *Business Economics, Washington,* 30(3): 67–72.

Weyant, J. and Yanigisawa, Y. (1998), 'Energy and industry' in Rayner, S. and Malone, E. (eds) *Human Choice and Climate Change: Resources and Technology, Volume 2,* Columbus, Ohio: Battelle Press.

Wilhite, H., Nakagami, H. and Murakoshi, C. (1996), 'The dynamics of changing Japanese energy consumption patterns and their implications for sustainable consumption', *Human Dimensions of Energy Consumption 1996 ACEEE Summer Study on Energy Efficiency in Buildings,* Washington DC: ACEEE 8.231-8.238.

Wilhite, H. and Lutzenhiser, L., (1998), 'Social loading and sustainable consumption', *Advances in Consumer Research,* 26: 281–7.

Wilhite H., Nakagami, H., Masuda, T., Yamaga, Y., and Haneda, H. (1996), 'A cross-cultural analysis of household energy-use behaviour in Japan and Norway', *Energy Policy,* 24(9): 795–803.

Wilk, R. (1995), 'Learning to be local in Belize: global systems of common difference' in Miller, D. (ed.), *Worlds Apart: Modernity through the prism of the local,* London: Routledge.

Wilk, R., (1999), 'Towards a useful theory of consumption', *European Council for an Energy Efficient Economy Summer Study Proceedings,* Paris: ADEME.

Wilkie, J. (1986), 'Submerged sensuality: technology and perceptions of bathing', *Journal of Social History,* 19(4): 649–64.

Wilson, C. (1954), *The History of Unilever: Volume 1,* London: Cassel & Co.

Winkler, C. G. (1989), *The Well Appointed Bath: Authentic plans and fixtures from the early 1900s,* Washington DC: The Preservation Press.

Woolgar, S. (1991), 'Configuring the user: the case of usability trials', in Law, J. (ed.), *A Sociology of Monsters,* London: Routledge.

Wright, L. (1960), *Clean and Decent: The fascinating history of the bathroom and the water closet, and of the sundry habits, fashions and accessories of the toilet, principally in Great Britain, France, and America,* New York: Viking Press.

Wright, L. (1964), *Home Fires Burning: The history of domestic heating and cooking.* London: Routledge & Kegan Paul.

Zavestoski, S. (2001), 'Environmental concern and anti-consumerism in the self-concept: do they share the same basis?', in Cohen, M. and Murphy, J. (eds), *Exploring Sustainable Consumption: Environmental policy and the social sciences,* Amsterdam: Pergamon.

Zdatny, S. (1999), *Hairstyles and Fashion: A hairdresser's history of Paris 1910–1920,* Oxford: Berg.

Zerubavel, E. (1979), *Patterns of Time in Hospital Life,* Chicago: Chicago University Press.

Zmroczek, C. (1992), 'Dirty Linen: Women, Class and Washing Machines, 1920s–1960s', *Women's Studies International Forum,* 15(2): 173–85.

Index

Abernathy, W., 14

Ackerman, M., 27, 28, 51

air-conditioning, 53–7, 62, 63, 67, 76, 189
  buildings and, 34, 39–40, 54–5, 65–7, 76, 133
  history, 29–30
  in America, 45–6, 49–51, 73
  in Japan, 50–1, 69, 73
  nature and, 27–8
  resistance to, 54
  thermal research and, 30–4

Akrich, M., 15, 47

Albaum, M., 130

Aldridge, A., 140

Allen, R., 194

American Consumers Union, 140, 142, 143–4, 146, 151–2

Anson, R., 145

Appadurai, A., 16, 47, 72–3

Armstrong, David, 33

ASHRAE (American Society of Heating Refrigeration and Air-Conditioning Engineers), 22, 74, 83, 93
  standards, 32–4, 36–40

ASHVE (American Society of Heating and Ventilating Engineers), 30
  automobiles, 50, 68, 71, 176

Baker, Nick, 34, 37

Baranzini, A., 5

Bardwick, J., 23–4

bathing, 2, 16, 95–6, 98–116, 190
  as expression of societal propriety, 116
  discourses, 108
  pinwheel model, 112, 114–15
  stories, 109–11, 115

bathrooms
  as index of civilization, 100
  as therapy, 103–5, 108
  design 98, 103, 104–5, 113
  history, 93–4, 98–102, 106–7
  in America 95–6
  in Britain, 96

Beck, U., 28

Becker, H., 38

Bedford, T., 34–5

Bell, M., 172

Bendix, 143

Berner, B., 128

Biermeyer, P., 131

Bijker, W., 15, 46, 50, 57, 58, 59–60

Bischof, E., 125

Boardman, B., 46

Bode, Matthias, 127, 129

Bordass, W., 36

Borg, N. 57

Bourdieu, P., 49, 53, 102, 162

Bowden, S., 142

Brager, G., 29, 34, 36–8, 40

Breedveld, K., 181

Burke, T., 88, 89, 100